ENVIRONMENTAL POLICIES: AN INTERNATIONAL REVIEW

THE CROOM HELM NATURAL ENVIRONMENT –
Problems and Management Series

Edited by *Chris Park, Department of Geography, University of Lancaster*

THE ROOTS OF MODERN ENVIRONMENTALISM
David Pepper

In Preparation:

THE PERMAFROST ENVIRONMENT
Stuart A. Harris

Environmental Policies

AN INTERNATIONAL REVIEW

Edited by
CHRIS C. PARK

CROOM HELM
London • Sydney • Dover, New Hampshire

Croom Helm Ltd, Provident House, Burrell Row,
Beckenham, Kent BR3 1AT
Croom Helm Australia Pty Ltd, Suite 4, 6th Floor,
64-76 Kippax Street, Surry Hills, NSW 2010, Australia

British Library Cataloguing in Publication Data

Environmental policies: an international review.
1. Environmental policy
I. Park, Chris C.
304.2 HC79.E5

ISBN 0-7099-2062-8

Croom Helm, 51 Washington Street, Dover,
New Hampshire 03820, USA

Library of Congress Cataloging in Publication Data
Main entry under title:

Environmental Policies.

Includes Bibliographies and index.
1. Environmental policy–addresses, essays,
lectures. I. Park, Chris C.
HC79. E5E57846 1986 333.7 85-22370
ISBN 0-7099-2062-8

Printed and bound in Great Britain by
Biddles Ltd, Guildford and King's Lynn

CONTENTS

CONTRIBUTORS

D. Briggs	Department of Geography, University of Sheffield, Sheffield S10 2TN, UK.
J. Formby	Centre for Resources and Environmental Studies, Australian National University, GPO Box 4, Canberra, ACT 2601, Australia.
A.W. Gilg	Department of Geography, University of Exeter, Exeter EX4 4RJ, UK.
S.L. Kayastha	Department of Geography, Banaras Hindu University, Varanasi 221005, India.
M.G. Marcus	Climatology Laboratory, Arizona State University, Tempe, Arizona 85287, USA.
T. Nakano	Ohzenji 450-29, Asao-ku, Kawasaki City, Japan.
C.C. Park	Department of Geography, University of Lancaster, Lancaster LA1 4YR, UK.
R. Sandbrook	International Institute for Environment and Development, 3 Endsleigh Street, London WC1H ODD, UK.
G. Wall	Department of Geography, University of Waterloo, Waterloo, Ontario N2L 381, Canada

ACKNOWLEDGEMENTS

This book reflects the work and commitment of a number of people whom it is my great pleasure to acknowledge with thanks. I am indebted to the contributors for their willing participation and sustained enthusiasm; their endeavours have made this compilation both possible and enjoyable. Peter Sowden, at Croom Helm, first suggested the idea of a series on environmental management, and he has shown commendable interest in both this book and the host series.

The fine appearance of the text owes much to the skills, dedication and reliability of Jean Burford, who typed the camera-ready copy with speed and accuracy and who merits a medal for doing so.

I am grateful to Colin Pooley for making available the resources of the Department of Geography at the University of Lancaster during the final stages of preparation of the book. Deserving of special thanks is Clair Hutson whose meticulous proof reading skills are matched by her patience and enduring interest, and who gave so freely of her time. I am also indebted to Peter Mingins who drafted the figures for chapters 4 and 8 with his usual skill and effectiveness.

My wife Angela maintains a healthy and sustained indifference to all matters environmental, but she offered me encouragement and forbearance in abundance. These I quietly accepted and acknowledge with gratitude.

Chapter One

ENVIRONMENTAL POLICIES IN PERSPECTIVE

Chris Park

INTRODUCTION

Recent years have witnessed mounting concern over the state of the environment. This has embraced a variety of environmental changes such as pollution, depletion of natural resources, declining environmental quality, and extinction of species. Growing awareness of these critical changes has encouraged the introduction of more sustainable patterns of activity at all scales from the local to the global.

In the chapters which follow, authors review the environmental problems and evaluate the policies designed to tackle them in a selection of countries and at a range of scales. The book offers an insight into the scale, nature and possible causes of the contemporary environmental problems in the chosen countries (chapters 2, 3 and 5 to 8), and a perspective on how the national decision-makers view them and seek to solve them.

Inevitably many themes (in terms of both problems and solutions) recur from country to country, and this highlights the need for exchange of ideas and dialogue between environmental decision-makers in individual countries. It also provides a context for recent international (chapter 4) and global (chapter 9) environmental initiatives.

The aim of this chapter is to review the need for national environmental policies, and to provide a background against which the policies of individual countries might be set.

ENVIRONMENT - UNITY AND FUNCTION

'Environment' is taken to refer to the sum total of the biological, chemical and physical status and character of the natural world. It is the fabric of the biosphere, and as such it embraces both living (biotic) and non-living (abiotic) features, along with the processes, cycles and interrelationships which influence these.

The biosphere is a sensitive, open system and changes in one part of the system can be transferred - through space and time - to other parts of the system (e.g. most pollutants are extremely mobile through natural environmental cycles and flows). The integrity and survival of the whole system is more important than the preservation of component parts.

The environment has traditionally been seen as a public good, available in almost unlimited supply, and free for use (generally without restrictions) by all who desire to use it. It is an exploitable asset, to be carefully allocated among competing users. The environment offers both natural resources (which have some tangible, practical value - such as minerals and water) and non-utilitarian resources (which do not - such as landscape and wilderness). It has three main functions (Siebert et al, 1980):

(a) it serves as a public consumption good (e.g. air and landscape),
(b) it provides basic inputs for production processes (e.g. raw materials) and
(c) it is used as a receptor of wastes (e.g. air and water pollutants).

Cottrell (1978, p.7) notes that:

> *the natural environment has been largely ignored in conventional accounts of economic processes, and the earth has been commonly regarded as a free reservoir and bottomless rubbish dump.*

Environmental management is required beause of the wide range of demands being made on all parts of the environmental system. Many of these demands are not compatible with others, and some of them lead to serious, long term and at times irrevers-

ible changes in the environment. The paradox is highlighted by O'Riordan (1971, p.176):

> *the environment is to be all things to all men. It is to be life supporting, it is to be useful and it is to be beautiful.*

The challenge of environmental decision-makers is to introduce policies which make it possible to realise all three goals simultaneously. The ultimate objective behind such management is the long term survival of humanity. As Ward and Dubos (1971) conclude:

> *the depletion of natural resources is... one of the chief reasons of uncertainty concerning the continued ability of the earth to support human civilisations.*

THE ENVIRONMENTAL PREDICAMENT

The environmental problems faced by individual countries are components of a global problem, often referred to as the 'Environmental Crisis'. The use of the term crisis is not without purpose, because it is designed to highlight the critical nature of the present problem. A crisis can be defined as '...a crucial stage or turning point... an unstable period...a sudden change, for better or worse...' (Collins English Dictionary, 1979).

Black (1970) maintains that the term 'crisis' implies some sudden decisive change, which is perhaps not fully representative of the gradual, incremental development of many contemporary environmental problems. Berry (1972) also stresses that many such problems are chronic and pervasive, rather than acute. It might be more correct to refer to the recent problems as elements of an 'Environmental Predicament' rather than a crisis.

There is accumulating evidence, particularly since the 1960s, that many forms of human activity are having long-term and wide-ranging impacts on the environment (see Table 1.1). For example, the World Conservation Strategy (Allen, 1980) singles out for particular attention the problems of soil erosion, desertification, loss of cropland, pollution, deforestation, ecosystem degradation and destruction and extinction of species and varieties.

TABLE 1.1 Some negative environmental changes observed during the 1970s

ATMOSPHERE

* slow rise in carbon dioxide levels (due to use of fossil fuels and forest clearance)
* acid rain established as product of long distance transport of sulphur oxides and nitrogen oxides (burning of fossil fuels)
* uncertainty about depletion of ozone (supersonic transport, release of chlorofluorocarbons)
* increasing stratospheric particulates

MARINE ENVIRONMENT

* localised contamination of some areas - rising mercury levels, increased sewage, washout of agricultural chemicals, oils, metals
* high input along some rivers of pollutants - such as iron, manganese, copper, zinc, lead, tin, antimony
* increased exploitation of sea bed mineral resources (especially oil)
* wide distribution of organochlorine pesticides and PCBs, with some evidence of declining levels of DDT and PCB

INLAND WATERS

* increased pollution of some water bodies, from nutrient enrichment (eutrophication) and acidification (acid rain)
* deteriorating state (pollution) of many underground aquifers
* rising concern over environmental impacts of large man-made lakes

LITHOSPHERE

* increased annual production of almost all non-metallic minerals
* moderate increases in production of most metals

TERRESTRIAL BIOTA

* growing concern over declining soil stability and fertility
* growing concern over loss of species and populations of plants and animals
* clearance of tropical rain forest - in the order of 11 million ha per year; faster in Africa than in Asia and Latin America

TABLE 1.1 (continued)

* increasing desertification - in tropical deciduous forests, savannas, grasslands, steppes and areas with Mediterranean climate
* concern over impacts of acid rain on temperate evergreen and broadleaf deciduous forests
* increased threat to Arctic tundra (search for oil and gas)

AGRICULTURE AND FORESTRY

* widespread food shortages - over 450 million people chronically hungry or malnourished during the decade
* increasing production requires new land for cultivation (land intake)
* transformation of agricultural land to other uses - world wide estimates to be between 50 and 70,000 sq.km per annum
* widespread soil degradation - erosion, salinization, alkalinization, chemical degradation
* salinization in arid and semi-arid areas
* desertification - in the order of 60,000 sq.km of land destroyed or impaired per annum; affecting 600-700 million people
* concern about side effects of agricultural chemicals on the environment - over 54 million tons of nitrogenous fertiliser used per annum. Pollution of surface and ground waters, threat to aquatic life, adverse effects on animals, fish, birds

POPULATION

* world population in 1980 = 4,400 million, an increase of 700 million since 1970
* annual rate of population increase (1975-80) = 1.72 percent. This represents an additional 1 million people every 5 days
* moderation of population growth - but growth continues in many countries faster than public services (e.g. education, health care, sanitation, transportation) can be provided
* large migration streams of humans between countries

Source: summarised from Holdgate, Kassas and White (1982)

Some human impacts (such as the deliberate conservation of species) are beneficial to both man and environment. However, many (such as the felling of the tropical rain forest), benefit man in the short term at the expense of long term environmental stability and sustainability. The Global 2000 Report to the President of the United States (1980) concluded that:

> *if present trends continue, the world in 2000 will be more crowded, more polluted, less stable ecologically, and more vulnerable to disruption than the world we live in now. Serious stresses involving population, resources and environment are clearly visible ahead...*

The Historic Dimension

Environmental problems are not new. History provides a rich compendium of environmental control over man, through natural processes such as floods, droughts and volcanic eruptions. Natural environmental change provides a backcloth to the very development of culture and society, and a context for patterns of human endeavour. For example, Wendland and Bryson (1974) conclude their study of the timing of changes in culture and environment (climate) through the Holocene with the observation that:

> *the fact that the cultural discontinuities mostly follow rather closely those of the palaeo-botanical record suggests that there has been a distinct climatic impact on the cultural history of man.*

Cases of environmental disturbance by man in the past are legion, and one example will suffice (examples from individual countries are given in the following chapters).

Deforestation is a traditional form of land management practised throughout the settled world over the last four millenia (Sagan et al, 1979). Localised clearance for land preparation has occurred in many countries (e.g. North America up to A.D. 1600), and agricultural expansion has promoted desertification in the Sahara and Arabia (since 5000 B.C.), in India, Pakistan and Sumeria (2000 B.C. to A.D. 400) and Peru (around 1200 A.D.).

Major phases of forest clearance have occurred in China (2000 B.C. to A.D. 1950), the Mediterranean basin (500 B.C. to A.D. 500), West and Central Europe (A.D. 1000 to 1900), the United States (A.D. 1800 to 1900).

Deforestation of the tropics (Africa, Indonesia and South America) has continued since agriculture began. Forest clearance can promote a variety of environmental impacts, including localised changes in hydrology and climate, loss of productive soil, and silting of rivers and lakes (Goudie, 1981).

Recent Changes

If many environmental problems are not new, then what is new is the accelerating pace and changing character of the human impact on the environment. Malone (1976) argues that there are four new ingredients to the environmental debate:

(a) realisation that new hazards are more than ever before the side-effects of human activities,
(b) increasing uncertainty in linking observed effects with possible causes,
(c) mounting evidence that the cumulative effects of small impacts over long time periods may reach significant proportions before they are detected, and
(d) accumulating evidence of the global distribution and significance of many environmental problems.

The new dimensions of environmental problems are at times alarming. The examples of species extinction and pollution highlight the nature of recent changes.

Rates of extinction of plant and animal species are clearly rising (Table 1.1), to such an extent that Myers (1980) has visions of a global 'sinking ark'. Silverberg (1973) indicates that in the period 1801 to 1850, only two mammals became extinct; between 1851 and 1900 this had risen to thirty. Recent estimates suggest that some 25,000 species of plants and over 1,000 species of animals - out of about 1.6 million species of wildlife known and named (Secrett, 1984) - are currently threatened with extinction. The problems of species extinction within member states of the European Community are explored in Chapter 4.

A further cause for concern is the evidence of rising levels of environmental pollution (Table 1.1). The observed trends are particularly serious in the light of better understanding of the possible links between pollutants and human health. For example, there is evidence to link prolonged exposure to high levels of carbon monoxide (derived from vehicle exhaust emissions) with deterioration of visual and manual functions, and declining intellectual abilities (Wolf, 1971). Relationships between air quality and some aspects of human health (such as lung cancer and bronchitis) are well established, and recent concern has focussed on the possible health effects of prolonged exposure to lead (again from vehicle exhausts), which might be linked with some forms of mental retardation (Warren, 1974).

Possible links between nuclear radiation and human health - such as in suspected increased incidences of some cancers (e.g. leukaemia) - have also been keenly debated and explored (Rowland and Cooper, 1983). Acute health effects occur within minutes or hours of exposure to high levels of some pollutants (e.g. the accidental release of toxic gas from the Union Carbide factory at Bhopal in India, December 1984, which killed 2,500 people - see chapter 7). Chronic health effects develop over years of exposure to modestly increased concentrations (e.g. lead and carbon monoxide from vehicle exhausts, a recurrent problem in modern Japan - see chapter 8).

The changing concentrations and distributions of air and water pollutants give rise to much concern, and the problems of air quality are addressed in most chapters which follow. Informed decision making is not assisted by the lack of detailed knowledge of the effects on human health of many chemicals released into the environment. There are some 3.5 million chemicals known, of which about 25,000 are in significant production. However, only about 6,000 of these have been tested for carcinogenicity (cancer causing) in humans (Edmunds, 1981). About 700 new chemicals appear on the market each year.

Emergent Themes

The nature of the 'Environmental Predicament' naturally varies from country to country, and this is reflected in the themes selected by authors in this book. At the global scale there is ongoing debate over which are the most urgent problems, which are the most important, and what factors influence observed patterns and changes. There are four key priority areas at the global scale (see chapter 9):

(a) sustainable conservation of resources,
(b) preservation of nature,
(c) prevention of pollution, and
(d) control of population growth.

The first three themes are addressed in the following chapters, but the emphasis given to each varies from chapter to chapter in accordance with perceived significance, designated priorities and observed patterns of change.

Population growth per se is beyond the terms of reference of this book (see, for example, Ehrlich and Ehrlich, 1972). It is clear, however, that many environmental problems are being compounded by continued population growth and the attendant pressures to increase food production and resource availability (Table 1.1). The World Conservation Strategy (Allen, 1980) concludes that:

> *the escalating needs of soaring numbers have often driven people to take a short sighted approach when exploiting natural resources.*

For many of the world's underprivileged, the struggle to survive in the face of poverty and starvation is of paramount importance. It is estimated that of the two thirds of the world's population who live in the Third World, some 20 percent are undernourished (i.e. they do not receive enough calories per day) and a further 60 percent are malnourished (i.e. they have serious dietary deficiencies in one or more essential nutrients, usually protein) (Ehrlich and Ehrlich, 1972). What use long term environmental policies in developed countries to them?

THE COUNTRIES IN PERSPECTIVE

In order to make this book manageable in size, but allow space to explore some representative national environmental policies in detail, it has been necessary to limit the treatment to six individual countries (the United States, Canada, the United Kingdom, Australia, India and Japan), one international federation (the European Community) and a global overview. The treatment is thus of necessity selective, but it does offer a valuable opportunity to explore some common themes in a sample of countries and at a variety of scales.

The World Bank (1984) classifies countries on the basis of national economies (Table 1.2). The United States, Canada, United Kingdom, (and all other member states of the European Community), Australia and Japan are all 'industrialised market economies'. As such they share demographic and socio-economic characteristics typical of western developed nations at large - including relative affluence, urban dominated societies, low levels of population growth, high levels of energy use, and dominantly service based economies (Table 1.3). India, in contrast, has a 'Low Income Economy' (Table 1.2), and hence a markedly different demographic and socio-economic profile (Table 1.3).

The main emphasis throughout the book is environmental policies in capitalist countries with market economies, most of which can be regarded as 'developed'. The countries all have largely pluralist societies in which no particular political, ideological, cultural or ethnic group is dominant - they are democracies in which policy formulation is coloured by consensus views. Regular free elections of the governing political parties take place under a variety of electoral systems.

Notably absent from the book are countries with centrally planned economies (i.e. the largely socialist states), such as the USSR, Eastern European and many Central and South American countries. Missing also is any treatment of the developing countries of the Third World. These two areas of omission reflect in part the difficulties of securing informed, national environmental writers with access to non-classified information

TABLE 1.2 World Bank classification of countries

(a) Low Income Economies: GNP per capita in 1982 less than 410 US dollars. 34 countries. e.g. India, China, Ethiopia, Zaire

(b) Middle Income Economies: 60 countries
   i. Oil Importers - e.g. Brazil, South Africa, Zimbabwe
   ii. Oil Exporters - e.g. Mexico, Peru, Arab Republic of Egypt

(c) High Income Oil Exporters: 5 countries. e.g. Saudi Arabia, Libya

(d) Industrial Market Economies: 19 countries. e.g. USA, Canada, Australia, Japan, United Kingdom, all of Western Europe except for Portugal

(e) Eastern European Non-Market Economies: 8 countries. e.g. USSR, German Democratic Republic, Poland

Source: World Bank (1984)

and scope for unrestricted critical interpretation and evaluation of trends, policies and results.

The choice of countries also reflects the intent to focus on countries in which contemporary environmental problems have become central components of government decision making. For reviews of environmental problems and policies in the USSR see, for example, Gerasimov et al, (1971) and Komorov (1978), and for reviews covering developing countries see, for example, Deutsch (1978) and Pearson and Pryor (1978).

The emphasis on 'developed' countries is no accident. Chapman (1969, p.32) has suggested that:

> *as a society reaches some threshold of economic development, with its attendant scientific and technological capabilities, it can afford to concern itself less with materials and quantity, and more with the quality of life.*

TABLE 1.3 Some characteristics of the sample countries

Variable	USA	CANADA	UK	AUSTRALIA	INDIA	JAPAN
area (thousand sq.km)	9,363	9,976	245	7,687	3,288	372
population (million) (mid-1982)	231.5	24.6	55.8	15.2	717.0	118.4
average annual growth rate of population (%) (1970-82)	1.0	1.2	0.1	1.5	2.3	1.1
crude birth rate (per thousand) (1982)	16	15	13	16	34	13
crude death rate (per thousand) (1982)	9	7	12	8	13	7
urban population (% of total) (1982)	78	76	91	89	24	78
daily calorie supply per capita (1981)	3,647	3,321	3,322	3,210	1,906	2,740
GNP per capita (US dollars) (1982)	13,160	11,320	9,660	11,140	260	10,080
average annual growth rate of GDP (%)						
(1960-70)	4.3	5.6	2.9	5.6	3.4	10.4
(1970-82)	2.7	3.4	1.5	3.1	3.6	4.6
index of food production per capita (1969-71 = 100) (1980-82)	119	119	126	98	101	91
average annual growth rate of agricultural production (%) (1970-82)	1.7	2.0	1.9	2.5	1.8	-0.2
fertiliser consumption (x 100 grams per ha of arable land) (1981)	1,024	419	3,296	279	338	3,872
energy consumption per capita (x 1000 kg oil equivalent) (1981)	7,540	9,208	3,541	4,908	158	3,087
distribution of GDP (%) (1982)						
agriculture	3	4	2	6	33	4
industry	33	29	33	35	26	42
services	64	67	65	59	41	54

Source: based on data in World Bank (1984)

Countries with high standards of living (in both absolute and relative terms) can devote greater attention to the need for clean supplies of air and water, access to unspoiled landscapes, protection of ecological habitats and conservation of species than can countries with lower standards of living, more limited material comforts, and shortage of advanced economic infrastructure and government resources for investment.

Ophuls (1977) argues that environmental problems are perhaps most acute, and attempts to deal with them best developed and most successful, in the United States and Western European countries. The experiences from such countries are well represented in the chapters of this book.

In contrast, Vanderpool (1981, p.162) contends that the formulation of environmental policy has not been a central issue of national concern in the Third World and in Socialist Bloc countries of Eastern Europe, which:

> *have not been as environmentally conscious because they have emphasised the need for economic growth and development even at the expense of the environment. Concern with the environment is largely limited to interest in furthering the development of economic productivity.*

Thus whilst the following chapters largely reflect the views, priorities and actions of western countries with market economies, it is contended that the sample selected does provide a balanced perspective on policies in the countries with the greatest interest in long-term environmental protection. The chosen countries also offer a range of governmental and administrative structures, including 'classical' parliamentary structures on the Westminster line (e.g. in the United Kingdom), federal systems (e.g. in the United States and Australia) and the international European Community, each of which poses special problems for rational environmental decision making.

RETROSPECTIVE - A DECADE OF CHANGE

The main focal point of this book is contemporary environmental policies. Whilst authors were invited to review the history, background and context of contemporary environmental problems and policies within their countries, special attention was to be given to the recent (post 1970) past and to the present.

In many western countries, the roots for recent initiatives can be traced to the 1960s, which Sandbrook (1984, p.11) sees as a 'golden age' during which:

> *something had to be done to offset the "future shock", provide a "blueprint for survival", ensure that the "limits to growth" were recognised, and help to design a world where small was not only beautiful but possible.*

The 1960s were a period of relative abundance and rising affluence in many countries, and the 1970s (especially after the first OPEC oil price rises of 1974) were to signal the arrival of an age of austerity and relative scarcity which has continued at least up to the mid 1980s. The World Bank (1984, p.1) stresses that:

> *the recession of 1980-83 was the longest in fifty years. It increased unemployment, reduced investment, and undermined social programmes in almost every country in the world. It put great strain on the international trade and financial systems, and caused friction between governments everywhere.*

The Decision Making Climate

The 1960s were to see marked changes in attitudes towards the environment in many countries. These provided a catalyst for important changes in patterns and styles of environmental decision making. In the United States, for example, O'Riordan and Sewell (1981) detect a number of profound changes set against a background of clarifying national priorities in all aspects of environmental management. These changes include:

(a) the opening up of government activities towards more detailed public analysis and wider (though not widespread) participation,
(b) the reinforcement of the traditional role of representative elected politicians to make policy and take decisions, and
(c) the improvement of techniques and consultative devices with which administrative authorities

consider options and take advice.

Whilst the foundations of many recent environmental policies in a wide range of countries were laid during the 1960s, the 1970s were to witness a number of important social, economic and technological changes which provided the immediate impetus for contemporary policies. A number of key forces were at work during the 1970s and early 1980s, including:

(a) economic growth as the major national priority in the developing world,
(b) economic recession (and attendant problems of unemployment, changing productivity, money and commodity flows between countries, lack of investment by companies and governments, etc.) in many developed countries; note the decline in annual growth rate of GNP in most countries between 1960-70 and 1970-82 (Table 1.3),
(c) rising energy costs (especially after the first OPEC price rises of 1973-74 - which brought a four-fold rise in oil costs - and the second round of price rises in 1979-80),
(d) industrial efforts to introduce new production technologies, choose alternative materials, and treat waste so as to reduce if not eliminate harmful effects to people and ecosystems (and to reduce production costs). New technologies emerging (for waste abatement, waste avoidance and material recycling),
(e) introduction of a wide range of economic political measures in many countries to encourage the use of appropriate (environmentally sound) technologies,
(f) expanding demand for the enforcement of higher standards of environmental quality, coupled with public efforts to improve environmental quality, and
(g) the rise of environmentalism as an important social force, with pressure groups, lobbies and environmental campaigns mobilising citizen concern for the environment and seeking to influence individuals and decision makers in government and industry.

The contemporary problems and policies in individual countries must be set against this contextual background of the 1960s and 1970s. Many of these changes of the 1970s were not unique to the United

States or other individual countries - they represent the changing socio-economic scene world-wide, within which individual countries formulated their own specific environmental policies.

The links between economic climate and pursuit of environmental initiatives must not be seen as exclusively one-way, however. There is evidence (from the United States, for example) that environmental regulations may make a contribution to the slowdown in growth of industrial productivity (Christiansen and Haveman, 1981), so that environmental improvements might in some circumstances promote recession.

As well as providing the catalysts for contemporary policies, the last two decades saw the emergence of international initiatives designed to deal with both trans-national problems (e.g. trans-national transfers of air and water pollution between members states of the European Community) and problems at the global scale (e.g. rising carbon dioxide levels in the atmosphere).

Environmentalism

One hallmark of the 1970s was the mobilisation of public interest in the environment on an unprecedented scale. This theme is well documented elsewhere (O'Riordan, 1976; Pepper, 1984), but some comments are appropriate here. During the 1970s there were marked shifts in areas of public concern and interest, coupled with gradual changes in public attitude and political commitment in a number of countries.

These are reflected in a wide variety of ways, such as the increased membership of environmental groups (such as Friends of the Earth - see Wilson, 1984), and increased involvement and broader campaigning by activist groups (such as Greenpeace). The new mood is also reflected in political changes, such as the increased electoral and financial support for 'green' parties (especially in western Europe - see Chapter 4), and more overt interest in environmental issues shown by established parties (partly as a vote-catching issue and partly through growing genuine commitment to environmental protection and improvement).

Changing attitudes are also reflected in the media, through the amount of coverage given to environmental issues and the contexts in which they are covered. Analyses of media coverage can yield useful information on changing public attitude and concern. For example, Bowman and Fuchs (1981) found three groups of environmental topics dominant in the (US) mass circulation magazines of the 1970s - energy resource management, followed by water quality, population and general environmental issues, followed in turn by air quality and chemical additives.

In each case - public concern, political change, and media coverage - the extent to which observed events follow or influence public views and attitudes is open to some debate. It is also a matter of interpretation whether this new awareness of the 1970s arose largely as a result of specific environmental events, or as a reflection of general changes in society. Public awareness might also reflect the availability of popular literature, such as Rachel Carson's widely read SILENT SPRING (1962) on the ecological effects of DDT pesticides.

Doubtless specific pollution episodes, if widely publicised through the media, heighten public awareness and reinforce public concern about the environment. Notable events of the 1970s include the nuclear accident at the Three Mile island reactor at Harrisburg in the United States on the 28th March, 1979 (Bunyard, 1979), and the accidental release of dioxin - a by-product of the manufacture of the pesticide 2,4,5-T and one of the most toxic materials yet synthesised - from the Seveso Chemical plant near Milan in Italy in 1976 (Cook and Kaufman, 1982). The recent leakage of methyl isocyanide from the Union Carbide pesticide plant at Bhopal in India on the 3rd December, 1984 (see chapter 7) also brought environmental problems - and the human suffering often associated with them - into sharp perspective via world-wide media coverage.

It is doubtful whether specific incidents alone can account for the recent rise of environmentalism in many countries. Another catalyst has been the general tide of post-war cultural changes. Sandbrook (1984) isolates two key trends in this respect - growing concern for the rights of both nature and people (the latter illustrated by the birth of the United Nations), and the advent of welfare ideas (e.g. the welfare state, and international development agencies and aid programmes).

Progress and Retrogression

Whilst growing interest in, concern about, and knowledge of declining environmental quality was a hallmark of the 1970s, the decade did provide some cause for optimism (see Table 1.4). for example, there is evidence that in many countries the environmental policies introduced in the 1960s and 1970s are having positive effects in reducing pollution, encouraging resource conservation, restraining if not reversing the trends of declining environmental quality, and fostering the conservation of plant and animal species.

There is also evidence from many countries of technological research and development designed to reduce pollutant emissions and recycle resources Moreover, the world-wide economic recession of the 1970s has promoted a decline in demand for some natural resources (because they are simply too costly to be economically viable) and a concomitant search for sustainable and economically viable alternatives.

On the other hand, the increased scale and diversified nature of environmental research during the 1970s, at both national and global levels, yielded evidence of significant adverse changes in the physical environment. Valuable information on the state of the environment, based on monitoring and observation, became available in many countries and in some cases at the global scale during the decade in unprecedented quantities and of unprecedented quality.

Results (see, for example, Table 1.1) illustrate and reinforce some earlier concerns (such as the continued rise of atmospheric carbon dioxide levels pollution of oceans and inland waters, and loss of soil and productivity through erosion, desertification and increasing salinity). The available evidence also promotes concern in new areas of environmental change (such as the growing problem of acid rain, and the continued felling of tropical rain forests).

PERSPECTIVES AND INFORMATION

Environmental problems are the sole domain of

TABLE 1.4 Some positive environmental changes observed during the 1970s

ATMOSPHERE

* decreasing photochemical oxidants and levels of sulphur dioxide and suspended particulate matter in many cities (due to effective air pollution controls)

INLAND WATERS

* development of technologies for waste water treatment and recycling
* expansion of inland fisheries and development of aquaculture

LITHOSPHERE

* advances in methods used to reduce adverse effects of mining, treatment and transport of metallic and non-metallic minerals
* renewed interest in recycling and substitution of mineral resources

AGRICULTURE AND FORESTRY

* food production rising at up to 7% per annum; FAO estimate the need for a 60% increase in food/fish/forest production to maintain current consumption patterns to the year 2000 AD
* advances in genetic engineering and biotechnology

POPULATION

* decline in crude birth rates and in death rates in most countries
* decline in birth rate of 94 developing countries (1965-75) (especially in Asia and Latin America)
* widespread adoption of family planning programmes

Source: summarised from Holdgate, Kassas and White (1982)

no single discipline. All such problems are multi-dimensional, involving a wide variety of issues and spanning a wide range of subject areas. The identification and solution of environmental problems requires the synthesis of contributions from many different disciplines - including economics, ecology, sociology, physics, chemistry, engineering, systems, law, philosophy, ethics and politics.

Perhaps no one discipline is so well placed to provide the necessary holistic perspective as geography, with its nodal niche between the social and the natural sciences. This endows it with a unique vantage point from which to survey the many issues implicitly and explicitly involved in environmental decision making and policy formulation. Many of the authors of the following chapters are or were geographers.

Spectrums of Concern

Much of the environmental literature of the last two decades has been a blend of the sensational, the emotional and the rational. Clayton described the environmental movement in the early 1970s as 'a confused mixture of quasi-scientific concern and thorough-going sentimentality' (Clayton, 1971, p.83).

The views represented by the authors in this book reflect the growing informed 'scientific concern' of the 1970s and early 1980s, as a result of which rationality has largely displaced sensationalism within the serious environmental literature.

Whilst many conclusions in individual chapters are implicitly pessimistic, the treatment of environmental problems and prospects overall is one of realistic concern tempered with some signs of optimism. The feeling overall is a mixture of boom (success) and gloom (failure).

This balance reflects the middle ground of a wide range of views on the seriousness of contemporary environmental problems, which spans a complete spectrum from pessimism to optimism (see, for example, Pepper, 1984). Pessimists foresee an imminent environmental Doomsday. They are championed by the ecological prophets Ehrlich (1972) and Commoner (1972). The dynamic computer simulation modelling underlying 'The Limits to Growth' (Meadows et al, 1972) yielded inherently pessimistic forecasts of possible environmental futures if recent trends in resource use, population increase, pollution emission and consumer materialism are allowed to continue unabated.

The pessimist school believes that within our lifetimes will come the critical time of insufficient food, water, land, energy and other resources, unless present day trends and patterns of resource use are markedly altered. Solutions called for include radical changes in attitudes towards the environment (as a fragile and vulnerable 'spaceship earth'), changes in life-style (away from consumerism and materialism), and the implementation of rational, sustainable resource management strategies.

In contrast, the optimists believe that resourcefulness, human ingenuity, and technological innovation can postpone the 'crisis' indefinitely. Champions include Maddox (1972) who sees in the 'doomsday syndrome' signs of unwarranted sensationalism, crisis reactions and failure to allow for human endeavour and insight. Other optimists include Simon and Kahn (1984), who argue that population trends, agricultural prospects, energy resources and quality of environment are quite sustainable within 'The Resourceful Earth'.

Paradoxically the views of both optimists and pessimists are founded largely on the same basic body of information on the state of the environment. Divergence of views stems from interpretation of the data, speculation on causal factors, and adoption of intellectual and disciplinary perspectives.

Information and Monitoring

The shortage of reliable and detailed information on some aspects of the environment and in some parts of the world makes it difficult to draw firm conclusions about many trends and changes. The UNEP assessment of the changing state of the world environment between 1972 and 1982 (Holdgate, Kassas and White, 1982) was, of necessity, based on information which was at best partial.

Fairly good information exists on trends in atmospheric composition, food contamination and fresh water. Information is becoming available on forest cover, conditions of some seas, and land use patterns. However there is still, as yet, very incomplete data on rates of desertification, conditions of rangelands, farmlands and other major land uses, and little reliable data on ocean pollution and the condition of groundwater (Sandbrook, 1984).

Clearly a major prerequisite to the formulation of realistic environmental policies is the availability of high quality reliable information on the state of the environment and on rates and patterns of change through time. The collection, analysis, dissemination and synthesis of this information must be a major goal for environmental decision makers in the 1980s. The international co-operative research project 'Global Habitability' (Edelson, 1985) - aimed at investigating long term physical, chemical and biological changes on a global scale - is a welcome initiative in this respect.

Jeffers (1978) sees the lack of adequate survey of existing environmental systems as one of the most urgent problems to address. We know relatively little about current land uses and distributions of ecological features in many areas, and even less about patterns and rates of change. Many areas are not fully surveyed and others lack recent, reliable or compatible observations.

Because many serious environmental problems (such as acid rain and eutrophication) build up over long time periods, and others involve relatively small chemical, physical or biological changes, it is often extremely difficult to detect them before they reach critical proportions.

The prospects for collecting information on rates and patterns of environmental change look much brighter in the 1980s, with developments in remote sensing and environmental monitoring technologies, coupled with closer harmonisation of surveillance and monitoring schemes within and between countries and enhanced computer-based data storage, retrieval and processing systems.

ENVIRONMENTAL DECISION MAKING

Economics and Environment

There is little doubt that classical economic theory has played a significant part in shaping human attitudes to the environment. The links between economics and environment are fully reviewed elsewhere (e.g. Pearce, 1976; Cottrell, 1978), but some comments are appropriate here.

The economic system (in non-centralised economies) is founded on the notion of free enterprise in the private market place. In this context the environment has traditionally been seen as a public commodity, to be used at zero price. Until recently there has been no perceived need for public interference in the allocative workings of the private market place. Since the environment (e.g. clean air and water, unspoiled landscapes, natural habitats and survival of species) has been valued as an important national asset, intervention has been accepted as essential, and so environmental management and policy formulation have been encorporated into national political decision making.

Cramp (1975) isolates three basic assumptions of modern economic theory:

(a) the pursuit of efficiency via profit maximisation is both rational and right,
(b) efficiency in production takes priority over justice in distribution, and
(c) accumulation of capital in large units is acceptable if the pursuit of efficiency leads in that direction.

The net result is 'rational economic man', engaged in the pursuit of material wealth at the expense of long term environmental stability and sustainable life-styles. There appear to be at least four imporant corollaries of this viewpoint:

(a) material welfare and economic growth generally assume a higher priority than environmental protection or improvement in national political decision making,
(b) conservation and re-cycling of resources are adopted only where they can be defended as viable (or cost effective) on purely economic grounds,
(c) many aspects of decision making are founded on economic cost-benefit analysis (for a review of which see Haram, 1980), although many aspects of the environment (e.g. survival of rare species, availability of wilderness) cannot be measured in purely economic terms; such items are thus difficult to encorporate

into rational 'economic' decision making,
(d) in the pursuit of material wealth, the environment is often regarded as a 'free good', to be used at zero price. Thus many aspects of productive activity seek to externalise disbenefits (such as pollution) and internalise benefits (such as profits). The disbenefits are externalised by passing them on to society at large, whereas the benefits are internalised and thus enjoyed solely by the producer (or causer of the disbenfits). But to society at large, these externalities (disbenefits) - such as the discharge of polluting wastes from factories, the depopulation of seas by overfishing, and the overuse of national parks (Cottrell, 1978) - are a burden.

Externalities are in effect social costs met by society at large. With the arrival of welfare economics has come the demand that resource-using activities internalise as far as possible all social costs associated with them (Misham, 1971). One example of this is the 'polluter pays princile', based on economic policy mechanisms (Table 1.5). Hardin (1968) uses the analogy of common pasture land in medieval England to develop his argument about 'The Tragedy of the Commons', in which optimum net gain to all commons users is a function of sensible (and compromising) patterns of behaviour by all users of the resource.

In final analysis, Lorrain-Smith (1982) argues that environmental decision making is implicitly (if not explicitly) founded on economic criteria. He argues that the costs of environmental protection must be weighed against the costs of other goods and services that consumers want, given that consumers have finite amounts of resources (especially monetary resources) to allocate in fulfilling their desires.

The Decision Making Process

Environmental management is an inherently difficult area of decision making, based on complex, dynamic, multi-participant, multi-goal and ill-structured decision making contexts (Bradley, 1973; Shakun, 1981). The complexity arises partly because of the many factors involved, but also because of the difficulties of evaluating trade-offs between alternative means of proceeding.

Matthews and Perkowski (1975, p.214) note that all major environmental decisions are made in the broad context of meeting the different needs of society:

> *society cannot simply decide, and get, what kind of environment it wants; it must also decide what it is willing to give up, or to do in addition, so that it can effect the change in the status quo which will generally be required to produce a change in the environment.*

Policy decisions are not neutral or value free. The value system underlying decisions is a very important influence on how the decisions are made, and what factors are taken into account, and how alternatives are evaluated. Policy formulation is normative in the sense that it is concerned with recommendations and rules based on standards and values of society within that country.

Potter and Norville (1981) list a wide variety of values involved in environmental decision making - including aesthetics, democracy, efficiency, equality, freedom, material comfort, individualism, nationalism and science. Those persons involved in environmental decision making should strive to make explicit the contextual factors which govern their decisions - such as the values involved, the objective information available, and the compromises which would be necessary (Mann, 1981).

O'Riordan and Sewell (1981) argue that a proper policy formulation procedure should include the analysis of assumptions, definition of priorities and comparison of alternatives - although they point out that in many environmental organisations ameliorative and mitigating functions often assume greater importance.

Evaluation of alternatives is clearly a key issue in decision making. Few environmental issues are clear cut, and ultimate decisions are often founded as much on pragmatism as on absolute rationality. The complexity is illustrated by the case of pesticides regulation decision making

(Dorfman, 1982, p.25):

> *It is a tough regulatory decision in which the administrator, subject to very general legislative guidance, must use his judgement to choose among alternatives whose consequences for good and ill differ in a number of incommensurable ways and are only vaguely foreseeable.*

Many environmental problems are extremely complex, and it is difficult to establish a decision making machinery suitable for selecting between multiple goals. Such complex problems are best handled, according to the principle of 'bounded rationality' (Simon, 1957), by limiting the scope of analysis to things of manageable proportions. Manageability in these terms is conditioned by the quantity and quality of information available, and our mental abilities to deal with complex, multi-variate problems.

The 'bounded rationality' model of decision making is founded on the assumption that we select paths with a reasonable probability of achieving a need-satisfying goal - that is, we adopt a pragmatic approach and are satisfied with an acceptable (but generally sub-optimal) solution.

Some of the problems of evaluation of alternatives arise because the evaluation is generally made by administrators (with or without the guidance of scientific experts). It is the administrators task to assemble a wide range of relevant data, compile a check list of alternative policy instruments suitable for a given problem, and then use relevant scientific disciplines to interpret them and evaluate the probable consequences of each alternative.

Whether the evaluation is based on traditional cost benefit analysis (Haram, 1980) or other techniques, the decision making process must be systematic, rational, appropriate and accountable.

The rationality criterion is clearly of paramount importance. The level of rationality will depend on how the decision is made, on what basis, and by whom. The question of who makes the decision, in practice, is somewhat vexed. O'Riordan (1982,

p. 104-5) notes that:

> *institutions may prepare policy guides, but more often than not they embark on activities which by their very existence become policy. What eventually takes place therefore, is rarely the consequence of a single analytical plan; it will have evolved from innumerable decisions taken by unknown individuals or by committees whose opinion may be deeply divided at various levels of influence and authority.*

Matthews and Perkowski (1975, p.214) echo this observation:

> *there are really no formalised, comprehensive environmental management procedures...there are, instead, a myriad of individual and collective decisions by persons, groups and organisations throughout society, that result in impacts - both positive and negative - on environmental resources. Taken together, these decisions and the interactions among the people involved, constitute a process...that in effect results in the management (or mismanagement) of the environmental resources of our society.*

ENVIRONMENTAL POLICY FORMULATION

Projects, Programmes and Policies

Environmental decision-making spans a hierarchy of levels from the individual (place specific) project (e.g. the building of a nuclear power station at a named site), through the more general programme (e.g. a national nuclear power programme), to the overall policy (e.g. national energy policy). At each level within this hierarchy the goals and objectives change, along with the space and time scales involved and the nature of the environmental problems and dilemmas to be resolved.

A policy can be defined as 'a plan of action adopted or pursued by an individual, government, etc. ...' (Collins English Dictionary, 1979). However, as O'Riordan (1982, p.104) points out, the term policy is very elusive:

> *it may refer to a set of guidelines or principles against which possible courses of action can be evaluated, or it may relate to a declared statement of intent to do something, backed up by the provision of an enabling budget.*

Whether it is concerned with guidelines, actions or statements of intent, Shakun (1981) sees policy making as 'the design of purposeful systems to deliver values to participants'. The specific policy instruments chosen to deliver these values may be based on positive strategies (such as education and moral persuasion) and/or negative strategies (such as laws, regulations and taxes). The wide variety of policy mechanisms described in the following chapters fall into three main groups - moral persuasion, direct (legal) regulation, and economic incentives - as outlined in Table 1.5.

An environmental policy is thus a goal-seeking series of actions, designed to satisfy objectives normally defined by national governments. These objectives might include the conservation of species of plants and animals, the maintenance of high quality air and water supplies, and the prevention of unsuitable or high risk developments.

Vanderpool (1981) argues that environmental policy normally reflects the interaction between three processes - a concern to optimise the use of natural resources, a response to environmental lobbies and pressure groups, and a need (in advanced economic states) to gain control over the vital productive processes in society via comprehensive regulation.

Policy formulation must always be at least in part subjective, in that it will reflect the values, ideologies and standards of those involved in decision making, and of the institutional framework within which they must operate (Mann, 1981).

Scales of Concern

Environmental problems are no respectors of political, administrative or economic boundaries, and environmental policies can be formulated and implemented at a number of spatial scales. Four appear to be particularly relevant (Garlauskas, 1975; Siebert et al, 1980):

(a) Local : many policies must be developed to deal with environmental problems at the sub-national level. The three most common units of scale are topographic (e.g. a large drainage basin), ecological (e.g. a large forest), and political (e.g. a state, county or regional district). Such policies should logically reflect the broader national policies, modified where appropriate to take account of local factors and constraints.

(b) National : national policies are required to cope with many environmental problems which arise in individual countries, as a result of human activities within those countries. Examples include land use, development control and natural resource management. Such policies are also required to deal with pollutants which are emitted into the environment of one country and which are not diffused abroad. Environmental management is often more effective when based on unified and legally effective national organisations - such as the Environmental Protection Agency in the United States (see chapter 2), the Department of the Environment in England and Wales (see chapter 5), and the Environmental Agency in Japan (see chapter 8).

(c) Transfrontier : some environmental problems transcend national boundaries, and it is appropriate to deal with them bi-laterally or multi-laterally. Transfrontier policies are required where two or more adjacent countries are linked by an environmental system, and activities within one country affects environmental quality in the foreign countries. Examples include the release of sulphur dioxide from the UK and Germany which ultimately falls as acid rain over Scandinavia; and the use of the River Rhine by France, Switzerland, Germany and the Netherlands.

(d) International : some environmental problems (especially air and water pollution) are truly international in character. Sometimes these relate to a particular area (such as the Mediterranean, which receives pollutants from rivers in all surrounding countries). Often, however, they are global (such as rising levels of carbon dioxide in the atmosphere. Many of the most urgent problems are international, because political segmentation and differences in national objectives and ambitions prevent consistent international implementation of global environmental management strategies.

TABLE 1.5 Some Environmental Policy Mechanisms

a. MORAL PERSUASION: seeks to alter the preference functions of consumers and producers, so that environmental impacts are taken into account in private decisions.

b. DIRECT (LEGAL) REGULATION: involves the use of mechanisms (laws, licences, permits, registrations, directives) to discourage pollution beyond a pre-defined acceptable level.

   e.g. PERMIT SYSTEMS - under which firms are only allowed to produce or locate if they use an approved production or purification technology; EMISSION NORMS or STANDARDS - standards which specify permissible pollutant levels for fuels or equipment; this allows the individual decision maker to decide on the type of technology to be adopted.

c. ECONOMIC INCENTIVES: which seek to correct specific deficiencies in the allocative mechanisms of the private market system.

   e.g. SUBSIDIES - where government contributes to the cost of capital investment in pollution abatement activities, to relieve the financial burden on the individual or municipality (includes outright grant-in-aid; guaranteed loans; fast depreciation write-offs; tax or property assessment credits on new pollution control investments); DIRECT CHARGES - in the form of EMISSION FEES (taxes levied on pollution emissions, proportional to levels of emission - aimed at internalising social costs of pollutants); and FUEL TAXES (like Emission Fees, but levied on the input to polluting processes, thus easier to measure and administer).

Sources: based on Ducsik (1971), Siebert et al (1980)

The National Policy Context

Environmental policy formulation at the national level is both important and difficult. Complementing the inherent difficulties of decision making in such a broad area, are three practical problems which can only be addressed at the national level. These are:

(a) the need to ensure that national environmental policies are compatible (in objectives, practice, and impact) both with other national policies and with the government's desired direction of change,
(b) the competition to secure public funding to enable certain policy instruments to be adopted (e.g. tax concessions, grant aid for pollution abatement technology, sponsored research into environmental problems), and
(c) the need to consider the possible impacts of environmental policies on trade, investment and sector structure (at home and abroad).

These issues reinforce Lorrain-Smith's (1982, p.235) argument that 'environmental policy must be seen as a part of (not an alternative to) national economic policy'.

Environmental policies must be formulated alongside and be compatible with, if not supportive of, other national policies (e.g. social, economic, military and strategic policies). It is generally presumed, for example, that if policies to encourage economic growth conflict with the requirements of environmental protection, the former would normally prevail. During the late 1970s many western countries faced conflicts of policy priorities between industrial expansion and economic growth on the one hand, and increased environmental regulation and protection on the other.

Many policies which have an impact on the environment (whether positive or negative) are not formal 'environmental policies'. Nearly all national policies related to economic activities and physical planning will produce environmental impacts, some of which may be acceptable (or even worthy of promotion) and others not so. It is therefore encumbent on decision makers to harmonise the national policies which are formulated and implemented, to ensure as far as possible that environmental considerations are taken into account at all stages of the policy process.

The International Dimension

There can be marked variations between countries in environmental policy formulation and implementation, because of variations in the nature and perceived seriousness of the problems and variations in procedures for the selection and ranking of major policy areas. Policy formulation cannot be divorced from politics. Indeed, at the national level it is the key tangible product of political decision-making.

Many national policies (environmental and others) have potential international implications. For example, some environmental policies can distort economic comparative advantage and thus affect overseas trading flows and prospects, pricing policies, sector structure, resource allocation and location of industry (Koo, 1974; Siebert et al, 1980).

There are both theoretical (Pethig, 1976) and empirical (Wood, 1982) grounds for concluding that some aspects of environmental policy can distort levels of competition between countries. For example, some policies may confer competitive advantages to some countries or states (where permission to proceed with potentially hazardous or environmentally damaging developments or projects is granted), at the expense of others (where permission is withheld, in accordance with prevailing national environmental policies).

Another international dimension of national policies is what Siebert et al, (1980) refer to as 'environmental imperialism', or the export of pollution. If restrictive environmental policies are introduced in the home country (to reduce the production of certain commodities which produce much pollution), then foreign (especially Third World) countries can become more competitive in the production of those commodities. Consequently they tend to specialise in this form of productive activity, which leads to increasing pollution and declining environmental quality.

National environmental policies are not unrelated to broader issues within the North South debate. The Brandt Report (1980) also highlights how many environmental problems in the Third World can be traced back, ultimately, to various forms of national policies within the developed world. Hourcade (1978) highlights three areas of particular concern:

(a) national aid policies; in which the sums allocated to environmental protection at the international level are drawn in part from the reserves intended as aid for development,
(b) the possibility of neo-protectionism by industrialised countries (via the imposition of arbitrary quality standards for products), and
(c) the transfer of unmodified (and inappropriate) techniques and technologies to the Third World.

The dependence of many countries on raw materials and natural resources of other countries creates yet more international inter-dependence. Ashby (1978) regrets that 'competition for scarce resources will undoubtedly exacerbate the natural hostility between nations with different ideologies', and fears the likely temptation of nations into war or serious international blackmail consequent upon an uneven distribution of key resources between countries.

A further international dimension is the spread of environmental concern, understanding and initiatives from country to country. There are signs of international diffusion and assimilation of environmental awareness and of concern to implement sustainable environmental management strategies, in particular from the United States to other countries (e.g. Canada and Australia).

The direct and indirect transfer of policy directions and procedures between countries is indicative of an invisible college of informed decision makers. This has helped to ensure that policy directives are compatible between countries, even if details (such as permissible levels of pollution) vary from country to country. It has also paved the way for increasing formal international collaboration in environmental policy formulation (see chapter 9), and for global initiatives in monitoring and fundamental research.

THE NATURE OF ENVIRONMENTAL MANAGEMENT

Management of the environment constitutes one of the most difficult but also one of the most important areas of planning intervention in market economies. Intervention in the free market system is required where market forces are an imperfect basis on which to allocate resources. This often arises on three grounds:

(a) national responsibility - such as matters of national security, or national welfare of the community (e.g. where standards of living, unemployment or prices are involved),
(b) key resource allocation - such as in the provision of goods and services of major importance to the community (e.g. health care, education, coal and gas), and
(c) equity of resource allocation - such as in government views on what ought to be rather than what presently is, founded on value judgements made in the interests of the community as a whole (e.g. equity in opportunities to enjoy informal outdoor recreation).

The ultimate objective of environmental management is to govern the allocation of environmental resources and quality in a manner most consistent with the goals and values of society (Ducsik, 1971). However, whether this is best achieved by direct or indirect intervention is a matter of debate.

Garlauskas (1975) argues that environmental management is a direct form of intervention, promoted by the need to manipulate inter-dependencies between environmental processes and problems. This view presupposes that there is one 'best' or 'optimal' goal hierarchy within environmental management, which is determined on the basis of environmental quality.

Lorrain-Smith (1982), in contrast, favours an indirect interpretation. He argues that there is no environmental management as such, because there is no absolute definition of environmental quality. Environmental quality is a relative notion, determined by a balance between consumer demand and levels of satisfaction. Consequently, he argues, the goal of environmental management is not environmental quality per se, but consumer welfare; it attempts to control the economy in order to avoid or correct 'mistakes' which reduce consumer welfare via impacts on environmental quality.

Environmental management is complex because tactical objectives must be met alongside strategic ones. Critical tactical (operational) factors include the need for consistency in regulation between different policies, fairness of the decision making process, and the formulation of rules that promote efficient and equitable use of society's resources in order to protect the nation's environment (Magat, 1982). The strategic objectives are the societal goals (expressed in terms of desired environmental changes) towards the achievement of which the policies have been designed.

Further complexity arises from the fact that environmental protection can never be an absolute objective. Most forms of activity have possible adverse impacts on environment and human health and welfare. Consequently it is not realistic for regulatory authorities to strive towards absolute control or absolute safety. Environmental policies often seek optimal solutions to complex problems, at levels commensurate with other key national objectives (e.g. economic recovery and growth) and in ways which do not introduce unacceptably high social and economic costs.

A key prerequisite to the successful formulation, implementation and review of environmental policies is appropriate institutional and organisational support. The scale, complexity and significance of many environmental problems demand that they are dealt with at the highest levels within the national political decision making machinery, and this in itself can produce operational problems. Large organisations commonly suffer from a range of inherent limitations, including rigidity and the difficulties of collectively changing values and directions (Brenner, 1973).

Murphy (1977) argues that extreme caution is needed to prevent bureaucracy from simply institutionalising environmental problems rather than trying to solve them. He sees three main requirements:

(a) hierarchical chains of command, with a clear

role for local control,
(b) injection of knowledge into the judicial process for environmental protection, and
(c) public participation in environmental bureaucracy.

The potential for institutionalising rather than solving problems is very real. A closely related theme is the extent to which political decision making reflects (at least in part) national consensus as well as ideological commitment.

Consensus Politics and State Legitimacy

The individual countries covered in this book share two important characteristics - they are pluralist societies (characterised by competition between rival elites or interest groups), and state activities within them are founded on the principles of representative democracy.

In representative democracies periodic free elections offer an effective choice between ruling parties (with differing ideologies). In such cases the elected body of representatives - whether it be a parliament, congress or national assembly (Bullock and Stallybrass, 1977, p.161) - has:

> *the right of legislation, right to vote taxes and control the budget, and the right publicly to question, discuss, criticise and oppose government measures without being subject to threats of interference or arrest.*

These rights are incorporated in the formulation and implementation of all national policies, and they influence national commitment to international policies and initiatives.

Much national policy formulation reflects the processes of consensus formation and the struggle to preserve state legitimacy (as described, for example, by Vanderpool, 1981; Offe, 1976; and Frieberg, 1979). State legitimacy - in representative democracies - rests on:

(a) government ability - to manage society's affairs and crises in a rational manner, and to distribute costs and benefits of its actions equitably across the different political groups within that society, and

(b) government authority - to fo implement effectively a set of are binding on its members.

If the objective of state actions and po is to preserve belief in the legitimacy of state, then they must reflect some general agre ment (consensus) over appropriate key issues (such as policy priorities and instruments). The penalty for sustained failure to reflect such consensus would be failure to continue in office at the next election.

In pluralist societies, the formation of consensus reflects competition between groups to define what is in the public interest. O'Riordan (1982) argues that this perspective on the consensus process makes three assumptions, which in practice only partly hold true:

(a) that interests are freely able to form by coalescing around pivotal points of common purpose,
(b) that they can gain access to policy makers before binding commitments are made, and
(c) that they have a reasonable chance of influencing events if their arguments are strong.

In theory, all members of society have an opportunity to contribute to consensus formation, and hence to the formulation of national parties. In practice, however, consensus formation is elitist in that it is heavily influenced by the power dominant classes (often the wealthy, the educated and articulate, those with influence within the corridors of power). Thus the policies of the state often reflect the class interests and values of the elite groups.

In order to legitimate its authority, the state must act in ways which transcend the dominant class interests and which acknowledge the existence and interests of non-elite sectors of the population. Thus, it is argued, the state must manipulate the consensus process to:

(a) avoid conflict between sectors of the population,
(b) avoid public testing of the influence of elite groups, and
(c) maintain state legitimacy.

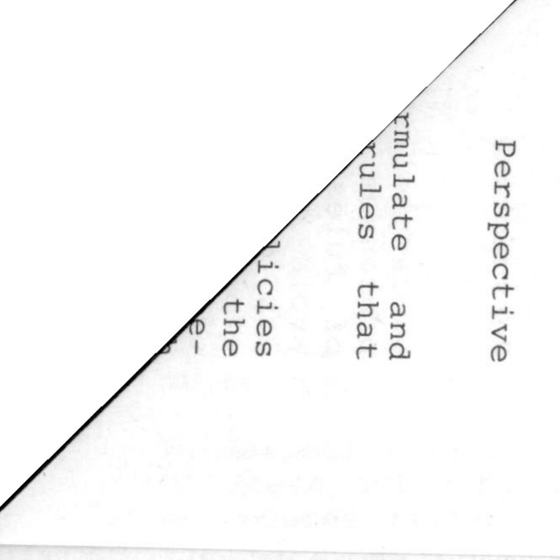

...es that state decision making ...d largely to develop a set ...es that allow the state to ...ems that might delegitimate ...Such 'problems' include the ...ental activism and the rise ...l) politics. Public concern ...ed - at least in part, and ...to national policies.

...3) sees the primary objective ...the formulation of strategic

> *seek to provide what appear to be optimally efficient, value-free solutions to the problems confronting the state. Such mechanisms mean that the state is often less concerned with the nature of society and with setting the goals for its future direction, and is frequently more concerned with maintaining the smooth functioning of the processes it is charged with creating and governing.*

The state thus becomes the manager of the public good. Both the state and consensus formation processes are regulated by procedures, and the creation and implementation of procedures become more important than a specification of desired products or consequences.

In short, the state must be seen to be doing things. If state activities and policies lead towards optimal solutions (e.g. optimal rates of resource use) and equitable distributions (of both benefits and losses), then so much the better. With this perspective, policy formulation is largely a normative process, designed to define approved ranges of what is acceptable in terms of resource exploitation and environmental quality.

CONCLUSIONS

This chapter has sought to provide a background against which the environmental policies of individual countries might be set. It is clear that whilst marked differences in the basis, orientation and implementation of environmental policies between individual countries must be expected, these normally reflect domestic national responses to problems broadly shared by many countries (the 'Environmental Predicament').

This book focuses on contemporary environmental problems, many of which are neither new to mankind nor peculiar to an individual country. However, the changing character, broader distribution, growing magnitude and increasing significance of many of the more pressing problems can often be related - at least in part - to socio-economic changes observed during the 1960s and 1970s. Other key ingredients incude the legacy of environmental legislation introduced over those decades, and the changing technological base in developed countries.

Recent years have witnessed a number of basic changes in understanding of, interest in, and concern for the environment. Typical trends include:

(a) increasing public concern over environmental quality (environmentalism),
(b) greater availability of reliable observational data on existing environments and on rates and patterns of environmental change,
(c) increasing scientific and academic interest in environmental problems and their solution,
(d) increasing political interest in environmental issues and the prospects of enhanced environmental management at both national and international scales,
(e) a better appreciation of the limitations of purely economic perspectives on environmental decision making,
(f) refinement of organisational and institutional dimensions of environmental decision making,
(g) the formulation of appropriate models of decision making in complex, multi-goal, value-based situations (including the 'bounded rationality' model),
(h) a better appreciation of the symbiotic links (in theory and practice) between environmental policies and other national policies (such as those to promote economic growth),
(i) mounting concern over the trans-national nature of many environmental problems (such as acid rain), and greater willingness to harmonise monitoring schemes, contribute to trans-national policy initiatives, and take a broader view on the links between

environment and development,
(j) greater awareness of the increasingly global nature of many environmental problems (such as changing carbon dioxide levels in the atmosphere), and of the need for rational and well co-ordinated international policies and initiatives,
(k) growing international recognition of the links between national environmental policies in developed countries, and possible environmental repercussions in developing countries; the environment-development debate belongs not only to the developing countries, and
(l) the availability of new perspectives on the role of consensus politics, elite groups and normative processes of policy formulation.

The scene is set. The final word of introduction belongs rightly to the Brandt Report (1980), which feared that:

> *few threats to the peace and survival of the human community are greater than those posed by the prospect of cumulative and irreversible degradation of the biosphere on which human life depends.*

REFERENCES

Allen, R. (1980) How to Save the World. Kogan Page, London
Ashby, E. (1978) Reconciling Man with the Environment. Oxford University
Berry, R.J. (1972) Ecology and Ethics. Inter-Varsity Press, London
Black, J. (1976) The Dominion of Man. Edinburgh University Press, Edinburgh
Bowman, T.S. and Fuchs, T. (1981) Environmental coverage in the mass media; a longitudinal survey. International Journal of Environmental Studies 18; 11-22
Bradley, M.D. (1973) Decision making for environmental resources management. Journal of Environmental Management 1; 289-302
Brandt, W. (1980) North-South; A Programme for Survival. Pan, London
Brenner, M.J. (1973) The Political Economy of America's Environmental Dilemma. Lexington Books, Lexington

Bullock, A. and Stallybrass, O. (1977) The Fontana Dictionary of Modern Thought. Fontana, London

Bunyard, P. (1979) Living on a knife-edge; the aftermath of Harrisburg. The Ecologist 9; 97-102

Carson, R. (1962) Silent Spring. Hamilton, New York

Chapman, J.D. (1969) Interactions between man and his resources, 31-42, in Committee on Resources and Man (editors) Resources and Man - a Study and Recommendations. Freeman, San Francisco

Christiansen, G.B. and Haveman, R.H. (1981) The contribution of environmental regulations to the slowdown in productivity growth. Journal of Environmental Economics and Management 8; 381-90

Clayton, K.M. (1971) Reality in conservation. Geographical Magazine 44; 83-4

Commoner, B. (1972) The Closing Circle. Cape, London

Cook, J. and Kaufman, C. (1982) Portrait of a Poison - the 2,4,5-T Story. Pluto Press, London

Cottrell, A. (1978) Environmental Economics. Arnold, London

Cramp, A.B. (1975) Notes towards a Christian critique of secular economic theory. Institute for Christian Studies, Toronto

Deutsch, K.W. (1978) Ecosocial Systems and Ecopolitics. UNESCO, Paris

Dorfman, R. (1982) The lessons of pesticide regulation, 13-29, in W.A. Magat (editor) Reform of Environmental Regulation, Harper, New York

Ducsik, D.W. (editor) (1971) Power, Pollution and Public Policy. MIT Press, Cambridge Massachusetts

Edelson, B.I. (1985) Mission to planet earth. Science 227; 367

Edmunds, S.W. (1981) Environmental policy - bounded rationality applied to unbounded ecological problems. 191-201, in D.E. Mann (editor) Environmental Policy Formation, Lexington Books, Lexington

Ehrlich, P.R. (1972) The Population Bomb. Pan, New York

Ehrlich, P.R. and Ehrlich, A.H. (1972) Population, Resources and Environment. Freeman, San Francisco

Frieberg, J.W. (editor) (1979) Critical Sociology.

Irvington, New York

Garlauskas, A.B. (1975) Conceptual framework of environmental management. Journal of Environmental Management 3; 185-203

Gerasimov, I.P., Armand, D.L. and Yefron, K.M. (1971) Natural Resources of the Soviet Union - their use and renewal. Freeman, San Francisco

Global 2000 (1980) Report to the President of the United States. US Council and Environmental Quality/Pergamon, Oxford

Goudie, A. (1981) The Human Impact. Blackwell, Oxford

Haram, M.S. (1980) Cost benefit analysis; an inadequate basis for health, safety and environmental regulatory decision making. Ecology Law Quarterly 8; 473-531

Hardin, G. (1968) The tragedy of the commons. Science 162, 1243-8

Holdgate, M.W., Kassas, M. and White, G.F. (1982) The World Environment 1972-1982. Tycooly, Dublin

Hourcade, J.C. (1978) Another way out. Mazingira 7; 63-9

Jeffers, J.N.R. (1978) The ecology of resource utilization. Journal of the Operational Research Society 29; 315-21

Komorov, B. (1978) The Destruction of Nature in the Soviet Union. Pluto Press, London

Koo, A.Y.C. (1974) Environmental repercussions and trade theory. Review of Economics and Statistics 56; 235-44

Lorrain-Smith, R. (1982) The nature of environmental management. Journal of Environmental Management 14; 229-36

Maddox, J. (1972) The Doomsday Syndrome. McGraw Hill, London

Magat, W.A. (1982) Introduction. 1-12 in W.A. Magat (editor) Reform of Environmental Regulation. Harper, New York

Malone, T.F. (1976) The role of scientists in achieving a better environment. Environmental Conservation 3; 83-9

Mann, D.E. (editor) (1981) Environmental Policy Formation; the impact of values, ideology and standards. Lexington Books, Lexington

Matthews, W.H. and Perkowski, J.C. (1975) Integrating scientific knowledge for professional education in environmental management. Environmental Conservation 2; 213-22

Meadows, D.H. et al (1972) The Limits to Growth.

Universe, New York
Misham, E.J. (1971) The post war literature on externalities; an interpretative essay. Journal of Economic Literature 9; 1-28
Murphy, E.F. (1977) Environmental bureaucracies appraised. Ekistics 44; 157-63
Myers, N. (1980) The Sinking Ark. Pergamon, Oxford
Offe, C. (1976) Political authority and class structure. in P. Connerton (editor) Critical Sociology. Penguin, New York
Ophuls, W. (1977) Ecology and the Politics of Scarcity. Freeman, San Francisco
O'Riordan, T. (1971) Environmental management. Progress in Geography 3; 172-231
O'Riordan, T. (1976) Environmentalism. Pion, London
O'Riordan, T. (1982) Institutions affecting environmental policy. 103-40, in R.T.N. Flowerdew (editor) Institutions and Geographical Patterns. Croom Helm, London
O'Riordan, T. and Sewell, W.R.D. (1981) From project appraisal to policy review. 1-28 in T. O'Riordan and W.R.D. Sewell (editors) Project Appraisal and Policy Review. Wiley, London
Pearce, D.W. (1976) Environmental Economics. Longman, London
Pearson, C. and Pryor, A. (1978) Environment North and South; an Economic Interpretation. Wiley, New York
Pepper, D. (1984) The Roots of Modern Environmentalism. Croom Helm, London
Pethig, R. (1976) Pollution, welfare and environmental policy in the theory of competitive advantage. Journal of Environmental Economics and Management 2; 160-9
Potter, H.R. and Norville, H.J. (1981) Social values inherent in policy statements; an evaluation of an energy assessment. 177-89, in D.E. Mann (editor) Environmental Policy Formation. Lexington Books, Lexington
Rowland, A.J. and Cooper, P. (1983) Environment and Health. Arnold, London
Sagan, C., Toon, O. and Pollock, J. (1979) Anthropogenic albedo change and the earth's climate. Science 206; 1363
Sandbrook, R. (1984) Opening the environmental debate. 11-21, in D. Wilson (editor) The Environmental Crisis. Heinemann, London
Secrett, C. (1984) Wildlife - an international perspective. 163-86, in D. Wilson (editor)

The Environmental Crisis. Heinemann, London

Shakun, M.F. (1981) Policy making and meaning as design of purposeful system. International Journal of General Systems 7; 235-51

Siebert, H. et al (1980) Trade and Environment; a theoretical enquiry. Elsevier, Amsterdam

Silverberg, R. (1973) The Dodo, the Auk and the Oryx. Penguin, London

Simon, H.A. (1957) Models of Man. Wiley, New York

Simon, J.L. and Kahn, H. (editors) (1984) The Resourceful Earth. Blackwell, Oxford

Vanderpool, C.K. (1981) Environmental policy and social impact assessment ideology. 161-75, in D.E. Mann (editor) Environmental Policy Formation. Lexington Books, Lexington

Ward, B. and Dubos, R. (1971) Only One Earth. Penguin, London

Warren, H.V. (1974) Environmental lead; a survey of its possible physiological significance, Journal of the Biosociological Society 6; 223-38

Wendland, W.M. and Bryson, R.a. (1974) Dating climatic episodes of the Holocene. Quaternary Research 4; 9-24

Wilson, D. (editor) (1984) The Environmental Crisis. Heinemann, London

Wolf, P.C. (1971) Carbon monoxide; measurement and monitoring in urban air. Environmental Science and Technology 5; 212-5

Wood, C. (1982) Implications of the European EIA initiative. ECOS - A Review of Conservation 3; 25-9

World Bank (1984) World Development Report 1984. Oxford University Press, London

Chapter Two

ENVIRONMENTAL POLICIES IN THE UNITED STATES

Melvin G. Marcus

INTRODUCTION

Any attempt to explain environmental policy in the United States must begin with an appreciation that the topic is complex, confusing, replete with contradictions, and probably not explainable in the first place. The fabric of policy is woven from an amazing array of threads, each exerting significant control on the system. They include jurisdictions, land tenure, public attitudes, lobbies, litigation, economics, and the occupant of the White House, to name but a few.

To identify and separate each of these is difficult but discussion of two topics is essential to a basic understanding of how policy originates and is implemented. These are the history and development of environmental attitudes and actions in the United States; and the structure and operation of American government and its associated bureaucracy. These, in turn, are reflections of ongoing socio-economic and political forces. This chapter is organised to provide a background to these two topics and then to describe and evaluate recent environmental policy in the United States.

HISTORY AND DEVELOPMENT OF ENVIRONMENTAL ATTITUDES AND ACTIONS

There are many contradictions and ironies in the ways that Americans have perceived, used, and managed the landscape. On the one hand, the early settlers were struck by the extraordinary beauty and bounty of the land, but on the other they set out to subdue and exploit it. Stuhr finds irony in the fact that "people who had always been denied land and its resources were not, after settling in America, protectively appreciative of it" (Stuhr, 1973, p.69). From the very begining the new Americans wanted to have their cake and to eat it too.

Initially, reactions to expansion and exploitation were scattered and often self-serving. Thus the trappers and frontiersmen who had made their living by careless exploitation of wildlife were the first to decry the passing of the American wilderness into the hands of farmers, livestock raisers, and lumbermen. Much of what might be viewed as early manifestations of an environmental movement were in reality reactions of advocates committed to particular economic pursuits and lifestyles.

It is commonly stated that human society interacts with environment in one of three ways: man over nature, man under nature, and man with nature (Kluckholn and Strodtbeck, 1961; Burton and Kates, 1964). The pre- and post-revolutionary populations of North America were represented by all three of these world views. Many early immigrants, and especially the peasant societies of Hispanic origin, subscribed to the man under nature philosophy, whereas Eskimos and some American Indians believed that humans lived in harmonious interaction with nature. In contrast, the majority of European immigrants came out of an industrialising society and the Judeo-Christian tradition which favoured a man over nature attitude. This latter group soon dominated American development, both philosophically and numerically.

Manifest Destiny and Intellectual Transition

The doctrine of Manifest Destiny (an expansionist attitude based on the richness and seeming boundlessness of the land) was pervasive in America for over 100 years. Manifest Destiny ideally suited the national land tenure policy, which was to put as much of the land as possible into the hands of the people. This was accomplished by sales, grants, and straighforward give-a-ways. At the same time the government satisfied its needs by simultaneously responding to socio-economic pressures for land and, through settlement, establishing sovereignty over contested southern and western lands.

The government during this period managed to remove

itself as much as possible from issues of land management or regulation. Thus many of the property and water laws established in pioneer communities on an ad hoc basis were eventually accepted as state and federal law. Manifest Destiny has not yet wholly disappeared from the national consciousness. The immense energies given to the settlement and agricultural and industrial development of the resource base have imprinted it on the American ethos.

A counterpoint perception, focusing on the concept of 'the balance of nature', began to emerge in the mid-nineteenth century. It is, however, somewhat restricted to the writings and lectures of an intellectual few. The cornerstone was surely George Perkins Marsh's Man and Nature (1864), later retitled The Earth as Modified by Human Action. Marsh has been represented as: "...the first American to lay down for the populace the broad principles of conservation...based upon the doctrine of ecological balance" (Hawkes, 1960, p.11).

A small but influential coterie of intellectuals and conservation-minded scientists began to attract public attention and to influence nineteenth century politicians and decision-makers. These were pioneers who preceded the later environmental movements in the United States. The transcendental writings of Henry David Thoreau, Ralph Waldo Emerson, and others - which expounded the benefits of communion with the natural world - laid the philosophical groundwork whereby many Americans made at least the intellectual transition from a resource exploitation ethic to an aesthetic environmental ethic. This latter approach, which usually encouraged a preservational attitude, was further enhanced by the lectures and publications of environmentalists such as naturalist John Muir, editor-conservationist Robert Underwood Johnson and artist-writer George Catlin.

Scientist-conservationists held a different view. They saw nature in terms of its utility to humans, and so they approached resource management in terms of principles of sustained yield. By the turn of the century, their influence was great and they began to realise their goals in the blossoming of the first major period of environmental action; i.e. the presidential tenure of Theodore

Roosevelt. Because the history of such conservational, preservational, and environmental movements is thoroughly treated elsewhere (Graham, 1971; Hawkes, 1960; Manners and Mikesell, 1974; Nash, 1967, 1968), it will suffice here to describe only briefly the sequence of changing environmental attitudes and policies that have characterised the past eighty or ninety years in the United States.

Theodore Roosevelt and Early Federal Efforts

The administration of Theodore Roosevelt (1901-1908) was the first concerted attempt by a federal administration to exercise broad scale control over the land. Roosevelt - himself an avid outdoorsman - was a highly visible and persuasive politician and, for the first time, there was public awareness of major environmental problems and policy.

Roosevelt was much influenced by dedicated but practical naturalists and scientists. Typical of these were politician-forester Gifford Pinchot, geologist John Wesley Powell, soil scientist Nathanial Shaler and wild life champion George Bird Grinnell. Roosevelt's tenure was characterised by a rush of environmental actions - including the organisation of national and international conservation commissions and conferences, and the passing of important legislation relating to wildlife, forests, fish and water. This period was also an important turning point wherein the federal government consciously moved from a policy of general land dispersal to the beginnings of planned land withdrawal.

While the public was widely aware of the President's hunting adventures, they paid less attention to the increasing federal role that he was developing in the management and ownership of western lands. The emergence of government as a significant creator of environmental policy, and the increasing importance of nature and outdoor oriented organisations (such as the Audubon Society and the Sierra Club) were results of the efforts of a relatively few individuals. Not surprisingly, these tended to be highly educated persons who also could afford leisure to experience nature. Clearly, the early U.S. environmentalists were an elitist group.

Contemporary opponents of protective environmental policies argue that little has changed in this respect. The evidence suggests, however, that there has been continuously expanding public support for intelligent environmental actions.

The New Deal: The Government as Resource Manager

World War I brought an abrupt halt to practically all conservational measures. If there was an environmental policy, it was to exploit the environment as quickly as possible to support the war effort.

Post-war administrations sustained this policy for twelve further years under the flag of laissez faire economic growth. This exploitation came to a halt with the advent of the Great Depression in 1929, but it was the inauguration of Franklin Delano Roosevelt as President in 1933, which ushered in a new era in American environmental policy.

A number of natural disasters in the 1920's and early 1930's, each closely interrelated with human uses of the land, had already primed the nation to support conservational measures. Floods regularly wrought destruction along American river systems and the devastating Johnstown (Pennsylvania) flood - perhaps the best known of this century - focused public attention on the problem. The depletion of Pacific Coast salmon fisheries and accelerated soil erosion in the southeastern states exacerbated the situation. Finally, a devastating drought spread across the Great Plain to create the legendary Dust Bowl. Coupled with the near-complete collapse of the economy, a political climate existed in which Roosevelt was able to initiate radical changes in national and environmental policy.

Roosevelt's tenure, especially the first two terms, saw the initiation of massive national and regional projects designed to combine preservational and utilitarian conservation goals. These were introduced under the aegis of his "New Deal", as an effort to simultaneously alleviate unemployment, regenerate a collapsed economy, and create a national programme of integrated resource management. The effort was comprehensive and, as Nash (1968, p.147) states:

> *During the 1930s no resource escaped consider-*

> *ation as a subject for conservation. More significant still is the fact that, although the approach was comprehensive, the record of achievement in the conservation of any single resource surpassed that of any previous administration.*

The impact of the New Deal years on the United State's environmental policies, as well as its political and socio-economic structure, has been lasting and controversial. A particularly significant step was the placement of much greater control of environmental management and decision-making in the hands of the federal government. Tremendous regulatory and administrative powers were given to both the traditional agencies (such as the Departments of Agriculture and Interior) and newly created ones (such as the employment-oriented Works Progress Administration, and the regional Tennessee Valley Authority (TVA)). The TVA, depending on one's point of view, was either a pace-setting example of integrated watershed planning and management or a socialistic attack on the free market system and jurisdictional rights of individual states.

The TVA was but one of many programmes that approached land planning from a regional perspective, often using river basins as the rational management unit. Simultaneously, there was an ever-increasing return of marginal and sub-marginal areas into the federal pool of public domain lands. This explosion of resource-based activity carried with it the creation of a massive new federal bureaucracy which has proliferated to the present.

The existence of this federal infrastructure has had significant and sometimes contradictory effects. For example, the pure size and inertia of many agencies perpetuates philosophical and operational policies, despite ongoing changes of party and personality in the executive branch.

Public Participation and Expanding Federalism

It appears that environmental/conservational cycles in the United States follow in periods of roughly a third of a century, with eight to ten years of environmental commitment and rather frantic activity, followed by twenty to twenty-five years of inaction or even retreat from accomplishments of the earlier effort (Marcus, 1981).

This occurred between the Roosevelt eras and again between 1940 and the late 1960s. It is almost as if each generation has to rediscover the fragile relationship between man and landscape.

In any event, following the resource exploitation associated with both World War II and the twenty subsequent years of post-war boom, a new environmental groundswell swept the nation. This time, however, the causes and manner of its emergence were different. Two factors stand out. First, the new environmentalists led, not followed, politicians and decision-makers in the drive for new national policies and legislation. The movement's energies came from a grass roots constituency, much of it youthful and vocal. Second, the country's educated population base had expanded dramatically, providing the environmental cause with a larger and more diversified clientele. The old pejorative label of environmental elitism had been significantly weakened.

This new environmentalism, while it had peaked by 1973, set the tone for the 1970s and 1980s. The struggles over current environmental policy are essentially a battle between those who accept and those who reject the legacy of that era; contemporary policy merely reflects the state of that battle. Although the particulars of this policy will be addressed later, its recent roots require discussion because American environmental action must be appreciated in the context of a complex convergence of political and socio-economic forces.

Rachel Carson's (1962) Silent Spring is generally seen as the benchmark event. Her book, which showed significant links between the agricultural use of chemicals and insecticides and the well-being of the entire faunal hierarchy, had an immense impact. Graham has fairly represented it as the first "ecological" book to reach a wide audience and as prompting the federal government to take action against water and air pollution - as well as against persistent insecticides - several years before it otherwise would have moved (Graham, 1971, p.315).

Environmental policies were not, however, changed immediately. The 1960s were a complex period in American history: counter-cultures multiplied, university students were for the first time a major political force, the civil rights movement was at its peak, urban ghetto discontent sometimes erupted in riots, and there was a continuous furor over the U.S. military commitment in Vietnam. Environmental issues took a back seat, not coming into focus until after a series of "Earth Days" on university campuses in 1968 and 1969. By then a populist base was ready to take on environmental issues with zeal and experience garnered in pursuit of other causes. They knew how to organise, they knew how to bring political pressure, and they joined liberally-oriented environment or nature organisations in droves.

There is no doubt that the press and television contributed to the situation. Genuine enough issues existed and the media and environmentalists concentrated on three:

(a) the 1969 oil spills from offshore wells along the Santa Barbara (California) coast, which took a costly (and well-televised) toll of birds and sea life,
(b) the ongoing eutrophication of Lake Erie, and
(c) the impending construction of a trans-Alaskan oil pipe line across a 1200 km spectrum of unstable and fragile landscape.

Public pressure was intense and in 1969 Congress, with the blessing of the Nixon administration, passed the National Environmental Policy Act (NEPA) (PL 91-190). The National Environmental Policy Act was really a general statement of purpose (PL 91-190):

> *To declare a national policy which will encourage productive and enjoyable harmony between man and his environment; to promote efforts which will prevent or eliminate damage to the environment and biosphere and stimulate the health and welfare of man; to enrich the understanding of the ecological systems and natural resources important to the Nation; and to establish a Council on Environmental Quality.*

A major result of this legislation was the creation of the Environmental Protection Agency (EPA) and the concomitant requirement for Environmental Impact Statements (EISs) for any project falling under the areal, regulatory, or fiscal jurisdiction of the national government. The following years saw a proliferation of laws, regulations, and court decisions which collectively enhanced the intent of NEPA.

The bloom of environmental legislation carried through to the mid 1970s, but in growing conflict with reactive social and economic forces. The inertia of post-NEPA laws has managed, however, to maintain a higher profile of environmental activity than was typical of the anti-conservational periods following the two Roosevelt administrations. The structure and functional behaviour of American government are significant factors in this regard.

GOVERNMENT AND POLICY IMPLEMENTATION

The organisation and philosophy of American government significantly affect the manner in which environmental policy is realised and implemented. The subject is extremely complex, but a brief and simplified description is necessary to put current policies and actions in perspective.

The hierarchical structure of governments and their associated functions vary from state to state, county to county, and locality to locality; only the umbrella of the federal government remains constant. Thus while national laws, regulations, and policies may set patterns and limits generally, each lower unit has considerable autonomy and hence an ability to act and enact independently. There is an assumption, however, that federal policies override those of states and municipalities; this has led to a history of recurring battles over so-called "states' rights".

National environmental regulations tend to supercede such rights, although state and local statutes may expand and/or strengthen requirements. As a result, some states and municipalities (through either inaction or litigation) may attempt to set aside the national intent, while others - such as California - may implement even more stringent regulations.

Any project which crosses political boundaries

- such as a pipeline, power transmission line, or highway - will encounter changing environmental regulations from one jurisdiction to the next. This confusion of requirements is often attacked as counterproductive to economical resource development. A dramatic example was the 1979 cancellation of a SOHIO Corporation pipeline which had been intended to carry Alaskan crude oil from California to refineries in Texas. SOHIO executives claimed that they were simply unable to cope with the hundreds of environmental regulations that beset them - ranging from municipal ordinances at tanker offloading in Long Beach, to federal protection of endangered species that might be encountered along the route. On the other hand, environmentalists saw this as a smokescreen to obscure the real reasons for cancellation, which they claimed were economic and related to the world petroleum market.

The National System

The government of the United States is organised into a three-part check and balance system consisting of executive, legislative and judicial branches. Any policy (and its implementation) is the product of usually complex interactions between these units. While synergistic in concept, it is expected that the branches will sometimes take adversarial roles. Environmental policy has been one of the most difficult topics handled by the three branches in recent years. This is not only because of the immense differences of opinion that characterise the public sector, but also because of conflicts between and within government agencies.

The passage of the National Environmental Policy Act, which was signed into law on New Year's Day, 1970, illustrates how the system works. Enacted in response to accelerating environmental degradation and concommitant public demands for action, Congress set a "motherhood and apple pie" statement of environmental concern into law. As O'Riordan has pointed out "There is little doubt that few, if any, Congressmen and even fewer resource managing agencies had any idea of its likely impact on environmental policymaking that New Year's morning " (O'Riordan, 1976, p.282).

NEPA has since become "our national charter for protection of the environment" (Council for Environmental Quality, 1978), and the mechanism whereby the Environmental Protection Agency (EPA) was created. This agency, with its mandate to enforce environmental regulations and its requirements for Environmental Impact Statements, has since intruded itself into almost every facet of American life.

Yet the initial law was only a few pages in length and mostly rhetorical in context. It remained for the administrative branch to develop a management system to implement the law and to establish a regulatory system compatible with it. As the appropriate agency (in this case EPA) develops a program, it is "tested" through publication of proposed procedures and requirements in the Federal Register. Anyone who monitors the Federal Register (and it is a monumental publication of tens of thousands of pages) may respond with suggestions or challenges. In the best of worlds, these prove useful in officially declaring the final regulations or procedures, which are then also published in the Register.

Conflicts over Appropriations

Implementations of policy requires money which must be obtained through co-operative efforts of the administration and Congress. Either can scuttle a program by withholding or minimising appropriations. The National Climate Act of 1978 (Pl 95-367) is an interesting case in point. Passed during the last months of a devastating three-year drought in western and midwestern states, it was intended to focus efforts on the generally neglected areas of agricultural, industrial, and urban climatology as well as climatic change.

After passage, however, two issues weakened the Act: Public and congressional interest quickly declined when the drought waned; and the established meterorology leadership (composed largely of atmospheric physicists and/or traditional station forecasters) showed little enthusiasm for the law and its mandate. If anything, given ongoing cuts in government spending, the Climate Act was viewed as threatening to existing forecasting and global modelling programs.

A situation thus developed whereby Congress no longer had reasons to make climate a priority appropriation and the National Oceanic and Atmospheric Administration (NOAA) had no interest in pressing the case. As a result, the environmental policy inherent in the National Climate Act has never been realised because interest was not sustained by administration, legislature or public. The program is perpetuated in law, but languishes. Its appropriations are only a few hundred thousand dollars annually and the Act's best hope for revival is recurring drought or some other climatic hazard sufficiently destructive to rekindle public concern.

The history of the Environmental Education Act of 1970 (PL 91-516) similarly illustrates how proposed policy can be eroded through the appropriation process. As with NEPA, PL 91-516 emerged at a time of high environmental consciousness in the United States. It was the realisation of a major environmentalist's goal: to enhance environmental awareness and management through incorporation of environmental education in the large fabric of the nation's formal and informal educational systems. Designed to provide policy guidelines and funding for development and diffusion of innovative educational methods, the Act would help instill a sense of interdisciplinary understanding of landscape in the American psyche from cradle to grave. An Office of Environmental Education was created to accomplish these goals. Unhappily neither the law nor environmental education lived up to initial expectations.

How did this happen? There is a litany of reasons, including:

a. discipline-based resistance to interdisciplinary activity,
b. unwillingness of the educational establishment, especially the elementary and secondary systems, to alter curricula,
c. absence of a corps of trained and experienced specialists to initiate new programs,
d. confusion of the larger purposes of environmental education with public relations campaigns to prevent forest fires, reduce litter, and recycle waste,
e. focus of programs on traditional natural science topics, to the exclusion of significant socio-economic and political relationships, and
f. lack of universally accepted core themes which give consistency and identity to the subject.

Given these obstacles, the bottom line remains that the Environmental Education Act was never properly funded. Congress authorised in excess of $155 million to be spent specifically on environmental education during the fiscal period 1971-1983. In reality, funds were appropriated sufficient only to operate the Office of Environmental Education and to finance some modest research projects (see Table 2.1). This failure of federal support had been anticipated as early as 1971 when Clay Schoenfeld pointed out in an editorial in the *Journal of Environmental Education*: "It is one thing for Congress to authorise monies: it is another thing for those monies in fact to be appropriated."

Only a few Congressmen seriously supported environmental education and the new Office of Environmental Education (which has since disappeared from the federal organisational chart) was an unwanted child within the multi-billion dollar Department of Education establishment. With no major pre-existing position in the federal system and a diffused public constituency, environmental education never had the necessary political or academic clout to garner large appropriations. Thus, what was initially seen as a significant national policy was found wanting by those who had to implement it. They (including both administrations and legislature) sentenced environmental education to a slow, wasting death by fiscal starvation.

This is somehow sadly summarised in my recollection of an important Program Director in the National Science Foundation's Educational Directorate angrily claiming that "there is no such thing as environmental education...it is not a discipline and there is no reason to support it".

Role of the Judicial System

Congress seldom enacts laws which spell out the details of its intent. As a result, as we have seen, it becomes incumbent on the assigned administrative agency to officially declare regulations and establish procedures. Because these are often viewed as "too strict" or "not strict enough" by opposing interests, it follows that courts are asked to review the regulations and to interpret the intent of Congress.

TABLE 2.1 Authorisations and Appropriations: Environmental Education (1,000s U.S. $)*

Year	PL 91-516		Year	PL 93-278		Year	PL 95-561	
	Auth.	Approp.		Auth.	Approp.		Auth.	Approp.
1971	5,000	1,928	1975	5,000	1,895	1979	5,000	3,500
1972	15,000	3,514	1976	10,000	2,543	1980	7,000	n.a.
1973	25,000	3,093	1977	15,000	3,483	1981	9,000	n.a.
1974	25,000	2,263	1978	15,000	3,500	1982	11,000	n.a.
						1983	13,000	n.a.

*By 1980, appropriations that had been authorised in the Environmental Education Act Amendments of 1978 were difficult to identify. This was because of the absorption and eventual disappearance of the Office of Environmental Education into the mammoth Department of Education.

Sources: U.S. Code (1976) and U.S. Code (1976) Supplement IV; Code of Federal Regulations (1981); The Budget of the U.S. Government: Fiscal Year Appendices (1973-1983).

Other litigation arises because the new regulations may be seen as in conflict with existing statutes and procedures. NEPA alone was responsible for 200 major law suits in its first three years (Platt, 1978). Resolution of such issues can give rise to delays of several years. Nevertheless the judicial role in the regulatory process is an important one: it serves to protect the public from over-zealous agencies on the one hand and from derelict ones on the other.

Two counterpoint examples of the judiciary's impact on implementation of environmental policy are illustrated by the Calvert Cliffs Decision and the Alabama Power Decision. The former strengthened the hand of the Environmental Protection Agency; the latter has seriously delayed full implementation of air quality standards.

In the Calvert Cliffs case, the proposed construction of a nuclear generation plant in Maryland was challenged as not being responsive to the intent of NEPA. The defendant, the Atomic Energy Commission (AEC), argued that the plans and site development had been initiated by January, 1970, and that the plant was subject only to pre-existing AEC regulations. The courts quashed this "grandfather clause" concept, ruling that proposed actions not completed by 1970 were fair game for the impact evaluation process. At the same time, the legitimacy of Environmental Impact Statements was established. Recall that neither EPA nor Environmental Impact Statements were explicitly created by the National Environmental Policy Act (although it was the vehicle by which they were created).

The Calvert Cliffs Decision not only verified that Environmental Impact Statements would henceforth be an essential component of agency decision-making, but it also broadened the scope of the EIS:

(a) to establish, as necessary, standards more strict than those of the initiating agency, and
(b) to require that non-environmental issues (e.g. socio-economic questions) be balanced against the environmental impacts.

These conditions subsequently diffused across the entire environmental assessment arena.

The Alabama Power Decision, on the other hand, has delayed the implementation of much of the Clean Air Act and its Amendments. During the 1970s, an extremely complex set of regulations and procedures was developed to control the emission and dispersion of polluting particulates and aerosols. Because airborne pollutants have high transport-ability, these regulations encompass large areas beyond the polluting sources. The rules have been formally designated, therefore, to establish both national ambient air quality standards and land classes within which differing maximum levels of pollution are permitted.

Construction and/or operating licenses will only be issued to facilities (generating 100 tonnes of pollutants per year) that can demonstrate - through several layers of analysis and reporting - that all potential impacts have been identified and that the project will provide means to mitigate them. Otherwise, no permit will be issued. The interrelationship between state and federal agencies and their regulations is critical during the licensing stage. Technically, each state is supposed to set and administer its own air pollution regulations; these rules, called a State Implementation Plan, are subject to EPA approval - which will not be forthcoming if standards do not equal or exceed the federal ones.

By mid-1979, about half of the states appeared to have established plans which would meet with EPA approval. A consortium of power companies took EPA to court, however, claiming that the regulations were, among other things, unreasonable and not in line with congressional intent. Adversaries also appeared to testify that the regulations were not strong enough. In December, 1979, the so-called Alabama Power Decision (U.S. Court of Appeals, 1979) was handed down, directing the Environmental Protection Agency to redraft its principal licensing regulations and standards. All state plans were put in abeyance subject to the arrival of the new federal rules.

Meanwhile, there have been several years of ad hoc decision-making and arguably poorer monitoring of air pollution. While the Court congratulated EPA on its efforts to improve the environment, the judicial process clearly has dampened those very efforts.

RECENT ENVIRONMENTAL LEGISLATION

Two ways to view the current condition of environmental policy in the United States are:

(a) in terms of the effect of environmental legislation enacted and amended during the 1970s, and
(b) from the perspective of current and ongoing political and socio-economic battles that characterise the environmental management field.

The former represents current, legal reality; the latter identifies the pushes and pulls that work to shape future policy. Sometimes, however, because the law trickles down slowly through a cumbersome bureaucratic hierarchy, the distinctions between reality and rhetoric are blurred.

Law as Policy

Insofar as existing laws represent policy, the United States remains strongly committed to rigorous controls over reckless exploitation and unthinking development of the resource base. The National Environmental Policy Act was only the first of a series of environmentally-related laws enacted during the 1970s. These cut across the spectrum of human uses of nature, ranging from control of pollutants to health and safety practices to protection of endangered flora and fauna. A selected sample of such federal laws is provided in Table 2.2. All hold the basic NEPA mandate in common; that is, to protect and conserve the quality of the ecosystem through careful regulation, management, and even retrieval of resources back into the public domain.

The degree to which these Acts have been an effective expression of policy varies. We have already seen how lack of either federal or public commitment weakened the Environmental Education Act and the National Climate Act. Conversely, other Acts have fared well because of strong, sometimes zealous, support by federal agencies and advocacy organisations. The Clean Air Act and the Endangered Species Act are good examples. Indeed, the latter has been so successful that a backlash has set in; there is now less willingness to see major projects halted for the protection of what many persons perceive to be obscure and insignifi-

TABLE 2.2 Selected Federal Laws which significantly influence Environmental Management and Reflect Environmental Policy

Law and Administrating Agency	Date	Selected Aspects
National Environmental Policy Act (NEPA), PL 91-190; Environmental Protection Agency	1970	Established Council for Environmental Quality; led to Environmental Protection Agency and Environmental Impact Statements to accompany development in any way related to federal land, licensing, or financing.
Air Quality Act, PL 90-148	1967	To protect and enhance the nation's air quality; set standards for designated pollutants; established visibility standards.
Clean Air Act, PL 91-604	1970	
Amendments, PL 93-15	1973	
PL 93-319	1974	
PL 95-95	1977	
PL 95-190;	1977	
Environmental Protection Agency		
Clean Water Act, PL 92-500	1972	Established national water quality standards, enforcement and research mechanics; focused primarily on surface waters.
Amendments PL 95-217	1977	
PL 95-576;	1977	
Environmental Protection Agency		

Continued...

TABLE 2.2 (continued)

Law and Administrating Agency	Date	Selected Aspects
Safe Drinking Water Act PL 93-523 Amendments, PL 95-190; Environmental Protection Agency	1974 1977	Established national primary drinking water standards, maintaining enforcement umbrella over contamination problems; primary focus on ground water.
Endangered Species Act, PL 93-740 Amendments, 16 U.S.C. 1532 Department of Interior Fish and Wildlife Service	1973 1978	316A and B laws deal with impingement and entrapment vis à vis thermal pollution, water screens, etc. Law generally deals with identification and inventory of threatened or endangered flora and fauna providing appropriate protective and mitigating measures.
Noise Control Act, PL 92-574 Environmental Protection Agency	1972	Governs community noise standards and problems; affects operations of both fixed and mobile equipment.
Wilderness Act, PL 88-577; Forest Service Department of Agriculture	1964	Established a National Wilderness System by withdrawal of wilderness areas with intent to preserve unimpaired; exceptions allowed for previous uses in some cases.

Continued...

TABLE 2.2 (continued)

Law and Administrating Agency	Date	Selected Aspects
Federal Land Management Policy Act PL 94-579; Bureau of Land Management	1976	Established review and inventory of all federal lands for determination of future use, jurisdiction, management, etc. Sect. 603 required review of all roadless areas of 2025 ha. or more for wilderness suitability.
Construction Safety Act PL 87-581 Amendments, PL 91-54; Department of Labor	1962 1969	Affects transmission line construction, operation, and procedures.
Federal Mine Safety and Health Act, PL 92-164 Amendments, PL 92-203 PL 95-239; Occupational Safety and Health Administration	1972 1972 1977	Established operational, protective standards for health and safety in mining; amendments provide black lung benefits.
Surface Mining and Control Act 30 U.S.C. 1201 Exec. Order; Department of Interior	1977	Sect. 710 gave complete authority to Reservation tribes to promulgate rules and regulations; allows land reclamation costs to be passed on to consumers, regulates mineral exploration.

Continued...

TABLE 2.2 (continued)

Law and Administrating Agency	Date	Selected Aspects
Resource Conservation and Recovery Act, PL 94-580	1976	Defines hazardous waste and how best to dispose, store, and transport it.
Federal Insecticide, Fungicide and Rodenticide Act Amendments, PL 94-140; Environmental Protection Agency	1972 1975	Controls selection and application of chemicals.
Hazardous Materials Transportation Act, PL 93-633; Department of Transportation	1975	Mandates training of shippers, transporters and receivers of hazardous materials; defines use of shipping documents, vehicle labels, containers, etc.
Toxic Substances Control Act PL 94-469 Environmental Protection Agency	1976	Cradle-to-grave control of toxic chemicals; affects marketing, distribution and uses.
Environmental Education Act PL 91-516; Amendments, PL 93-278 PL 94-273 PL 95-561; Office of Environmental Education	1970 1974 1976 1978	Establish education programs to encourage understanding of ecological balance and environmental quality.

Continued...

TABLE 2.2 (Continued)

Law and Administrating Agency	Date	Selected Aspects
National Climate Act PL 95-367 National Oceanic and Atmospheric Administration	1978	Impact assessment of socio-economic consequences of climate variation; process and prediction research; improved data and information services.

Source: Expanded from Marcus (1981).

cant species of fish and fowl.

No act more clearly demonstrates the conflicts that exist between commitment to policy and marketplace realities than the Clean Air Act (CAA) and its several Amendments. The essential intent of the CAA is to insure that air (as a finite resource) will remain relatively healthy and unpolluted. Potentially, it is one of the most powerful pieces of environmental legislation that has been enacted in the United States. Within the law and its formally declared regulations, the federal government has the ability to delay, prevent, or transform the nature of many kinds of resource extraction, energy production, industrial development and construction.

The past fifteen years of air quality regulations, however, reveal the public ambivalence that accompanies efforts to implement policy. Everyone is in favour of clean air, especially when they are breathing it...until it impinges adversely on their life style or income. Clean air is expensive in an urbanised, industrialised society. For example, the United States leads the world in energy consumption, much of it from coal-fired power plants. These are high intensity pollution sources and the cost of pollution abatement at these plants is immense. Inevitably it is reflected in everyone's monthly rates bills.

Since power plants are often hundreds of kilometres from areas of consumption, an "out-of-sight, out-of-mind" principle comes into play: the public becomes less committed to improvement of air quality and more dedicated to a reduction of their electric rates. It takes a diligent regulatory agency to persist in the face of such sentiments. It is in such situations that environmental advocacy groups (such as the Sierra Club and the National Wildlife Federation) perform a watchdog function and shore up the government's resolve.

Any number of similar cases can be cited. There are communities which are economically dependent on mining and smelting; continuing operations and employment are the primary concern of the local population, not clean air or the host of other health, safety, and environmental regulations that affect them. These tend to loom important only after some hazard has taken its toll. And then there is the automobile. It is the primary pollution source in most American cities but also one of the most difficult to control. Codes vary from state to state and federal emision standards simply do not do the job. Because costs are passed down to individual car owners, the public tends to resist tougher regulations; many, in fact, go to great lengths to circumvent existing ones.

Thus policy is being constantly bent and reworked, often in response to the public mood, attitudes of the current administration, and the state of the economy. Also, the implementation of policy is continually influenced by changing technology, new research results, vested interest lobbies, and (as we have seen with the Alabama Power Decision) litigation. In any event, unless the law is changed, the Clean Air Act and its Amendments remains in place as a national statement of environmental policy; its enforcement may wax and wane but its basic mandate remains a powerful deterrent.

A similar scenario could be written for almost any other piece of environmental legislation. There is almost always resistance to regulation, but policy is usually implemented and accepted if funding and commitment are present. In fact, laws, once in place, are not easily changed and a given policy may stand long after changing conditions have diminished its utility. A classic example is the perpetuation of the various Homestead Acts, which allowed citizens to take possession of public domain lands within certain constraints. Although these Acts played a major role in settling the American West in the late 19th Century, most arable land had been taken by 1900 and subsequent homesteaders occupied marginal lands. The resultant land damage was not seriously addressed until passage of the Taylor Grazing Act in 1934.

CURRENT ENVIRONMENTAL CONFLICTS

Environmental policy is in a continual state of flux as vested interests fight to alter its scope and power. Environmentalists seek more rigorous laws and regulations; others seek to weaken them. Such current environmental conflicts can be grouped into three broad areas:

(a) questions relating to the status and validity

of scientific research in the environmental field,

(b) the incumbent administration's philosophical position and its interpretation and enforcement of the law, and

(c) arguments over conflicting rights of government and private sectors.

All three areas are interdependent and changes in one area lead to changes in all the others.

Status of Scientific Research

Scientific studies of the environment are supposedly the basis upon which policy and regulations are established. Unfortunately the validity and rationale of many of these studies is often called into question. This is true both for regulatory standards (such as those for air quality or ground water toxins) and for scientific evidence that leads to the initiation of policy.

The former is exemplified by arguments against clean air regulations wherein it is held that:

(a) EPA pollutant diffusion models are inaccurate and unrealistic,

(b) there is not a demonstrable, direct link between maximum allowable pollutant levels and health,

(c) the nationwide application of a single set of standards does not take into account regional environmental differences.

The use of so-called scientific evidence to initiate new policy and legislation can also lead to controversy. For example, a major dispute currently rages over the sources and dispersion of acid rain. Everyone agrees that acid rain exists and that it is environmentally destructive. Although a majority of scientists appear to agree that the Midwestern and Great Lakes industrial belt is a primary culprit, many investigators argue that this is not clearly proven. One cannot help but note that significant reduction of acid rain sources would take a massive economic toll of the industries concerned.

The problem is often that the data base is insufficient to draw irrefutable conclusions. It is reminiscent of the early arguments over the health hazards involved in smoking. The evidence showed a probable connection between cigarettes and health; the tobacco industry argued it was not an absolute connection. Thus there is sometimes a tendency for the objectivity of science to become obscured by who is consulting for whom. Meanwhile, policy often waits in vain for conclusions of science that have been chiselled in granite.

Administrative Philosophy and Interpretation

In the United States the executive branch is subject to elective change every four years. The longest one person can serve in office is eight years, although that has not happened since the presidency of Dwight Eisenhower in the 1950's. There is thus the opportunity for frequent change of policy since even successive presidents from the same political party will vary in philosophy. The President's greatest power to implement change is through Cabinet and agency appointments. If persuasive and sufficiently committed to change, these appointees may overcome the inertia of the entrenched bureaucracy. The administration of Ronald Reagan has been particularly effective in this regard.

The successes of the Reagan administration were due partly to a general public backlash against what was seen as excessive government interference in resource development and industry. The root causes of this reaction are complex. Inflation, increased unemployment and rising energy costs during the previous administration were no doubt important issues. Inconsistent and sometimes unrealistic operation of the environmental regulatory system also contributed to public disenchantment.

Perhaps the appointments which have most significantly affected recent environmental policy were those within the agencies that manage land in the eleven conterminous western states and Alaska. Not counting Alaska, where the federal presence is almost overwhelming, federal ownership in the western states represents roughly 163 million of 305 million hectares (53.5 percent). The proportion ranges from a low of 35 percent in Washington to a high of 89 percent in Nevada. The Departments of Interior and Agriculture control the larger portion of this land through the Bureaus of Land Management and Indian Affairs (BLM and BIA) and the Forest Service (USFS) respectively.

Because BLM and USFS control the allocation of mining, grazing, and timbering rights on their land, agency interpretation of land management policies is critical. The Reagan appointees(particularly James Watt as Secretary of Interior) caused major shifts in management practices. Earlier administrations had worked towards increasingly restrictive conservation practices; the Reagan administration has moved to greater exploitative access of the private sector on public domain lands and it has released protected lands for development. These actions reflect a laissez faire, business oriented philosophy applied to environment. They also represent the imposition of a very specific interpretation of existing land, water and mining laws on the responsible agencies.

Two examples of change occurring between administrations are the disposition of federally owned coal reserves and the designation of wilderness areas. Earlier administrations, including those of both Republican and Democratic Parties, had assiduously protected large coal reserve areas from development. Secretary Watt, on the other hand, released thousands of square kilometres for private purchase of coal mining rights. This was done in the face of a national coal glut, little economic interest or demand on the part of the coal industry, and the spectre of untold environmental damage that would accompany the surface mining operations.

A similar shift occurred when the Federal Land Management Policy Act of 1976 (Table 2.2) was brought into law under the Republican administration of Gerald Ford and initially administered under a Democratic executive, Jimmy Carter. Both worked to maximise the number of roadless areas that might eventually be designated Wilderness Areas. The thrust of the Reagan administration, however, has been to reduce the number of parcels that might be so protected.

Environmental policy has few teeth without enforcement. Commitment to enforcement follows from administrative attitudes and interpretations. However, even the most ambitious environmental policemen are constrained by manpower and appropriations. The Forest Service, for example, is badly undermanned considering that it holds responsibility for enforcement of a battery of activities on USFS lands: grazing, watershed management, lumbering, wildlife control, mining and recreation. Enforcement cannot possibly come up to standard in such a situation.

Another important factor is that actual enforcement usually occurs at the local or regional level where departures from national policy are not unknown. Staff may simply make realistic adjustments to local conditions. On the other hand, some regulators may "look the other way" more often than is appropriate. American environmental policy has been subject to such interpretations involving inadequate enforcement of toxic waste removal. A scandal ensued and several senior staff of the Environmental Protection Agency (including the Director) resigned under pressure. The problem with such cases is that the public is never certain whether the appointees were overzealous in their interpretation of what they thought to be the administration's hidden agenda, or whether they accurately represent the President's position.

Rights and Jurisdiction

Questions of the jurisdiction and rights of federal, state and local government and the private sector have been argued since the beginning of the republic. Although debate has ebbed and flowed with changing political climates for 200 years, the overall tendency has been towards a reduction of state and municipal rights and a strengthening of the federal (i.e. the public's) position. This is particularly important to environmental policy in that land/water planning and management units can supercede state and other boundaries. This has obvious advantages for river management, national parks and forests, and hydro-electric grids. Conversely, the states are deprived of revenue when they cannot control lands for lease or sale.

Two recent cases in point are the court-awarded acquisition of offshore oil site control and revenue by the federal government, and the attempt by some states to acquire lands presently held by the Bureau of Land Management. The latter phenomenon has been most dramatically manifested in Nevada, where the state legislature has passed a law reclaiming federal land. The courts have yet to honour this so-called "Sagebrush Rebellion".

Lastly, the rights of private individuals and businesses remain in debate. The nation has moved gradually but inexorably towards a position whereby private interests must not only operate within prescribed constraints on public domain, but also behave in an environmentally sound manner on private property. Ground water and air quality rules, which protect adjoining areas, exemplify this trend.

CONCLUSIONS

Despite ever-changing laws, regulations, and attitudes, environmental policy in the United States has developed as a cornerstone of national governance. Given impetus by the administrations of Theodore and Franklin Roosevelt, environmental policy has been historically related to land tenure and water rights practices. As these resources became increasingly scarce and threatened, the role of federal management and intervention grew. Indeed, the United States was an innovator in the development of its National Parks system and the organisation of regional river basin projects. Both concepts have been successfully exported to many countries.

More recently, the National Environmental Policy Act of 1970 has been the benchmark legislation from which all other laws and regulations have flowed. Born of a grass roots movement, with advocates from the full spectrum of American society, it is the most significant of all environmental legislation because it philosophically commits the nation to maintaining the health and well-being of the total ecosystem. All the rest is nothing more than means to achieve those ends.

There is, perhaps, some irony in the fact that the most conspicuous resource consumer of modern times has asserted leadership in development of a national environmental philosophy, but the intent is sincere enough. The laws that have followed tend to stay in place, but they are always subject to change and repeal. The future will see a continuing struggle between those who would enrich the spirit of NEPA and those who would erode it.

United States

REFERENCES

Burton, I. and Kates, R.W. (1964) The perception of natural hazards in resource management, Natural Resources Journal, 3: 412-441

Council on Environmental Quality (1978) National Environmental Policy Act - Implementation of procedural provisions; Final Regulations, Federal Register, 43: 55978-56007

Graham, F., Jr. (1971) Man's Dominion: The Story of Conservation in America, M. Evans, New York

Hawkes, H.B. (1960) The paradoxes of the conservation movement, Twenty-Fourth Annual Frederich William Reynolds Lecture, University of Utah Press, Salt Lake City

Kluckholn, F.R. and Strodtbeck, F.L. (1961) Variations in Value Orientations, Row-Peterson, Evanston, Illinois

Manners, I.R. and Mikesell, M.W. (editors) (1974) Perspectives on Environment, Commission on College Geography Publication No. 13, Association of American Geographers, Washington D.C.

Marcus, M.G. (1981) Federal impacts on energy development and environmental management in the American west. In G.W. Hoffman (editor), Federalism and Regional Development, University of Texas Press, Austin, 528-566

Marsh, G.P. (1864) Man and Nature, Scribners, New York

Nash, R. (1967) Wilderness and the American Mind, Yale University Press, New Haven

Nash, R. (1968) The American Environment: Readings in the History of Conservation,Addison-Wesley, Reading, Mass.

O'Riordan, T. (1976) Environmentalism, Pion, London

Platt, R.H. (1978) Space and authority: the dimensions of institutional response. In K.A. Hammond, G. Macinko and W.V. Fairchild (editors), Sourcebook on the Environment, University of Chicago Press, Chicago, 101-122

Schoenfeld, C. (1971) The year of the Act, Journal of Environmental Education, 2: 49

Stuhr, D.C. (1973) The heritage of environmentalism, The American Biology Teacher, 35: 68-77

U.S. Court of Appeals for the District of Columbia (1979) Alabama Power Company, et al v Douglas M. Castle, as Administrator, EPA, et al, Respondents, Sierra Club, et al Intervenors.

No. 78-1006. Petitions for Review of Orders of the EPS (Judgment entered Dec. 14), Washington, D.C.

Chapter Three

ENVIRONMENTAL POLICIES IN CANADA

Geoffrey Wall

INTRODUCTION

This chapter deals with environmental policies and problems in Canada. It has four main aims:

(a) to place present day environmental policies into their historical contexts, by examining changing attitudes to the environment, staple theory and the British North America Act,
(b) to explore the role of international relations,
(c) to describe the Canadian approach to Environmental Impact Assessment, and
(d) to draw attention to some of those aspects of environmental policy which are distinctively Canadian.

Because of constraints of space, the treatment is of necessity selective. It is not possible, for example, to describe the Canadian environment in any detail; this is covered in geographical texts, such as those by Irving (1978), Krueger (1968), McCann (1981), Putnam and Putnam (1970) and Warkentin (1967) and in the map folio produced by Environment Canada (Simpson-Lewis et al, 1979). Neither is it possible to review the many large resource projects which have been undertaken in recent years, their environmental consequences, or the policies which have influenced them and which they spawned. Fortunately, there are also readily available publications on these topics (Bryan, 1973; Burton, 1972; Dwivedi, 1980; Krueger and Mitchell, 1977; Krueger et al, 1963; McBoyle and Sommerville, 1977; Mitchell and Sewell, 1981).

THE ENVIRONMENTAL AND CULTURAL CONTEXTS

An appreciation of the size and location of Canada is fundamental to an understanding of the resource possibilities and environmental problems faced by the country. With an area of just under ten million square kilometres, Canada is second only to the Soviet Union in size. It has an extremely long coastline impinging upon the Atlantic, Pacific and Arctic Oceans. Canada shares a 6,000 kilometre frontier with the United States to the south, and a boundary with Alaska in the north. The province of Newfoundland (including Labrador), which comprises only 4 percent of Canada, has an area larger than Great Britain and it would be possible to drown England a number of times in the Great Lakes.

Canada has a much greater lake area than any other country. The fresh water area of Canada is listed as 755,166 square kilometres, but most of the smaller ponds, non-permanent lakes and sloughs, seasonally flooded marshes and field depressions, and large areas of muskeg and wet tundra are not included (Laycock, 1967).

The vast area of Canada is home to a relatively small population of approximately 24 million people giving an extremely low population density (or man-land ratio) overall. But the overall density hides considerable variations. Most Canadians are urban residents, with approximately 30 per cent of the population living in the three metropolitan areas of Toronto, Montreal and Vancouver. Furthermore, most Canadians live in the south of the country within 200 kilometres of the border with the United States. Most are concentrated in the incipient megalopolis extending inland along the northern and western shores of Lakes Ontario from Montreal to Niagara Falls, and westwards to Windsor. Yeates (1975) has called this area "Main Street" in recognition of its importance and McCann (1981) has suggested that it is the "heartland", with the remainder of the country as the hinterland.

Given the large size and small population of Canada, one might expect it to be a resource-rich country. There is a large element of truth in this, because Canada is an exporter of resource products (wheat, timber and other forestry products, and minerals) and it has important fisheries, oil supplies and abundant fresh water. However, these supplies are not unlimited and they are often not conveniently located. Canada has only limited areas of high quality agricultural land: only 4.5 percent of soils have been classified by the Canada Land Inventory as having no significant limitations for crops and of these almost half are to be found in southern Ontario - where they are threatened by the expanding cities (Simpson-Lewis et al., 1979, p.8; Krueger, 1978). High quality agricultural land elsewhere also suffers from the pressures of urbanisation (Bryant et al., 1983).

As a northern country, growing seasons are short and growth rates of timber are slower than in many areas to the south. Regeneration of harvested timber is a long-term investment, if it occurs at all. Minerals may be located at a considerable distance from potential markets and their exploitation may be hampered by permafrost on land (Williams, 1979) and by inclement weather and ice-bound seas, particularly in the north. Thus many of the resources can only be won at considerable cost.

The large size and great diversity of the country have contributed to a strong sense of regionalism which is associated with cultural differences and economic disparities (Irving, 1978, pp. 269-340). The country is divided into ten provinces and the Yukon and Northwest Territories. The uneven distribution of resources and population mean that each jurisdiction has its own possibilities and priorities, and this sometimes creates tensions between the individual provinces and territories and between them and the federal government based in the capital city of Ottawa. These tensions are exacerbated by the concentration of French-speaking Canadians in Quebec and parts of the Maritimes, with English being the dominant language elsewhere.

There are also a large number of new Canadians who speak neither of these languages and natives now a minority of the population overall but a majority in many areas in the north, and their status has yet to be fully resolved. Native land claims and native rights to self-determination persist on the political agenda and the resolution of these issues is of fundamental importance to the future of the Canadian environment, particularly in the northern parts of the country.

HISTORICAL PERSPECTIVES

The environment of Canada has changed greatly over time as a result of human activities. These changes have both contributed to and reflected changes in attitudes towards that environment. Furthermore, decisions which were made in the past greatly constrain the planning and management opportunities which can be adopted today and which are possible in the future. This section will explore three topics with very different foci, but all of which have an historical component.

Changing Attitudes Towards the Environment

A brief intellectual history offers a background to the changing context in which Canadian environmental policies have evolved. "The geography of a place results from how we see it as much as from what may be seen there" (Watson, 1969, p.10). Thus began a study of the role of illusion in North American geography. Watson (1969, p.10) argued that:

> *Not all geography derives from the earth itself; some of it springs from our idea (sic) of the earth. This geography within the mind can at times be the effective geography to which men adjust and thus be more important than the supposedly real geography of the earth.*

Geographies of the mind are not fixed and immutable, although they have been slow to change, even in the face of seemingly overwhelming evidence that the conventional wisdom may be a myth. Man's evaluations of the potential of an area reflect both his goals and his aspirations, as well as the technology available to interact with and modify the environment. As goals and technology change, so the potential of an environment will receive a different evaluation (Zimmerman, 1964). For example, Wall (1982) has pointed out that many of the currently popular places visited for recreation were not always seen in such positive terms.

The earliest settlers of Canada did not evaluate

the land primarily on the basis of its potential for sustaining outdoor recreation. In the first instance, they were looking for places which might provide them with a livelihood for themselves and their families. Many of the currently popular recreational areas of Canada were evaluated and used very differently before they became resort areas. Some were initially regarded as being among the last places to which one would choose to go for fun.

Davies (1972) has argued that North American relationships with the land have been based on two myths: progress and overabundance. The former refers to North America's conception of progress as meaning increased material production at virtually any cost. The latter is based on the premise that the resources of the continent were inexhaustible, and that vast areas of wilderness existed and would continue to exist without any conscious effort to preserve them. Both situations encouraged the conquest of wilderness and this provided a measure of the degree to which man could assess his progress in his efforts to attain a "civilised" status.

The early American symbol of progress was that of the advancing frontier pushing back the wilderness. However, unlike the United States, "Canada began as a group of small, outpost communities set amidst a menacing continent which could be penetrated, but, unlike the American example, could not be pushed back" (Altmeyer, 1976, p.21).

The wilderness was also a place to be feared. It was the unknown, the home of wild beasts and savage men; a place to be avoided. Forced always to cling to the mother country for security, nature became - for Canadians - the evil antithesis of all they most cherished in European society: order, security, and above all, civilisation. According to Frye (quoted in Altmeyer, 1976, p.21), because Canadians did not make the psychological break with Europe through revolution, they could not face the harsh realities of North American nature with the same positive attitudes as Americans. However, there is ample evidence to suggest that early residents of the United States also feared the wilderness. Turner has suggested that in American folklore, in addition to tales of sudden attack and capture, "the only other equally horrifying occurrence was to vanish utterly into the huge maw of the wilderness, leaving no single trace, to be thus lost forever to history" (Turner, 1977).

According to Davies (1972), an appreciation began not in the wilderness itself, but in the densely populated centres. The wilderness was more likely to be viewed with favour when it was not ever-present; it would only be protected when the myth of abundance was displaced, and thus wilderness was seen to have a scarcity value. Appreciation of wilderness was partly a reaction against urban living which has been the lot of increasing proportions of Canadians. Thus it is argued that, in response to the changed social and environmental situations in which Canadians found themselves, attitudes towards the wilderness changed from being dominantly negative to being largely positive in character.

Three additional comments are in order concerning attitudes to nature. The two perspectives which have been presented above are generalisations, even stereotypes. They represent dominant perceptions at particular periods of time. In reality, there was considerable variation in views and a gradual change in emphasis between the two. Thus, for instance, Dahl (1973) examined the writing of a number of early nineteenth-century authors and identified the existence of both antipathy and appreciation. He suggests that such a feeling of ambivalence is to be expected in a period when attitudes to wilderness were in a state of flux. Secondly, such changes in attitudes should not be viewed simply as modifications which were indigenous to North America. Rather, they reflected prevailing European attitudes. The first immigrants to North America brought their social, economic and political heritage with them. They had preconceived ideas about nature. Their Judeo-Christian tradition identified wilderness as wasteland. The story of the Garden of Eden embedded the idea in western thought that wilderness and paradise were physical and spiritual opposites. Man, as the highest being in the creation, had the privilege and responsibility to use nature for his own ends and to improve on its natural state.

Taming the wilderness gave purpose and pride to life.

As Nash explained: "The driving impulse was always to carve a garden from the wilds to make an island of spiritual light in the surrounding darkness" (Nash, 1967). The stimulus towards wilderness appreciation was primarily an intellectual one, with firmly fixed roots in Europe. Romanticism and associated changes in landscape art promoted the positive appreciation of wild lands and gave a fashionable, intellectual base for the appreciation of wilderness. These trends in Europe have been described by Hussey (1927) and Moir (1964), and their importation to North America has been examined by Shepard (1967) and Nash (1967).

Thirdly, while it is possible to generalise concerning prevailing attitudes to the land, it should be remembered that people interact with the land at a variety of scales, as a nation and also as small groups or individuals. Just as we can recognise temporal changes in attitudes towards the land, so sub-groups of the population may have distinctive perspectives. For example, for residents of the cities of southern Ontario the Canadian Shield is a recreational environment - even a wilderness - which is threatened and which should be retained and conserved. On the other hand, for many residents of the Shield it is primarily a work environment and only secondarily a recreational environment. It may be described by the derogatory term "bush", which is present in abundance and which should be developed. Such variations mean that there are likely to be regional differences in resource evaluations and in preferences for policies.

Staple Theory

One way of viewing the historical geography of Canada is through the sequence of products which have been associated with European exploration and exploitation of the country and which have been major contributors to the economy. These products - which include fish, fur, timber, wheat and minerals and possibly oil and water - have been called "staples". Staples are raw materials which are unprocessed or only slightly processed and which are produced predominantly for export. Although other colonial countries (such as Australia) have had their economies dominated by a limited number of similar products, the topic has been of such concern in Canada that it has been elevated to the status of a theory. Watkins (1963) has suggested that:

> *The staple approach to the study of economic history is primarily a Canadian innovation; indeed it is Canada's most distinctive contribution to political economy. It is undeveloped in any explicit form in most countries where the export sector is or was dominant. The specific terminology - staples or staples approach, or theory, or thesis - is Canadian, and the persistence with which the theory has been applied by Canadian social scientists and historians is unique.*

Staple theory is an attempt to link economic history, economic growth and the exploitation of natural resources. In the words of Bertram (1963):

> *The staple model is essentially a theory of regional growth within the framework of an international economy. Export staples can be identified as industries based on agricultural and extractive resources not requiring elaborate processing and finding a large portion of their market in international trades.*

Most of the staple products (except for minerals) are derived from resources which are potentially renewable. The theory assumes that staple products are the leading sector of the economy and that they underpin the rate of growth of the economy. In the early years of colonisation, the large amounts of resources relative to labour and capital create a comparative advantage in resource-intensive products (staples). There is a small or non-existent home market and economic development is regarded as a process of diversification, through spread effects, around the export base.

In summary, the development of a staple economy requires a favourable man-land (resource) ratio, appropriate markets and importation of scarce factors of production - factors which were all present in Canada during early European settlement and which, it can be argued, are still present today.

Innis (1967, 1954) and Lower (1938, 1973) were

two of the more prominent Canadian writers on this theme and their work (both individually and in collaboration (1936)) on the cod fisheries, fur trade, forest industries and mining, did much to advance the theory. Their work is still essential reading for those interested in the exploitation of Canadian resources. The writings of Innis and Lower were preceded by those of the Scottish geographer Newbigin, who argued (in a rather deterministic manner) that the resources and physiography of New France - and in particular the relative locations of the St. Lawrence River and the Canadian Shield - were major contributors to the distinctive character of Canada as opposed to the United States (see Berger, 1976, pp. 92-94).

The exploration and exploitation of the interior of Canada and the export of its products required the development of an increasingly sophisticated communications system. Newbigin (1926), in her book Canada: The Great River, The Lands and The Men, suggested that the entire history of Canada hinged on the solution to the twin problems of maintaining access to the sea and internal expansion based on products that could find their outlet by way of the St. Lawrence. The parallel between the fur trade and the river on the one hand, with the wheat economy and the transcontinental railways on the other hand, was neither fortuitous nor insignificant. They both involved the conquest of a vast area of land and its integration into the Canadian economy.

In recent years it has become fashionable to criticise the sweeping generalisations of staple theory. For example, urbanism and regionalism are two phenomena which complicate matters. Nevertheless, it is still argued that Canadians tend to be "hewers of wood and drawers of water" for others and that the Canadian economy is dominated by outsiders. These topics are explored further later in this chapter.

The British North America Act

The British North America Act (BNA Act) of 1867 provides the constitutional setting for environmental and resource issues by stipulating the jurisdictions and responsibilities of the federal and provincial governments. Sections 91, 92, 95 and 109 are the key parts of the Act in this context (Burton, 1972, pp. 97-112). Section 91 states that the federal parliament will be the recipient and custodian of all residual powers.

Thirty-one areas of jurisdiction are listed in the Act specifically as being areas of federal responsibility (e.g. defence, postal services, prisons). Two of these are concerned directly with the environment - coastal and inland fisheries, and Indian affairs (which includes Indian land claims). In addition, federal regulations of trade and commerce may also have resource and environmental implications. Consequently, the federal government is paramount in two main groups of areas:

(a) those which are specifically listed, and
(b) all other areas which are not granted elsewhere to the provinces i.e. residual powers.

While it is clear that any new powers should accrue to the federal government, the distinction between new and existing powers is often far from clear. For example, should the setting of environmental quality standards be regarded as a new activity or merely as an extension of existing responsibilities for natural resources?

Provincial responsibilities are detailed in Sections 92 and 109. Section 92 describes 16 areas of provincial responsibility, three of which are related to the environment. These are:

(a) the management and sale of public lands, which includes large areas of forest,
(b) all local works projects (except shipping lines, railways and canals which are interprovincial or international), and
(c) all matters of a merely local or private nature.

Section 109 delegates lands, mines and minerals to the provinces. In other words, most natural resources are under provincial jurisdiction although there are exceptions. Interprovincial resources are under federal jurisdiction but, in practice, there is debate on authority and responsibilities. Such debate occurs, for example, in fisheries, interprovincial rivers and the resources of the seabed. Both levels of government have some jurisdiction over agriculture, with the federal government paramount. National parks post-date the BNA Act and so they are not mentioned in it. They are, however, still a federal responsibility.

In summary, with some notable exceptions, natural resources were intended to be under the jurisdiction of the provinces. In practice, there have been numerous conflicts over jurisdiction. The authority of the federal government over interprovincial and international transfers permits federal involvement in a very large number of environmental and resource issues, be it air quality, pipelines or trade in products.

The jurisdictional context of Canadian resources and environmental policy is further complicated by the fragmentation of responsibilities within the federal and each of the provincial governments. The net result is that a large number of agencies have an interest in and influence upon most resource and environmental issues. For example, a study of the recreational responsibilities in federal and provincial governments showed that 66 agencies in the federal government were concerned with recreation. Although the parts played by the 10 provincial governments varies markedly, 58 agencies in 19 different ministries were shown to be concerned with some aspect of recreation in Ontario alone (Burton and Kyllo, 1974).

Hall (1976) has suggested that this fragmentation of responsibilities gives rise to a number of major problems of co-ordination:

(a) the problem of the duplication of facilities,
(b) the problem of underprovision, particularly on the edge of large cities (like Toronto) where municipal governments have not been able to provide resources outside their boundaries and rural municipalities have insufficient resources to provide extensive facilities,
(c) resources are not evenly divided between the various levels of government. For example, the federal government is capable of raising large sums of money, but the provincial governments with their responsibility for crown lands have large resources, and
(d) it has been claimed that the public has problems in understanding the roles of different

agencies and the absence of a unified approach probably leads to difficulty in accepting the different standards of behaviour required in recreation areas of different agencies.

Burton and Kyllo (1974) added the following problems to those listed above - the existence of conflicts within and between federal and provincial governments; the lack of a rational distribution of the services between them; and the inadequacy of machinery for policy development, priority definition and general co-ordination within these levels of government. Furthermore, the role of the private sector remains unspecified. Nevertheless, in spite of these observations, Burton and Kyllo (1974) concluded that there is:

> *...little evidence of overlapping and duplication that has so often been feared; the primary problem has not been one of duplication but of services operating at cross purposes.*

There are also some signs of increased co-operation between the various levels of government. This is illustrated by the establishment of the Federal-Provincial Parks Conference, the Agreements for Recreation and Conservation scheme (formerly called the Byways and Special Places Programme), and the joint funding of the Harbourfront recreational complex in Toronto (Hall, 1976, p.38).

This recreational example could be duplicated in many other subject areas. For example, Burton (1972, pp. 101-102) has argued that conflicts in fisheries arise from the legitimate exercise of constitutional powers. Harrison and Kwamena (1981) have examined the overlapping powers in coastal management and somewhat similar studies have been undertaken, including those of northern resources development (Wonders, 1981), oceans (Draper, 1981) and weed control (McBoyle et al., 1978). One conclusion from these studies is that co-ordination of activities among agencies and, in some cases, rationalisation of their responsibilities, should be given a high priority.

INTERNATIONAL RELATIONS

The colonial history of Canada coupled with its contiguity with the United States have always added an international dimension to Canada's environmental problems. These factors have combined to create two problems of concern in Canada which extend beyond environmental matters, but have implications for the Canadian environment and its exploitation. These are foreign ownership of Canadian resources and industries, and relationships with the United States.

Foreign Ownership

As indicated in the section on staple theory, foreign exploitation of Canadian resources is not a new concern. Nonetheless, there have been temporal changes in the sources of foreign investment and the significance of foreign investment varies considerably between resource sectors (Forgeron and Wall, 1976). In 1900, 85 percent of foreign investment in Canada originated in Britain and 14 percent in the United States. By 1966, however, the situation had reversed so that only 11 percent came from Britain, 80 percent came from the United States and much of the rest came from Japan. Foreign investment was particularly high in the petroleum industry, but it was present in most resource sectors. The Gray Report on foreign investment concluded in 1972 that "the degree of foreign ownership and control of economic activity is already substantially higher in Canada than in any other industrialised country and is continuing to increase". Cutler (1970) has provided a useful overview of the problem.

However, opinions are far from unanimous on the nature and significance of the problems associated with foreign investment. Those who are most concerned fear that the domination of foreign companies is a threat to Canadian sovereignty because Canadians no longer make the crucial decisions over the location and timing of resource developments. Should one consume now or preserve for the future? They further argue that profits leak out of the country, that the export of raw materials (as opposed to their manufacture in Canada) represents a loss of job opportunities, and that the stability of economic activity is called into question if Canada is a branch plant economy. It is suggested that increased competition for resources drives up prices to the detriment of Canadians, and that the beneficiaries are a small number of foreign investors at the expense of the majority of Canadians. Those who disagree suggest that foreign investments are necessary given the scale of many projects, and they argue that such investments stimulate the economy and generate jobs which would not otherwise exist.

Government policy has vacillated between these two perspectives. For example, the Foreign Investment Review Act of 1974 was introduced to screen possible foreign takeovers. The Act also encouraged Canadian takeovers of foreign companies. Thus Petro-Canada was instituted to gain a greater control over Canadian oil and the proportion of foreign investment in oil has decreased accordingly. On the other hand, in the late 1970s there were attempts to attract foreign investment through the provision of financial incentives. This illustrates the dilemma between the two goals of ownership and development. Governments can control investments if politicians decide that the benefits outweigh the costs. Too much control could result in a loss of investment and retaliation.

Foreign ownership of land provides a good example of the nature of foreign investment problems and policies which have been taken in an attempt to resolve them. In some places, such as the Lake Erie shoreline and Prince Edward island, sufficient recreational land is owned by foreigners to cause local residents to feel that they are losing control over their own destiny. These concerns led to the establishment of a Royal Commission on Land Ownership and Land Use in Prince Edward Island and restrictions were placed on the purchase of land by non-residents of the province (Prince Edward Island, 1973).

A similar form of concern has been expressed over changes in the ownership of farmland in Ontario (Mage, 1982). Concern here appears to stem as much from absentee ownership as from foreign ownership *per se*, although it is difficult to make a clear distinction between them. The Ministry of Agriculture and Food estimated that only 0.7 percent of Ontario farmland was owned by persons who were resident outside of Canada in 1978. However, foreign ownership is not evenly distributed throughout the province and the area in foreign absentee ownership doubled from approximately 2,150 hectares in 1975 to 4,050 hectares in 1980. The significance of these figures is difficult to assess because it is not clear what proportion of foreign ownership is acceptable and at what threshold it becomes a problem.

At present, the rate of change appears to be of as much concern as the absolute area in foreign ownership. Relevant data are difficult to gain and in 1980 the Ontario government passed an Act to Require the Registration of Non-Agricultural Interests in Agricultural Land in Ontario. This Act requires all non-residents with holdings of over 10 acres (4 hectares) to register their ownership. This should generate a stronger statistical base for an evaluation of the significance of the problem. In addition, a special tax was instituted on the sale of land to non-residents. Seven of the ten provinces now have procedures to monitor non-resident land ownership and Alberta, Manitoba, Saskatchewan and Prince Edward Island have enacted legislation over the last decade.

Although steps are being taken to reduce foreign ownership of Canadian resources, it remains unclear if it is foreign ownership or what is done to the resources and environment which is the crucial problem. Whether it is better to regulate ownership or use is still a moot question.

Relationships with the United States

Although Canada is a large country, it shares a boundary (including Alaska) over 8,900 kilometres long with only one other country - the United States. This boundary bisects the Great Lakes, the world's largest reserve of fresh water, and it was drawn without respect for physical features. The international boundary is a contributing factor to many problems and irritants - it crosses mountains, forests, airsheds, watersheds and wildlife and fish migration routes so that when resources are exploited in one country there may be repercussions across the border. Furthermore, a project may seem beneficial when costs and benefits are weighed for one side alone, but it may be damaging from the perspective of the side which receives few benefits but must bear some of the costs.

There are numerous examples of such projects. One is the High Ross Dam in Washington state, which flooded scenic and environmentally sensitive areas along the Skagit River in Canada to provide electric power for residents of Seattle (Ross and Marts, 1975). Another is the Garrison Diversion, which offers the prospect of diverting polluted irrigation water from North Dakota across the border to Manitoba. A further example is the recent discussion of the possibility of diverting water from the Great Lakes southwards to meet the requirements of the American mid-west, and the likely ecological and economic consequences of the lower lake levels which would follow. Other examples focus on air quality. Relatively local air pollution problems - for example from Detroit to Windsor - have escalated into an international debate on acid rain, its causes and its effects.

While many trans-border problems are handled by normal diplomatic channels, it has been found useful to establish a number of formal mechanisms to facilitate the resolution of such problems. The most important of these arrangements is the International Joint Commission (IJC); "none has a broader mandate, greater independence or a larger or more impressive record of accomplishment" (Jordan quoted in Dwiveldi and Carroll, 1980, p.310). This institution is a rather unusual and fairly successful means of facilitating the resolution of international environmental problems and thus it merits further discussion. There is an extensive literature on the IJC and this section draws heavily upon the writings of Day (1972) and Dwived and Carroll (1980). The Great Lakes pollution example is distilled from Munton (1980).

<u>The International Joint Commission</u>: The IJC was created by the Boundary Waters Treaty of 1909. It was hoped that the Commission would help to avoid disputes regarding the use of boundary waters and to settle all questions between the two countries involving their rights, obligations and interests. More specifically the IJC was to have jurisdiction over the use, obstruction or diversion of boundary waters where the use on one side of the boundary would affect the level of the waters on the other side. Application for approval was to be made to the IJC before any work could be undertaken. The Commission was directed to give precedence to domestic and sanitary needs, navigation and uses of water for power supply and irrigation. Pollution and environmental preservation were of lesser concern at the turn of the century and they received little attention in the treaty negotiations. The IJC was authorised to order

that compensation be paid to all interests adversely affected by the project. In addition, more general matters (including pollution) could be submitted by the two governments for examination by the Commission. Recommendations were to be made jointly to both governments, although they were not to be binding. The IJC was also given powers of arbitration, but these have never been invoked.

The Commission draws upon qualified personnel from the two federal, provincial and state governments. It appoints boards with equal numbers of professional representatives from the United States and Canada. The boards are authorised to seek information and technical data and to submit their findings to the IJC. These findings are released for public comment, following which the Commission prepares its own report which makes recommendations to the two federal governments. If some or all of the recommendations are accepted, the IJC may be asked to provide surveillance over implementation through control boards.

On the positive side, the reports and recommendations of the Commission have generated a great deal of information which has often led to agreement. A large number and great variety of problems have been referred to the Commission which has been extremely successful in its fact-finding and monitoring roles. The IJC has been used to make detailed proposals to implement negotiations which have already been carried out (the sceptical might say to delay final decisions!). Above all, the IJC has maintained its impartiality and, in consequence, it is highly respected:

> *The commissioners have not approached these questions as two distinct groups of national representatives, each jockeying for advantages for its own side, but rather as members of a single tribunal, anxious to harmonise differences between the two countries, and to render decisions which would be substantial justice to all legitimate interests on both sides of the boundary, and particularly those of the common people (Burpee quoted in Dwivedi and Carroll, 1980, p.312).*

However, the IJC is not without its limitations. In particular, it cannot initiate investigations or studies and its terms of reference may restrict it to a consideration of only one aspect of a broad issue. Moreover the Commission has no enforcement powers. Burpee (quoted in Dwivedi and Carroll, 1980, p.330) summarises the value of the Commission with a back-handed compliment:

> *...the true measure of the Commission's usefulness to the people of the United States and Canada lies not so much in its positive as in its negative qualities, not so much in the cases it has actually settled as in the much larger number of cases that never come before it for consideration, simply because the Commission is there, as a sort of international safety valve and therefore the sting is taken out of the situation.*

Great Lakes Pollution: The problem of maintaining water quality in the Great Lakes provides an interesting example of the working of the IJC and of the difficulty of resolving environmental problems, particularly those which have an international component. The pollution of the Great Lakes provides complex environmental and jurisdictional problems, because it involves so many actors. These include federal, provincial and state governments; a binational agency (the IJC); a host of government officials, diplomats, administrators and scientists; an aroused public which includes pressure groups; and polluters from the public, private and corporate sectors.

The Great Lakes Water Quality Agreement of 1972 grew directly from a reference to the IJC in 1964. Early studies of water pollution problems in the Great Lakes were made by the IJC in 1912 and 1946. These resulted in a report published in 1950 which, when approved, set up common water quality objectives and a bi-lateral monitoring board for the lakes' connecting channels. However, the mounting evidence of basin-wide problems and especially the declining condition of Lake Erie, indicated that further action was necessary and prompted the 1964 reference. Two joint investigatory boards were set up - one for Lake Erie and one for Lake Ontario and the St. Lawrence River - but a 1965 interim report recommending limits on phosphorus input was set aside. The final report was released in 1969. This emphasised phosphates and eutrophication, and it documented the relative contribution of United States and Canadian sources. The report recommended immediate phosphate controls, a new set of water quality objectives, and the establishment of a new international board to co-ordinate activities and monitor the results.

Public hearings were held in eight cities which pitted government agencies against the detergent manufacturers; this resulted in the release of an additional report in 1970. Eventually negotiations took place between the two sides, but each country had different premises. Canada argued (under Article VIII of the Boundary Waters Treaty) that each side could contribute pollution up to 50 percent of the assimilative capacity of the lakes. This would mean that minimal adjustments would be necessary for Canada, but drastic reductions would be necessary for the United States as the major polluter. In contrast the United States argued (under Article IV) that both sides were obliged to take equivalent measures to control pollution. Failing to agree on this broad question, discussion then concentrated upon technical issues in the IJC report, such as oil and gas drilling, ship waste, dredging and emergency co-ordination.

Following a ministerial-level meeting in June 1970, a joint Canada-United States working group was set up in September 1970 to establish the terms of reference for ten sub-groups. These included water quality objectives and standards, institutional matters, environmental legislation, co-ordination of special programmes and of research, pollution from hazardous materials, agriculture, forestry and watercraft. However, Canadians became preoccupied with a back-up programme which was to provide Central Mortgage and Housing Corporation grants and loans for municipal sewage treatment and in September 1971 President Nixon recommended a return to phosphates. Nevertheless, an agreement was reached in April 1972 on common water quality objectives, compatible standards, commitments on implementing programmes to meet these objectives and procedures for monitoring results. This agreement was the result of six years of studies and two years of intensive negotiations.

The next major landmark in joint management was

the Great Lakes Water Quality Agreement of 1978. The United States and Canada agreed that municipal and industrial pollution abatement and control programmes would be in operation no later than the end of 1982 and 1983 respectively. The former date was selected because sewage treatment facilities in Detroit were expected to be in operation by that time. A more stringent set of phosphorus loading reductions was accepted, but the actual division of these loadings between the two countries remained to be negotiated. The discharge of toxic chemicals was to be largely eliminated and approximately 350 "hazardous polluting substances" were to be banned from the lakes. A new surveillance programme was accepted and tougher standards on radioactivity were introduced. The new agreement represented a concensus that municipal programmes were well under way but that industrial programmes required attention and controls needed to be extended to cover new concerns.

ENVIRONMENTAL IMPACT ASSESSMENT

Background and Context

Heightened public concern in Canada for the impact of human activities on the environment was, in part, a product of the international environmental movement of the 1960s and 1970s. In Canada the scale of some projects - such as northern pipelines, river diversions and hydro-electric schemes - were commensurate with the size of the country. The areas which experienced impacts of some projects (such as the James Bay hydro-electric project) exceeded the total area of some countries and their environmental consequences were not fully understood at the time. The scale of projects, coupled with an increased appreciation of their externalities among a vociferous public and a growing concern for equity (i.e. that those who benefit from development should cover the costs), resulted in a movement to require the completion of an environmental impact statement prior to the approval of projects. The National Environmental Policy Act of the United States, passed in 1969 (see Chapter 2), constituted a precedent in environmental legislation and Canada followed with its own environmental impact assessment procedure in 1973.

Environmental Impact Assessment (EIA) is defined by Munn (quoted in Mitchell and Turkheim, 1977, p.47) as:

> *...an activity designed to identify, interpret and communicate information about the impact of an action on man's health and well-being (including the well-being of ecosystems on which man's survival depends).*

Mitchell and Turkheim (1977, p.47) define EIA as:

> *...a legislative or policy-based concern for possible positive/negative, short/long term effects on our total environment attributable to proposed or existing projects, programs or policies of a public or private origin.*

These definitions suggest that the environmental impact assessments should be broad in scope, may be legally required and should result in the preparation of an environmental impact statement (EIS).

It has been argued elsewhere that countries have "coping styles" which predispose them to respond to problems in particular ways (Wall, 1976). In the case of environmental impact assessment, as in many other policy areas, Canada occupies a position which is intermediate between that of the United States and the United Kingdom. The American approach, based upon legislation backed up by the courts, has generated a large number of environmental impact statements - according to Mitchell and Turkheim (1977, p.49) 2,933 by June 1972 and 7,100 by 1975 - and it has also resulted in considerable litigation and its associated costs. In contrast, the United Kingdom does not have specific legislation or regulations requiring formal environmental assessment (see Chapter 5). The first Minister of Environment (quoted in Mitchell and Turkheim, 1977, p.48) stated in 1970 that each government department was expected to "pursue high quality decisions in terms of the environment" and that the legal requirement for environmental assessment "really makes a land fit for lawyers to live in with no great impact upon the environment itself".

<u>EIA in Practice</u>
Both federal and provincial governments in Canada

are involved in environmental assessment and they have adopted an administrative rather than a legislative aproach. At the federal level, the Environmental Assessment and Review Process was instituted in 1973. In theory, an EIA should be undertaken for all projects which are federally funded or in which federal property is involved. Projects which are likely to have "significant" environmental effects (although significance is not defined in the policy) are subject to the preparation of an EIS which is reviewed by an Environmental Assessment Panel. In practice, the minister has considerable power because he can determine if the effects are likely to be "significant", as well as the composition of the panel and the degree of public participation which is to be permitted.

The ministers involved have the final say concerning project approval and, in cases where there is a inter-ministerial disagreement, the matter is resolved by cabinet. The Minister of Environment (quoted in Mitchell and Turkheim, 1977, p.49) stated in 1974 that:

> *I hope, in the process, that we can avoid the delays and other pitfalls which a strictly legalistic approach would cause in this country...We will not hold up important developments which are clean from an environmental point of view and, in contrast to the situation which has developed in the United States, we will not bring the environmental assessment process into disrepute. We will not be charged with blocking everything.*

The provinces each have their own approaches and requirements. Space does not permit a full discussion (Mitchell and Turkheim (1977) provide a comparative review of provincial practices) and the single example of Ontario is considered here for illustrative purposes. The Ontario Environmental Assessment Act was proclaimed in October 1976. It referred only to projects proposed by the provincial government, but it was intended that private sector projects should be made subject to the Act at a later date (this has yet to happen - December 1984). The assessments are submitted to the Ministry of Environment which refers them to the Environmental Assessment Board. The Board, in turn, makes recommendations to the Minister. The Minister has discretionary powers and he can exempt projects from the process. He can also reject the recommendations of the Environmental Assessment Board.

Critics of Canadian procedures at both federal and provincial levels argue that the discretionary powers of ministers detract from the value of the Canadian approach. However, it is possible to argue that increased public concern over environmental quality has helped to ensure that environmental concerns receive some consideration in both public and private sector projects, even in the absence of legal requirements to prepare impact statements. At the same time, there are those who argue that this is not enough.

In tandem with the growth and institutionalisation of environmental impact assessment, there has been an increased acceptance of public participation in decisions concerning the environment. Various means of public participation have been employed to facilitate communications between planners and managers and the interested public (including pressure groups). Public participation has rapidly become part of the conventional wisdom, but there is little agreement on how best to proceed. The Berger Commission enquiry into the Mackenzie Valley pipeline is often regarded as a classic example of how to conduct a public participation programme, although the breadth with which Berger (1977) interpreted his mandate took some government officials by surprise. On the other hand, the initial ventures of some agencies into public participation have themselves generated controversy. For example, the early public participation programmes of Parks Canada, which is responsible for the national parks, came under criticism (Hoole, 1978; Kariel, 1979; McFarlane 1979). In the case of Kouchibouguac National Park, consultation rapidly turned into confrontation (Folster, 1980). Parks Canada learned from its experiences and it has become much more sensitive in its approach.

One can only applaud any attempt to solicit input from the public and to keep interested parties informed of developments. But one wonders how much can be achieved when set positions are taken with little prospect of compromise.

SUMMARY AND CONCLUSIONS

A selective approach has been adopted in this chapter because of the size of Canada, the diversity of its environmental problems, and the complexity of the institutional arrangements which have evolved to deal with them. Following a brief introduction to the geography of Canada, three historical perspectives on environmental problems are presented. It is suggested that attitudes to the environment have changed considerably over the years and these have provided a varying context in which environmental policies have evolved. Staple theory is highlighted as a peculiarly Canadian way of understanding the exploitation of the Canadian environment and the British North America Act receives considerable attention because it lays down the jurisdictional responsibilities over resources and environmental issues. History and geography have combined to give Canadian environmental problems an international flavour. Foreign ownership of Canadian resources and the juxtaposition of the United States have forced Canadians to devote attention to these issues and in some cases (such as the International Joint Commission) innovative responses have resulted. The final topic which is considered is environmental impact assessment and it is argued that Canada has developed a distinctive administrative "coping style", intermediate between that of the United Kingdom and the United States.

REFERENCES

Altmeyer, G. (1976) Three ideas of nature in Canada, 1893-1914, Journal of Canadian Studies, 11: 21-36

Berger, C. (1976) The Writing of Canadian History, Oxford University Press, Toronto

Berger, T.R. (1977) Northern Frontier Northern Homeland, James Lorimer and Co., Toronto (2 vols)

Bertram, G.W. (1963) Economic growth in Canadian Industry, 1870-1915, Canadian Journal of Economics and Political Science, 29: 162-184

Bryan, R. (1973) Much is Taken, Much Remains, Duxbury, North Sciutate, Mass

Burton, T.L. (1972) Natural Resource Policy in Canada, McClelland and Stewart, Toronto

Burton, T.L. and Kyllo, T.L. (1974) Federal-Provincial Responsibilities for Leisure Services in Alberta and Ontario, Ontario Research Council on Leisure, Waterloo

Cutler, M. (1975) Foreign demand for our land and resources. Canadian Geographical Journal, 90: Nos. 4,5,6 and 7

Dahl, E.H. (1973) Mid Forests Wild: A Study of the Concept of Wilderness in the Writings of Susanna Moodie, J.W.D. Moodie, Catherine Parr Traill and Samuel Strickland, c. 1830-1855, History Division Paper No. 3, National Museum of Man, Ottawa

Davies, E. (1972) The Wilderness Myth, unpublished M.A. thesis, University of British Columbia, Vancouver

Day, J.C. (1972) International Management of the Great Lakes - St. Lawrence Basin, Water Resources Bulletin, 8: 1120-1136

Draper, D. (1981) Oceans exploitation: efficiency and equity questions in fisheries management, 109-150, in B. Mitchell and W.R.D. Sewell (editors), Canadian Resource Policies: Problems and Prospects, Methuen, Toronto

Dwived , O.P. (editor) (1980) Resources and the Environment: Policy Perspectives for Canada, McClelland and Stewart, Toronto

Dwived , O.P. and Carroll, O.P. (1980) Issues in Canadian-American environmental relations. In O.P. Dwivedi (editor), Resources and the Environment: Policy Perspectives for Canada, McClelland and Stewart, Toronto, 306-334

Folster, D. (1980) Refusing to take yes for an answer, The Globe and Mail, May 31

Forgeron, K. and Wall, G. (1976) Foreign investment in the primary resource and manufacturing industries of Canada, Contact: Journal of Urban and Environmental Affairs, 8: 34-43

Hall, R.K. (1976) Outdoor Recreation Provision in Canada, Discussion Papers in Geography No. 2, The Polytechnic, Oxford

Harrison, P. and Kwamena, F.A. (1976) Coastal management in Canada. In B. Mitchell and W.R.D. Sewell (editors), Canadian Resource Policies: Problems and Prospects, Methuen, Toronto, 84-108

Hoole, A. (1978) Public participation in park planning: the Riding Mountain case. Canadian Geographer, 22: 41-50

Hussey, C. (1927) The Picturesque, Studies in a Point of View, Putman, London

Innis, H. (1954) The Cod Fisheries, University

of Toronto Press, Toronto (revised edition)
Innis, H. (1967) The Fur Trade in Canada, University of Toronto Press, Toronto (revised edition)
Innis, H. and Lower, A.R.M. (1976) Settlement and the Forest Frontier in Eastern Canada. Settlement and the Mining Frontier in Eastern Canada, Macmillan, Toronto
Irving, R.M. (1978) Readings in Canadian Geography, Holt, Rinehart and Winston, Toronto
Kariel, H.G. (1979) Public participation in national park planning: comment no. 1, Canadian Geographer, 23: 172-173
Krueger, R. (1968) Canada: A New Geography, Holt, Rinehart and Winston, Toronto
Krueger, R. (1978) Urbanisation of the Niagara fruit belt, Canadian Geographer, 22: 179-194
Krueger, R. and Mitchell, B. (1977) Managing Canada's Renewable Resources, Methuen, Toronto
Krueger, R., Sargent, F.O., de Vos, A. and Pearson, N. (editors) (1963) Regional and Resource Planning in Canada, Holt Rinehart and Winston, Toronto
Laycock, A.H. (1967) Water. In J. Warkentin (editor), Canada: A Geographical Interpretation, Methuen, Toronto
Lower, A.R.M. (1938) The North American Assault on the Canadian Forest, Ryerson, Toronto
Lower, A.R.M. (1973) Great Britain's Woodyard: British America and the Timber Trade 1763-1867, McGill-Queen's University Press, Montreal
MacFarlane, R. (1979) Comment No. 2 in public participation in national park planning, Canadian Geographer, 23: 173-176
Mage, J. (1982) Absentee foreign ownership of farmland: trends, problems and issues with specific reference to Huron-Bruce Counties, Geographical Inter-University Resource Management Seminars, 12: 1-16
McBoyle, G., Mock, T. and Wall, G. (1978) Weed control legislation in Ontario, Journal of Environmental Management, 6: 223-243
McBoyle, G. and Sommerville, E. (editors) (1977) Canada's Natural Environment, Methuen, Toronto
McCann, L.D. (editor) (1982) Heartland and Hinterland, Prentice-Hall, Scarborough
Mitchell, B. and Turkheim, R. (1977) Environmental impact assessment: principles, practices and Canadian experiences. In R.R. Krueger and B. Mitchell (editors), Managing Canada's

Renewable Resources, Methuen, Toronto, 47-66

Mitchell, B. and Sewell, W.R.D. (editors) (1981) Canadian Resource Policies: Problems and Prospects, Methuen, Toronto

Moir, E. (1964) The Discovery of Britain: The English Tourists, 1540-1840, Routledge and Kegan Paul, London

Munton, D. (1980) Great Lakes water quality: a study in environmental politics and diplomacy. In O.P. Dwivedi (editor), Resources and Environment: Policy for Canada, McClelland and Stewart, Toronto

Nash, R. (1967) Wilderness and the American Mind, Yale University Press, New Haven

Newbigin, M. (1926) Canada: The Great River, the Lands and the Men, Christophers, London

Prince Edward Island (1978) Royal Commission on Land Ownership and Land Use Report, Charlottetown

Putnam, D.F. and Putnam, R.G. (1970) Canada: A Regional Analysis, J.M. Dent, Don Mills

Ross, W.M. and Marts, M.E. (1975) The High Ross Dam project: environmental decisions and changing environmental attitudes, Canadian Geographer, 19: 221-234

Shepard, P. (1967) Man in the Landscape: A Historic View of the Esthetics of Nature, Ballentine, New York

Simpson-Lewis, W., Moore, J.E., Pocock, N.J., Taylor, M.C. and Swan, H. (1979) Canada's Special Resource Lands, Map Folio No. 4, Lands Directorate, Environment Canada, Ottawa

Turner, F. (1977) The terror of wilderness, American Heritage, 28: 59-65

Wall, G. (1976) National coping styles: policies to combat environmental problems, International Journal of Environmental Problems, 9: 239-245

Wall, G. (1982) Changing views of the land as a recreation resource. In G. Wall and J. Marsh (editors), Recreational Land Use: Perspectives on its Evolution in Canada, Carleton Library Series, No. 126, Carleton University, Ottawa, 15-25

Warkentin, J. (editor) (1967) Canada: A Geographical Interpretation, Methuen, Toronto

Watkins, M.H. (1963) A staple theory of economic growth, Canadian Journal of Economics and Political Science, 29: 141-158

Watson, J.W. (1969) The role of illusion in North

American geography: a note on the geography of North American settlement, Canadian Geographer, 13: 10-28
Williams, P.J. (1979) Pipelines and Permafrost: Physical Geography and the Circumpolar North, Longman, London
Wonders, W.C. (1981) Northern resources development. In B. Mitchell and W.R.D. Sewell (editors), Canadian Resource Policies: Problems and Prospects, Methuen, Toronto, 56-83
Yeates, M. (1975) Main Street, Macmillan, Toronto
Zimmerman, E.W. (edited by H.L. Bunker) (1964) Introduction to World Resources, Harper and Row, New York

Chapter Four

ENVIRONMENTAL PROBLEMS AND POLICIES IN THE EUROPEAN COMMUNITY

David J. Briggs

INTRODUCTION

The ten member states of the European Community cover a land area of some 1.67 x 10^6 km^2. This area is politically, socially and economically diverse. Politically, each state retains independence at a national level, and within each state considerable regional autonomy survives. Socially and economically, the Community encompasses both heavily industrialised and urbanised regions (mainly in the north), and rural, agricultural areas (which dominate the south). .

The environment of the Community is similarly disparate. Its territory ranges from a latitude of 61°N in the Shetlands to 35°N in southern Crete; from a longitude of 11 °W in western Ireland to 28° E in eastern Greece. In consequence, its climate varies from cool temperate maritime to warm temperate continental, and from alpine to Mediterranean. Associated with this climate diversity is a distinct vegetational zoning. According to Ozenda (1979) the Community can be divided into four main phyto-geographical domains: the Atlantic in the north and west, the Subatlantic in central areas, the Mediterranean in the south and the Central European in the east. Within these broad zones, however, there occurs considerable local variation - related to physical factors such as topography, geology, soils and microclimate, and human factors such as past and present land use. Thus the territory of the Community provides habitats for a large number of species - an estimated 6,000 plant species, 50,000 invertebrates, almost 400 birds, about 130 mammals (including bats) and 60 freshwater fish (Nature Conservancy Council, 1982).

This wide range of environmental and socio-economic conditions is reflected in an equally wide variety of environmental problems. Urban and industrial areas are subject to problems of pollution; in coastal and intensively used agricultural areas there are widespread problems of erosion; almost everywhere there is pressure upon wildlife and landscape quality. Many of these problems are a result of economic development. Despite recent recession, the overall trend within the Community is towards expansion and intensification of both agriculture and industry (Table 4.1).

These developments are, in part, a product of specific Community policies and actions. Regional policy, for example, is focused on improving the economic status of less-favoured areas. Industrial policies are aimed at reducing unemployment and making the Community more self-sufficient by increasing output. Energy policies are geared towards reducing the Community's dependence on external sources. Both through its pricing policy and through specific grants to aid farm modernisation, the Common Agricultural Policy acts to encourage intensification and extension of farming. All these policies may affect the environment both locally and more widely. Moreover local, regional and national policies also have an impact on the environment.

Environmental problems, therefore, arise at a variety of geographical scales, and they need to be tackled at a variety of administrative and political levels. Community policy on the environment is thus aimed at resolving those problems considered to have European significance: either because they affect environmental resources or features of European or trans-national importance, or because they result from the Community's own policies. Community environmental policy must consequently be seen as being nested within a broader hierarchy of policies, ranging from the local to international scale.

THE DEVELOPMENT OF A COMMUNITY ENVIRONMENTAL POLICY

The general framework of the European Community's policy on the environment was laid down in 1973 in a Declaration of the Council on an 'Action

TABLE 4.1 Indices of Economic Development in the European Community (1975-1980)

	1975	1976	1977	1978	1979	1980
Total energy consumption	100	105	106	109	113	109
Energy consumption per capita	100	105	106	108	112	108
Numbers of motor vehicles	100	105	108	111	117	121
Total agricultural production[a]	100	99	103	108	112	115
Total irrigated area	100	87	97	100	101	106
Tractors and combines	100	102	103	105	107	110

Notes: a. Source - Commission of the European Communities (1982)

Source: OECD (1985)

Programme on the Environment'. This stated the basic objectives and principles of reducing pollution, avoiding damage to the environment and maintaining the ecological stability of the environment. Since then, this policy has been continued in two Resolutions (in 1977 and 1983), introducing what have become known as the Second and Third Action Programmes of the Environment.

The development of this policy, however, has not occurred in isolation. Two specific factors have guided and stimulated the policy: the growing strength of public opinion on the environment, and the existence of separate, and in some cases conflicting, national environmental policies.

Public attitudes to the environment

Political awareness of environmental concerns seems relatively rarely to be a direct response to ecological problems. More commonly, political perception develops as a result of public pressure. Such has been the case to a large extent in the European Community, where the attention devoted to environmental policies, and the nature of those policies, have been markedly influenced by public opinion.

The growth of environmental interest among the public in Europe can be traced back to the late 1960s, reaching a peak in the early 1970s. The strength of environmental interest in the Community at that time was indicated by an opinion poll of the then nine member states. Asked in 1973 to list some ten problems of national or global concern according to their relative importance, respondents cited pollution as the major problem, ahead of inflation, poverty and unemployment. Similar surveys in 1976 and 1978 confirmed this attitude, with nature conservation and pollution control being listed among the three most important concerns.

More recently, public opinion on the environment has been assessed by a wider survey of the ten countries in the Community (Riffault, 1982). Attitudes were found to vary between local and national or global issues; only 20-30 percent of interviewees were greatly concerned about their immediate neighbourhood, while 70-80 percent were worried about general environmental problems. Considerable differences exist between individual member states, however. Residents in Denmark, Ireland, the Netherlands and the United Kingdom tend to be less worried about the state of the local environment than those in Belgium, Greece, Germany and Italy. Conversely, concern about national and global environmental problems was least in Belgium and Ireland, and greatest in the Netherlands, Germany and Italy. The problems perceived by the public also varied from country to country. Air pollution, for example, was considered relatively unimportant in the United Kingdom, but serious by both Greek and Italian respondents; water pollution was cited as a major concern in Germany and the Netherlands, but of less significance in the United Kingdom and Belgium.

These environmental concerns have not been confined simply to passive opinion; they have also been given increasing political expression in recent years. Thus, by 1984 the so-called 'Green' parties had begun to have noticeable electoral success at national level in a number of member states and, in the elections to the European Parliament of that year, these parties gained some 10 percent of the seats in Strasbourg. Even before then, however, awareness of these public attitudes had begun to influence environmental policy making in the European Community.

National policies on the environment

In the light of this strengthening public concern with the environment, it is not surprising that the development of environmental policies in the European Community has become a major priority (in political if not financial terms). The political and administrative structure of the Community, however, is such that policy development is not a simple linear process, but it involves action at several different levels and on several different fronts - not all of them always compatible. National and regional autonomy, for example, means that individual member states and regions have their own environmental policies, which vary markedly in terms of comprehensiveness and authority.

Thus, in 1982, all member states except Italy had national legislation to protect wild flora. The number of species listed, however, ranged from 700 in Greece to 4 in Denmark (Nature Conservancy Council, 1982) - a variation which cannot wholly be related to differences in ecological conditions or conservation need. The efficiency of protection also varies, due to both differences in legislation and inadequacies in enforcement measures. Many bird species which are under legal protection are still widely subject to hunting and egg collecting in remoter areas of the Community, notably in Italy. Similarly, despite national protection in some states, several species of migratory birds and bats are still threatened because of lack of protection elsewhere - not only in the European Community but also in Africa, and, in some cases, Asia.

Similar problems occur in relation to pollution. The nature, rigour and enforcibility of pollution control varies significantly from one member state to another, although the pollutants themselves are often highly dispersible and unconstrained by national boundaries. Thus national legislation on vehicle exhausts has traditionally varied considerably from country to country, whilst controls on SO_2 emissions have also varied at a national level.

Scope and implementation of Community environmental policies

Given the disparate attitudes and policies of member states to questions of environmental protection and improvement, the general aim of the European Commission has been to develop a co-ordinated policy on the environment at Community level. As has been stated, the general objectives of this policy were established in the First Action Programme on the Environment, adopted on 22nd November 1973. The principles on which this policy were based - and which have underlain Community policies since - included:

i. prevention is better than cure, and thus priority should be given to developing protective measures,

ii. the polluter pays, such that the polluter is made financially responsible for making good any damage to the environment,

iii. environmental policy must be compatible with economic and social development and it should be integrated into economic and social policies,

iv. individual member states must take care to avoid damaging the environment in other states or in the Community as a whole, and

v. Community environmental policy should aim mainly at co-ordinating and harmonising national policies without hampering progress at a national level.

In this context, the First Action Programme specified three main objectives:

i. to reduce and prevent pollution and nuisances,

ii. to protect the environment and natural resources and improve the quality of life, and

iii. to take part in international initiatives to solve environmental problems at a wider scale.

Subsequently, the Second Environmental Action Programme restated and extended these aims (Official Journal of the European Communities, 13th June 1977), emphasising the need for research and data collection on the environment, and stating the intention of the Commission to develop a system of environmental impact assessment. The Third Environmental Action Programme (Official Journal of the European Communities, 17th February 1983) repeated the general objectives and stressed the link between environmental and economic considerations. In response to the growing concern about unemployment and resource depletion, therefore, environmental policies were seen as a means of conserving scarce resources for future use and creating employment by developing environmentally compatible industries and technologies.

Whilst the environmental action programme lay down the framework for Community policy on the environment, the implementation of these policies must generally be carried out by the member states themselves. Consequently, the broad outline of policy embodied in these programmes needs to be translated into more detailed obligations and legal instruments, specifying the action to be taken by the member states. This is achieved mainly through the adoption of Directives. These are texts which are binding upon the member states and they include (in most cases) precise targets that must be met in the timescale indicated. Implementation of the Directives then involves two further steps at national level: adoption of the necessary legal instruments (e.g. Acts of Parliament), and application of these in the field. As will be noted later, these requirements are not always fulfilled, and as a result Community policies are sometimes not enacted as originally foreseen.

Environmental Problems and Policies

The themes of integration and the need for holistic approaches to the environment which run through environmental policies in the Community make it difficult to separate these policies satisfactorily into distinct groups. Many of the Directives are aimed at co-ordinating different types of action on a range of different problems. In broad terms, however, it is possible to relate these initiatives to the three main threads of Community policy on the environment: reducing pollution, conserving natural resources and protecting the environment.

POLLUTION CONTROL

Problems of environmental pollution have long been of considerable concern within the Community, and much attention has been given to developing instruments for pollution control. The basic principle underlying Community policy in this area is that pollution can best be controlled by specifying 'standards' for emissions to the environment (emission standards) or for ambient pollution levels in the environment (quality standards). Where necessary, these can be introduced with progressively greater rigour through time, so that pollution is reduced in a step-by-step manner.

This approach is somewhat contentious (most notably in Britain), and disputes about appropriate emission and quality standards and ways of achieving these have in some cases delayed implementation of Community policy.

Air pollution

One of the most emotive aspects of environmental concern in recent years has been the problem of air pollution. Before the late 1950s, the main concern was with particulate pollution, arising largely from the combustion of coal. Following events such as the London smog of 1954, many countries introduced clean-air zones in cities and attempted to control the use of coal for both domestic and industrial purposes. As a result of these policies, smoke levels were already declining in many European countries by 1970. Since then, however, the significance of other atmospheric pollutants has been increasingly appreciated, and attention has been diverted to the effects of sulphur dioxide, nitrogen oxides and heavy metals such as cadmium and lead. In the light of these developments, the European Community has adopted a number of instruments to control air pollution.

A major concern today is with the effects of atmospheric acidification (the so-called 'acid deposition' or 'acid rain' problem). The processes by which acidification takes place are complex and, as yet, incompletely understood, but they generally involve oxidation of compounds of sulphur and nitrogen (Cox and Penkett, 1983). These compounds are derived mainly from power plants, industrial and commercial activity and vehicle exhausts. Due to inadequacies of available data, the levels of emission and atmospheric concentrations of both SO_2 and NO_x (general oxides of nitrogen) over mainland Europe remain uncertain. Data provided by OECD (1979, 1985), for example, suggest that SO_2 emissions have declined in the Netherlands, Germany and the United Kingdom since 1965, whilst they have risen markedly in France and Italy (see also Figure 4.1). Semb (1978), on the other hand, estimated that total SO_2 emissions in Europe rose from 16 x 10^6 tonnes in 1960 to about 27 x 10^6 tonnes in 1977, largely as a result of increased oil combustion. Similarly, OECD data indicate a progressive rise in NO_x emissions in France, Germany, Italy and the Netherlands over the last 15-20 years.

The effects of atmospheric acidification are also uncertain, and have been the subject of detailed and often vituperative political debate. Evidence is accruing, however, to show that acidity is transferred by rainfall and dry deposition to terrestrial and aquatic ecosystems, with consequent adverse impacts upon wildlife. The most dramatic effects have been claimed in Scandinavia: Morling (1981) monitored conditions in 21 Scandinavian

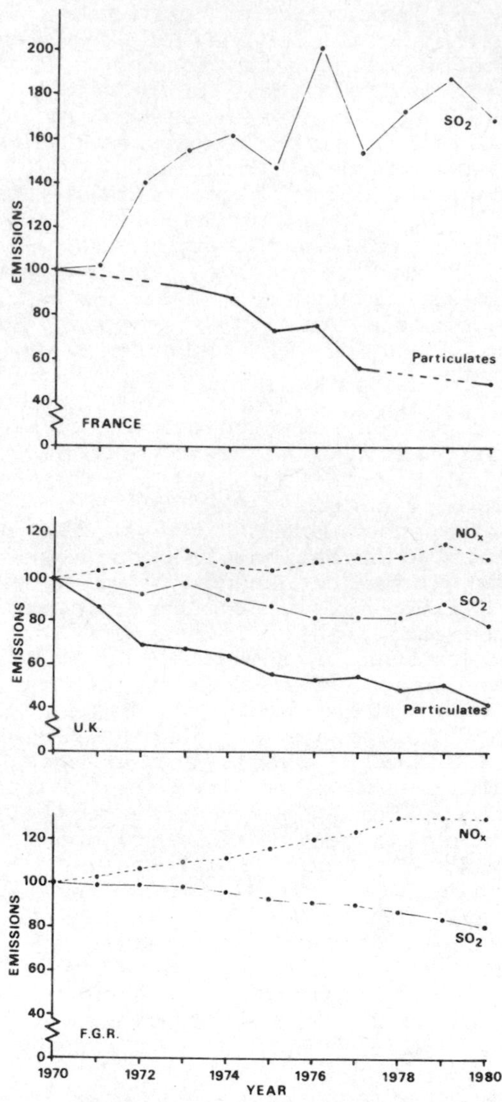

FIGURE 4.1 Trends in SO_2, NO_x and particulate emissions in selected member states, 1978-80

Note: index values based on changes since 1970(100)

Source: based on data from OECD (1985), Ministère de l'Environnement (1982), DOE (1983)

lakes from 1966 to 1979 and found that pH declined in almost all of them by 0.9 - 2.2 pH units, while sulphate concentration increased by 6 - 13 mg l^{-1}. It is also estimated that a total of 1771 fish populations have been lost from the four southernmost counties of Norway as a result of acidification (Muniz and Leivestad, 1980). Similar effects have been detected in the European Community. Hultberg (1983) reviewed a number of studies showing increased levels of acidity in lakes in Belgium, Denmark, the United Kingdom and Italy, and he suggested that in Germany losses of trout populations between 1940 and 1964, and carp between 1970 and 1980, may have been due to acid deposition.

Impacts on forest trees and soil fertility are claimed to be equally significant (Ulrich, 1983). Environmental Resources Ltd., (1983) estimated that 2 million ha of forest in Germany has been affected, representing an annual loss of U.S. \$0.2 x 10^9, whilst as much as U.S. \$1.0 x 10^9 per annum may be lost due to damage to agricultural crops. Nevertheless, Evans (1982), amongst others, has argued that results to date do not demonstrate a direct and deleterious effect on forest growth under field conditions.

Other impacts of atmospheric pollution have been equally contentious. The effects of high levels of lead intake on human health are well known, but the subclinical effects of lead from traffic exhausts on children in urban areas has been fiercely debated (Raphael et al, 1975; Roels, 1974). Similarly, other heavy metals such as nickel, asbestos, cadmium and mercury may be washed from the air and become concentrated in aquatic ecosystems, where they can accumulate in foodchains. Rauhut (1980), for example, estimated that 263 tonnes of the 5156 tonnes of cadmium released into the European environment in 1975 entered the atmosphere, and much of this was probably washed into aquatic ecosystems.

At a wider scale, changes in the composition of the atmosphere may have significant climatic and ecological effects. Increased levels of carbon dioxide have been cited as a cause of climatic change during the present century (e.g. Bach <u>et al</u>, 1979), and further increases in CO_2 may lead to further significant change. This, in turn, may alter the productive potential of the environment, resulting in changes in agricultural output. As part of a project to assess the effects of CO_2 enforced climatic change, Briggs and Coleman (in press) employed a crop-environment model to estimate likely effects of a doubling of atmospheric CO_2 on agricultural productivity throughout the Community, for a number of different climatic scenarios. Results indicated that biomass production would be likely to increase (by up to 30-50 percent) in central-eastern areas and the uplands, but show little change or a small reduction (by up to 20 percent) in the southern and more arid regions of the Community. Associated with this, small changes in runoff potential were estimated: increases of up to 90mm y^{-1} in eastern and northern areas, and decreases of up to 60mm y^{-1} in the south and west.

Given the significance of the impacts of air pollution on both the ecosystem and the quality of life, it is not surprising that much effort has been devoted to policies of pollution monitoring and control. Monitoring is of particular importance in this context, for although many countries have a network of stations measuring smoke, SO_2 and - less widely - other atmospheric pollutants, there are severe problems of inconsistency, incompatibility and incompleteness of the information. Different stations often use different measurement techniques, and many stations have not operated continuously or for sufficient periods of time to show clear trends.

Moreover, the siting of monitoring stations has been far from random, and often the sites are chosen to monitor a specific source; changes in atmospheric pollutants measured by these stations may therefore have little general significance and the network as a whole does not provide a representative picture of pollution levels in the Community. This may explain why SO_2 levels have appeared to decline at many stations, while SO_2 emissions at a national level have increased.

With this in mind, the European Commission has established a programme for the exchange of information on atmospheric pollution (Commission of the European Communities, 1979) and has set up some 400 additional monitoring stations in order to improve the comprehensiveness and compatibility of air pollution data. At the same time, research is being undertaken to improve and standardise measurement techniques.

More direct action to control air pollution has generally involved the adoption of Directives, which set emission limits. Thus a Council Decision in 1980 (80/372) limited the production of chlorofluorocarbons in the Community, specifying a 30 percent reduction (from 1976 levels) in the use of these aerosols by 31st December 1981. Similar standards are being introduced to control exhaust emissions from vehicles. This Directive, initially introduced in 1970, has undergone four amendments and is currently being further amended. It defines permitted levels of CO, hydrocarbon and NO_x and it is now being extended to additional substances.

Lead contents of petrol have also been limited by the Directive (78/611) adopted in 1978, which set a limit of 0.4 mg 1^{-1} for super grade fuel, whilst average and ambient lead levels in the air have been limited to a concentration of 2mg Pb m^{-3} by a Directive adopted in 1982 (82/884). A Directive of 1980 (80/773) lays down standards for SO_2 and particulate concentrations in the atmosphere. Further Directives have been proposed to define limit values for emissions of nitrogen dioxide (83/498) and to introduce specific pollution control measures in industrial plants (83/173).

Water pollution

Pressures on water resources come from a wide range of different, and often conflicting, activities. Water is used not only for domestic consumption and industrial purposes, but also for irrigation, as a medium for waste disposal and as a transport medium. In addition, water serves vital ecological functions and provides important habitats for wildlife. Moreover, as with the atmosphere, the various components of the hydrological system are intimately and intricately interlinked, so that effects on one part of the system are rapidly spread to others; in particular, pollutants entering streams tend to be carried into the seas which thus act as sinks for many polluting substances. These effects have become more acute in recent decades as a result of increased industrialisation, intensification of farming, and expansion of tourism.

One of the main sources of stream pollution is

agricultural activity. Partly because of national policies, but also due to the Common Agricultural Policy, farming within the Community has become increasingly dependent on inputs of chemicals. The use of pesticides has doubled since 1970, while fertiliser applications have increased by 25 percent (Figure 4.2). Grazing intensities

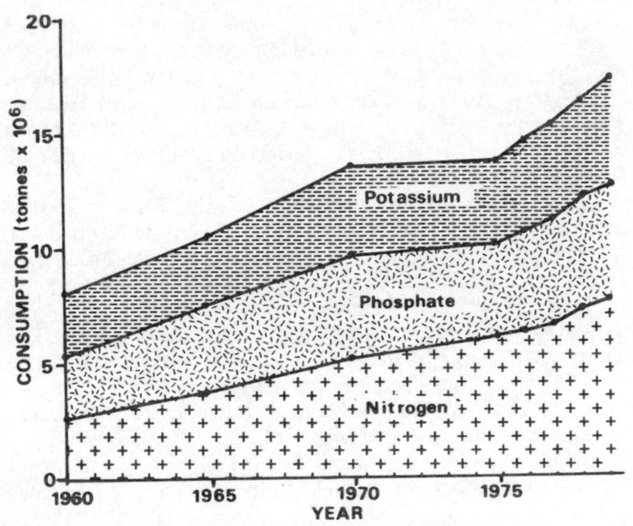

FIGURE 4.2 Trends in fertiliser applications in the European Community, 1960-79

Source: based on data from OECD (1985)

have also increased in many grassland areas, with consequent problems of waste disposal and runoff from feedlots and silos. The number of pigs, for example, rose at a rate of 7 percent per annum between 1973 and 1979 (Commission of the European Communities, 1982).

Rates of effluent generation from domestic and industrial sources show more complex changes in recent years. The total quantities of effluents produced have risen in all member states: in

Germany it increased by some 17 percent between 1953 and 1975, in Luxembourg by 51 percent between 1973 and 1977, and in France by 31 percent between 1974 and 1978 (SOBEMAP, 1981). At the same time, however, treatment facilities have been expanded not least in response to Community policy. Capital expenditure on sewage treatment rose in almost all countries between 1970 and 1982, with the result that the net load of effluents discharged to streams decreased (Figure 4.3).

It is difficult to isolate the effects of these different processes on stream water quality. In many cases the overall trend is towards improved water quality, reflecting the success of both national and Community policies. In England and Wales, for example, the length of grossly polluted streams has declined from 5280 km in 1958 to 3250 km in 1980 (Department of Environment, 1983). In France, the proportion of measured streams classed as polluted (<u>hors classe</u>) by toxic substances fell from 37 percent in 1973 to 2 percent in 1980 (Ministère de l'Environnement, 1982).

These changes are reflected by trends in many specific parameters of stream water quality. As part of a Community Decision (77/795) on the exchange of information on the quality of surface fresh water, for example, water quality data have been collected for selected stations in each member state (Commission of the European Communities, 1980a). The run of data is so far too limited to allow the recognition of general trends, but it appears that while nitrate levels are widely increasing, BOD and chlorine levels are declining in many rivers.

Nevertheless, there are many exceptions to these basic trends. Nitrate levels have more than doubled in the Witham and Stour in England between 1958 and 1980 (Departments of Environment, 1983), have shown similar increases in many rivers in Ireland between 1972 and 1978 (An Foras Forbartha, 1981) and have increased by 59 percent from 1970 to 1980 in the Rhine at Koblenz (International Commission for the Protection of the Rhine Against Pollution, 1980). Similarly, many lakes are showing evidence of eutrophication (nutrient enrichment) due to increased inputs of nitrates and phosphates. In Britain, the Norfolk Broads have been the subject of particular concern, while

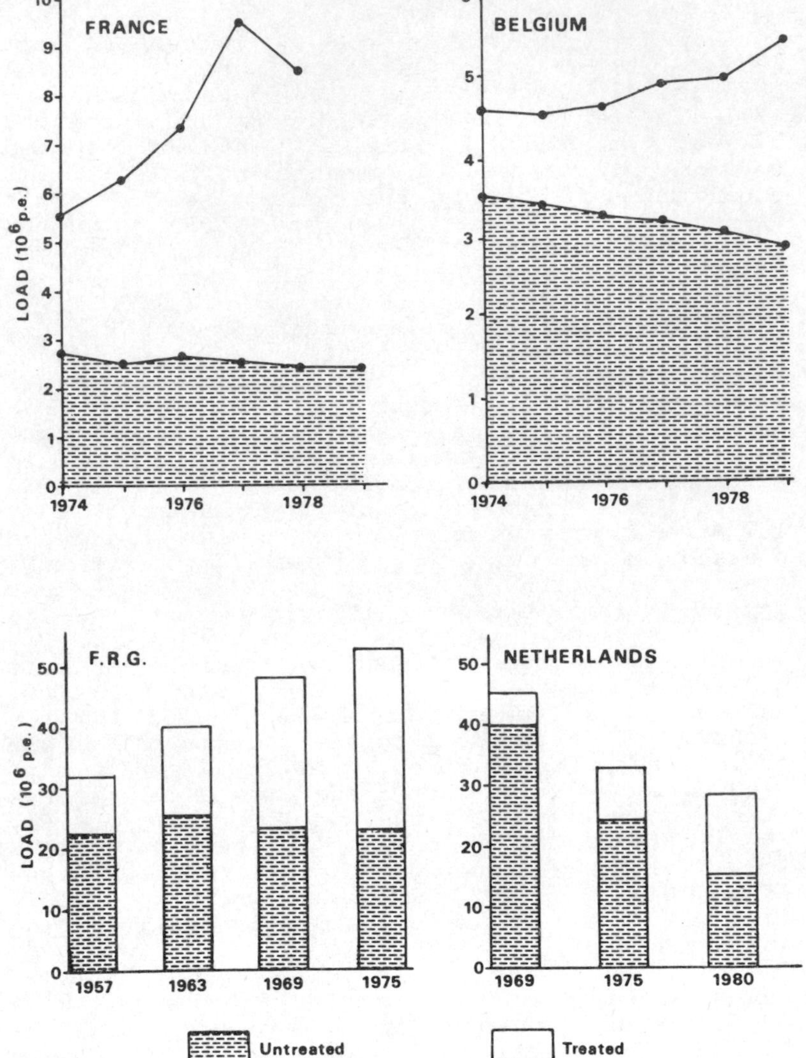

FIGURE 4.3 Trends in effluent discharges to streams in selected member states

NOTE: p.e. = population equivalent

SOURCE: based on data from Ministère de l'Environnement (1982), SOBEMAP (1981)

in the Netherlands nitrate levels are increasing rapidly in the Ijssel (OECD, 1985).

The effects of water pollution are not confined to stream and lake waters. Groundwaters also may be contaminated by agricultural chemicals, industrial effluent and domestic wastes. Nitrate fertilisers represent a particular problem, and much attention in Britain has been devoted to investigating claims of increased NO_3 levels in the aquifers of the Chalk and Triassic sandstones (e.g. Young and Gray, 1978; Foster et al, 1982). It is known that nitrate profiles beneath intensive agricultural land show a marked peak (with concentrations on occasions above the WHO 'safe' limit of 11.3mg l^{-1}). It is not clear, however, whether this reflects a dynamic balance between rates of surface input and loss by denitrification at depth, or whether it is evidence of a pulse of polluted water moving downwards into the acquifer as a result of changes in fertiliser practice. Nevertheless, in recent years similar fears have been expressed in Denmark and the Netherlands.

Concern has also been growing about the effects of coastal and marine pollution. Data on coastal water quality is scarce, but qualitative observations on marine pollution imply increasing problems, especially in the Mediterranean and adjacent to heavily industrialised areas in the North Sea. The preamble to the European Coastal Charter (Conference of Peripheral Maritime Regions, 1982), for example, stressed the combined problems of pollution by hydrocarbons (mainly as a result of accidents and oil spillage) and 'telluric' pollution due to inputs from industry and agriculture. The magnitude of this latter problem is illustrated for waters in the north-west of the Community by the data in Figure 4.4. This shows the activity of caesium-137 in 1974; as can be seen high levels of Cs occur in many littoral areas, most notably off the coast of the English Lake District. These appear to be a product mainly of wastes from nuclear processing plants such as that at Sellafield (formerly called Windscale) in Cumbria. Broadly similar distributions are shown, however, by zinc, nickel, copper and cadmium (see also MAFF, 1981), reflecting the inputs of industrial effluents and sewage.

The significance of pollution by hydrocarbons

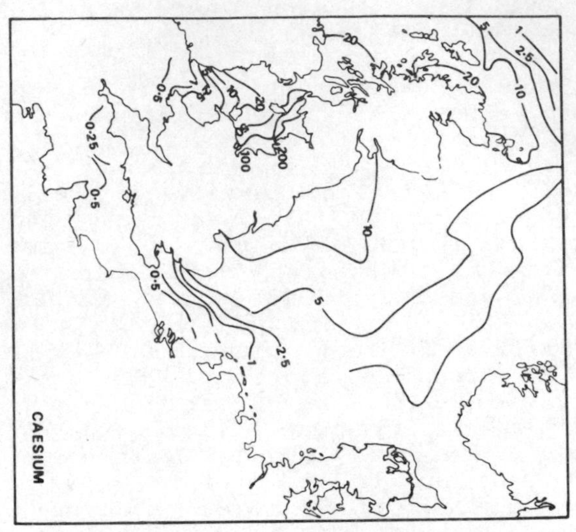

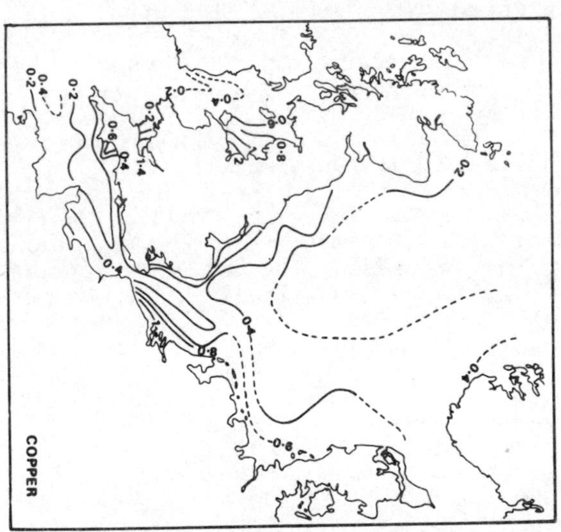

FIGURE 4.4 Distribution of caesium-137 and copper in the North Sea, 1974

SOURCE: after MAFF (1981)

is more difficult to assess. Many of the most serious effects are associated with individual major accidents (e.g. the grounding of the tanker Amoco Cadiz in 1978), but a large number of smaller accidents probably go unrecorded. In 1982, a total of 37 incidents of offshore oil slicks, 18 oil spillages in ports and 5 beach pollution incidents were reported from France, Denmark, Belgium and Italy (Wardley-Smith and Dixon, 1983). A further 31 spills were reported in British ports during 1981-2 (Wardley-Smith and Dixon, 1982). In most cases the causes of the pollution were unknown, though non-tanker vessels were the source of the majority of incidents which could be traced.

As has been indicated, action to control water pollution has been taken at both a national and Community level, and many of the trends in pollution levels and emissions are - at least in part - a product of these initiatives. At a Community level, policy has been directed mainly towards establishing rigorous emission and quality standard. One of the main components of this policy has been the Directive on Dangerous Substances (76/464), the objective of which was to provide a framework for controlling water pollution. It specifies two lists, the first (List I) consisting of the most toxic substances for which strict emission limit values are to be defined and applied to all effluents. The second list (List II) comprises less dangerous substances which are to be controlled by national agreed quality standards.

Like many Community Directives, it has not been without its problems. From the start, the United Kingdom government objected to the principle of limit values, and - following lengthy discussions in Council - the Directive was only adopted on the basis of a compromise. This permitted member states not to apply the limit values if they wished but, instead, to control List I substances by implementing environmental quality standards agreed by Council (see Haigh 1983 for a fuller discussion). Moreover, specification of limit values for List I substances was to be made by a series of 'daughter' Directives dealing with individual groups of toxic chemicals; until these were adopted all the substances concerned were to be treated as List II substances.

In practice, very few 'daughter' Directives have

been implemented, and limit values have been defined only for mercury discharges from the chlor-alkali electrolysis industry (82/176) and for cadmium (83/513). Further Directives dealing with discharges of aldrin, dieldrin and endrin (79/243), mercury from sources not already covered (83/838) and HCH and lindane (83/422) are currently (end of 1984) under discussion. In addition, a Directive has also been adopted controlling wastes from the titanium oxide industry (78/176). This obliges member states to monitor existing processing plants with a view to initiating decontamination programmes, and to establish a system of authorisation for disposal operations.

Numerous other Directives have been introduced, defining quality standards for water resources. They cover drinking water (75/440, 79/869 and 80/778), groundwater (80/68), bathing waters (76/160) and waters important for freshwater fish (78/659) and shellfish (79/923). Although somewhat less contentious in principle, considerable discussion has nevertheless attended many of these Directives (Haigh, 1983). The geographical areas to be subject to the quality standards are often defined not by the Commission but by the individual member states. This leaves considerable scope for avoiding (or at least minimising) the obligations of the Directives. In the case of the 'Freshwater Fish' Directive, for example, Haigh (1983) states that "Some member states have not designated any waters and in those countries the Directive is therefore effectively inoperative". Similarly, Wathern et al, (1983) found that implementation of the Shellfish Directive in the United Kingdom had been circumvented, and only those waters which already met the standards defined in the Directive have been designated.

In the same way, the United Kingdom has drawn up a restricted list of 27 beaches designed as traditional bathing areas used by large numbers of people, for inclusion under the Bathing Waters Directorate - the list excludes both Blackpool and Brighton (perhaps the two most popular bathing beaches in the U.K.)! Of these 27 beaches, four have since been exempted by national derogations from complying with the ten-year time limit for improvements to bathing water quality. Thus, although Directives have been adopted and, notionally, implemented, their application in the field is often emasculated, so that their effects on the environment may be limited.

The Community has also adopted several Decisions setting out policies on marine pollution. Notable among these are Decisions to combat oil pollution and pollution from land-based sources in the Mediterranean (81/420 and 83/101). A proposed Directive is now being discussed to specify methods for dealing with accidential oil spillages at sea, whilst the Community is also active in many international initiatives on marine pollution (e.g. the Paris Convention of 1974 and the Barcelona Convention of 1976).

Noise pollution

Noise pollution comes from a wide variety of sources, including industry, aircraft, domestic activities and recreation. Probably the most widely perceived source of noise pollution, however, is road traffic. Community policy has thus been directed at reducing noise pollution from traffic to an acceptable level. The general framework of this policy was set out in a Directive (70/157) adopted in 1970, and since then a series of more specific Directives have been introduced, defining noise limits for various groups of vehicles.

Initially, the aim was to reduce noise levels of all groups of vehicles to between 82 and 91 dB(A). However, recent technical developments in vehicle design and manufacture have enabled these targets to be lowered, and an amendment was therefore adopted in 1977 redefining the targets for different types of vehicle. A limit of 80 dB(A) (i.e. decibels at a standard frequency of noise), for example, was set for cars, 81-85 dB(A) for buses and 81-88 dB(A) for heavy lorries. At the same time, the intention was stated of reducing noise from all vehicles to no more than 80 dB(A) by 1985. In practice, these objectives have proved over-ambitious, and in 1983 a further amendment was proposed, again redefining the noise levels and extending the date for implementation to 1988 9.

RESOURCE CONSERVATION

In adopting the Third Environment Action Programme in 1983, the Council of Ministers (Official Journal of the European Communities, 17th February 1983;

p.46) stated:

> *...the common environmental policy is motivated equally by the observation that the resources of the environment are the basis of - but also constitute the limit to - further economic and social development and the improvement of living conditions. It aims therefore not only to protect human health, nature and the environment but also to ensure that natural resources are well managed..*

It later goes on to specify that environmental policy must, amongst other things, be concerned:

> *...to economise certain raw materials that are non-renewable, or of which supplies can be obtained only with difficulty, and to encourage the recycling of waste and the search for less polluting alternatives.*

This explicit concern with resource conservation is thus a relatively recent addition to the Community's environmental policy. As the preceding quote shows, however, it is closely related to the more deeply established objectives of minimising or eliminating pollution, and has thus been implicit in many earlier actions.

Waste disposal and recovery

The area which has received most attention is the recycling of wastes. This reflects the dual objectives of reducing pollution by these substances and avoiding the profligate exploitation of raw materials. The problem created by wastes is acute. The Commission of the European Communities (1984) notes that about 2,000 million tonnes of waste are produced annually in the Community (Table 4.2). Of these, 20-30 million tonnes are toxic and dangerous wastes. The total capacity of disposal facilities for these substances, however, is only 7-10 million tonnes; consequently, at least 50 percent of the toxic and dangerous wastes are available to cause pollution. Moreover, at present only some 35 million tonnes (2 percent) of wastes are recycled although it is estimated that 50 percent or more are recoverable. About 80 percent of the remainder are disposed of on land. Considerable potential thus exists to reduce

TABLE 4.2 Waste Production in the European Community (1983)

	(million tonnes)
Agricultural waste	950
Sewage sludge	350
Mining waste and ash	250
Municipal waste	240
Demolition rubble	170
Industrial waste	160
Other wastes	200

Source: Anon (1984)

losses of both land resources and raw materials.

In the light of these circumstances - and against the background of a major international oil crisis - the Community adopted a Waste Oils Directive in 1975 (75/439). This aimed to ensure the safe collection and disposal of waste oils "as far as possible...by recycling (regeneration and/or combustion other than for destruction". At the same time, a more general framework Directive on Waste (75/442) was agreed, with the objective of encouraging the recycling of wastes and providing for the authorisation of firms responsible for collection, recycling or disposal. Implementation of this Directive is to be monitored by a three-yearly report on waste disposal to the Commission.

More recently, three related Directives have also been adopted, dealing with polychlorinated biphenyls and polychlorinated terphenyls (76/403), titanium dioxide (78/176) and toxic and dangerous wastes (78/319). This last Directive lists 27 substances for which safe disposal methods must be developed, and it places a general obligation on member states to encourage the re-use of toxic wastes.

Current policy on wastes has been summarised in an internal document of the Commission (Anon, 1984). This estimates that 12,000 million ECUsy^{-1}

(European currency units per year) could be saved on raw material imports by waste recycling, while a further 1,250 million ECUsy^{-1} would be saved on waste disposal costs. It then outlines future objectives, including the:

> *...recovery of all agricultural wastes for re-use in agricultural activities... recovery of all sewage sludge for use in agriculture...recovery of paper, glass and metals for recycling...total recovery of rubber waste...total recovery of demolition and construction rubble... (and) total recovery and recycling or incineration of waste lubricating oils...*

Land resources

The need to conserve land resources and to develop methods of rational management of the land was stressed in the Second Action Programme on the Environment. Pressures on the land have been increasing, because of both intensification of agriculture and impacts from non-agricultural developments such as urbanisation, afforestation, mining and tourism.

Between 1970 and 1980, for example, the total area of utilisable agricultural land declined at a rate of about 0.5 percent per annum (representing a total loss of about 450,000ha), mainly as a result of urbanisation and afforestation (Commission of the European Communities, 1982). Sound data are lacking, but soil erosion and pollution are also considered to be increasing (Commission of the European Communities, 1974). These problems are of particular concern in the Mediterranean areas where good quality agricultural land is scarce and geographically fragmented, where many soils are inherently susceptible to erosion, and where pressures from urban growth and tourism are expanding rapidly due to economic development in the region (e.g. the planned Integrated Mediterranean Programme).

Nevertheless, to date, direct action to conserve land resources at a Community level has been limited, and the Community's role has mainly been to collect data in specific problem areas. Thus studies have been conducted of mountain areas (Danz and Henz, 1981) and the recently submitted proposal for an exploratory environmental information system in the Community (83/525) includes plans to map land use, agricultural land quality and risk of soil erosion in the Mediterranean region (Commission of the European Communities, 1983).

ENVIRONMENTAL PROTECTION

From the start, a keynote of Community environmental policy has been the protection of the environment from adverse effects of development and land use. The need for such action is clear. Over recent decades many habitats and landscapes have been damaged - often irreparably - by agricultural, industrial and urban development. Between 1950 and 1980, for example, the area of wetlands declined in Germany from 2471 km^2 to 1174 km^2, a loss of 52.5 percent; in the Netherlands 49.2 percent of wetlands (713 km^2) were lost over the same period (OECD, 1985). Similarly, many species of mammals, birds, reptiles, amphibians and fish are declining in numbers or are threatened with extinction (Table 4.3).

The sources of these threats are numerous. The Nature Conservancy Council (1982) cite increased uses of pesticides, habitat disturbance by tourism, habitat destruction by drainage, cultivation and urbanisation, and collecting as the main causes of plant species decline in the European Community (Figure 4.5). Likewise, Brown (1976) stressed the effects of pesticides, hunting and habitat loss on the population of raptors (birds of prey). Bat species are particularly threatened by the use of fumigants to treat timber, and by disturbance of roosting and breeding grounds (e.g. caves and trees) by tourists and hunters (Nature Conservancy Council, 1982).

Given these threats to the ecosystem, the European Community has taken a range of initiatives to protect endangered habitats and wildlife species. Particular attention has been given to controlling commercial exploitation of wildlife, and thus, in 1981, a Regulation was adopted banning the import of whale and certain other cetacean products (Reg 348/81). Trade in certain products derived from seal pups has similarly been restricted (Directive 83/129, and the Commission of the European Communities (1984) note that in anticipation of implementation of this Directive a substantial

TABLE 4.2 Threatened Wildlife Species in the European Community (1980)

	Numbers (and percent) threatened					
	Denmark	France	Germany	Italy	Netherlands	U.K.[a]
Mammals	20(41)	44(43)	51(59)	13(13)	29(48)	12(24)
Birds	41(22)	124(47)	134(45)	60(14)	71(40)	24(12)
Freshwater fish	17(10)	-	35(20)	70(14)	11(22)	8(22)
Reptiles	0(0)	16(50)	8(67)	24(52)	6(84)	2(33)
Amphibians	3(21)	15(50)	11(55)	13(46)	10(67)	2(33)
Invertebrates	155(1)	-	-	2308(4)	-	424(2)
Vascular plants	371(28)	403(10)	764(29)	-	-	144(8)

a. 1983 data (source: DOE, 1983)

Source: OECD (1985)

reduction in the number of seal pups killed has already occurred. Likewise, the Community has drawn up a Regulation implementing the Washington Convention (Reg 3626/82). This both confirms and extends the proposals of the Convention on International Trade in Endangered Species, held in March 1973, and bans or restricts trade in listed wildlife species.

Various instruments have also been adopted to protect wildlife habitats and to give more general protection to individual species. Thus, in 1975, the Community accepted a Recommendation (75/66) proposing that member states acceded to the Ramsar Convention on the conservation of wetlands and the Paris Convention on the protection of birds. This was followed by the adoption of the Bird Directive (79/419), obliging member states to maintain populations of all "naturally occurring" bird species in the wild state in the Community at a level appropriate to "ecological, scientific and cultural requirements, while taking account of economic and recreational requirements". The Directive listed 74 species of bird considered to be endangered and for which specific measures should be taken to conserve their habitats. This requires member states to identify habitats most suitable for protection and, in these areas, to take action to avoid pollution or damage that might adversely affect bird populations. In addition, all trade in these species is prohibited, while a further 72 bird species are listed which are subject to strict controls on hunting and collecting.

More recently, three Decisions have been adopted which conclude international conventions on the protection of wildlife and habitats. The Canberra Convention on Antarctic marine living organisms (81/691) aims to limit exploitation of Antarctic marine fauna, especially krill. The Berne Convention on wildlife and natural habitats (82/72) sets out to "conserve wild flora and fauna and their natural habitats, especially those species and habitats whose conservation requires the co-operation of several States, and to promote such co-operation" (Official Journal of the European Communities, 10th February, 1982, p. L 38/3). Similarly, the Bonn Convention on migratory species (82/461) encourages the protection of migratory species of wild animals "the conservation status

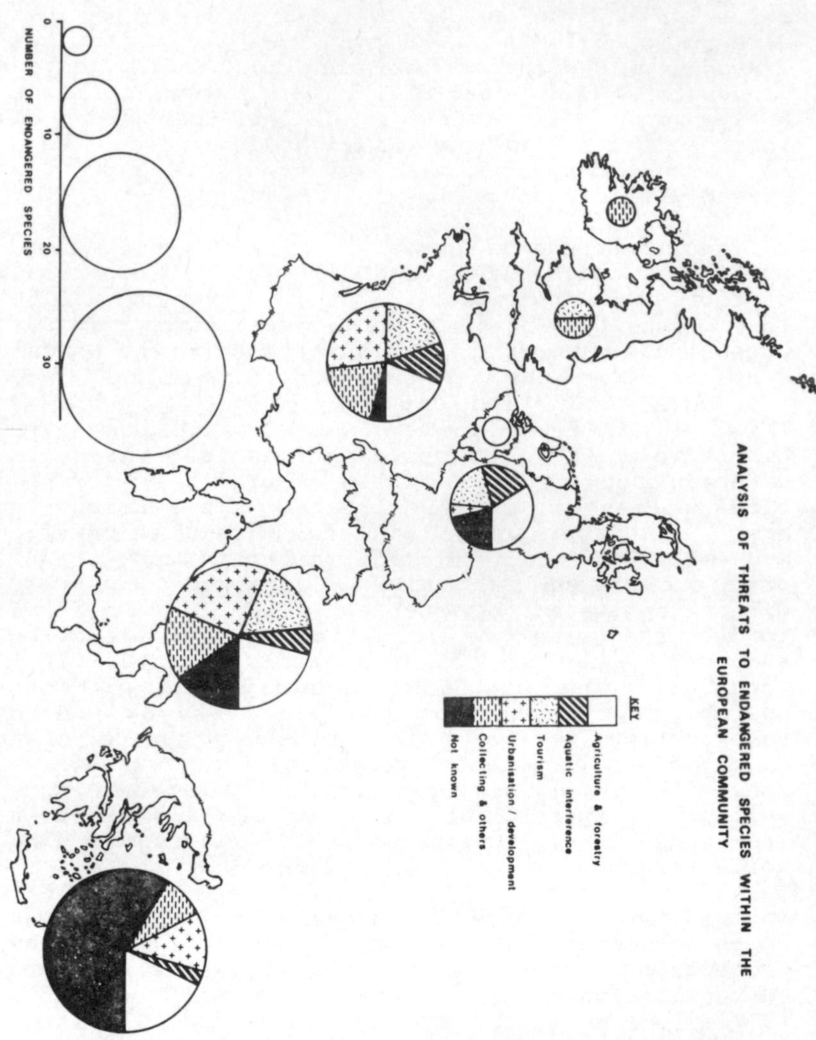

FIGURE 4.5 Sources of threats to plant species in the European Community

SOURCE: based on data from Nature Conservancy Council (1982)

---

of which is unfavourable" (Official Journal of the European Communities, 19th July 1982, p. L 210/12). Immediate protection is called for in the case of 40 species (15 mammals, 20 birds, 4 reptiles and 1 fish) listed in Appendix 1, while "agreements" to protect a further 26 species or groups of species should also be arranged.

Environmental impact assessment
The protection of the environment from the effects of economic development in any co-ordinated and preventive fashion, can only be achieved if the ability exists to predict the impacts of planned projects or development programmes before approval is given for them. Without this, the Community's environmental policy will inevitably be largely defensive and ameliorative. In stressing the need for a preventive policy, therefore, the First Action Programme on the Environment (Official Journal of the European Communities, 20th December 1973, p. C 112/3), stated:

> *Effects on the environment should be taken into account at the earliest possible stage in all technical planning and decision-making processes...It is therefore necessary to evaluate the effects on the quality of life and on the natural environment of any measure that is adopted or contemplated at national or Community level.*

This, however, is no easy task. It involves identifying aspects of the environment which are considered to be worthy of protection or evaluation; defining the potential impacts on these of planned developments; describing these impacts in a way which allows them to be incorporated into the decision-making process; and specifying the measures which need to be taken if the adverse impacts are to be minimised or avoided.

Traditionally, the performance of this task has been left to planners and politicians, acting upon their individual experience and intuition. Since the 1960s, however, numerous techniques have been developed to formalise the procedure. Methods of sieve mapping and potential surface analysis, for example, have been devised to help identify areas or sites of particular significance and to specify the nature of potential environmental impacts. Cost-benefit analysis has been used to provide an econometric evaluation of the impacts.

But the most far-reaching development has undoubtedly been the use of environmental impact assessments (EIAs). Having been devised and first implemented in the U.S.A. (see Chapter 2), these have now been adopted by a large number of states (Lee, 1983), and the European Commission has attempted to introduce the same approach within the Community. Thus, in 1980, a proposal was submitted to Council for the "assessment of the environmental effects of certain public and private projects".

Perhaps, more than in any other single instrument, the fate of this proposal highlights the problems of environmental policy development in the European Community. The proposal (Commission of the European Communities 1980b, p.2) envisaged:

> *The preparation, through the co-operation of developers of the project, the authorities and the public, of the most complete information possible on the major effects of a project on the environment, to assess the magnitude of these effects and to examine possible alternatives to the proposed project and lastly to provide the measures to minimise the adverse impacts.*

Projects to be subject to these evaluations comprised industrial, mining, energy, commercial, residential, agricultural and infrastructural developments. These were divided into two groups. The first (Annex 1 projects) included developments such as extraction of bituminous shale, petroleum refining, cement manufacture, forging, slaughter houses and primary rubber production, all of which were considered to affect the environment under any circumstances: these were to be subject to 'full assessments'. The second (Annex 2 projects) were considered to affect the environment only under particular circumstances, and thus they would be subject to impact assessments only when certain thresholds (e.g. size, output) were exceeded. These included projects such as cultivation of natural land, extraction and purification of natural gas, pesticide production, boilermaking, tanning and flood relief schemes. The criteria by which these Annex 2 projects were to be selected for impact assessments were to be defined by the individual member states.

Despite the circumstances that EIAs were already established features of planning procedures in a number of member states (including France and Luxembourg) and were being considered for implementation in Germany, the proposal met fierce resistance. Objections included claims that the proposals would infringe national competence in planning decisions, would be too costly to implement, would delay developments and would deter investment. In addition, there was much disagreement over the range of projects to be included. As a consequence, by 1984 the Directive had still not been adopted, and the proposals had been progressively diluted until they provided no more than a general framework for impact assessment.

Because of this loss of impetus regarding the proposals for a system of environmental impact assessment in the Community, it is now doubtful whether the objective of making the environmental policy fully preventive and integrative can be achieved. Without such a system it is difficult to see how the effects of planned developments can be identified and evaluated in time to allow co-ordinated action to be taken either to amend the project or to protect the environment. Even if the current proposals are accepted, however, it is not certain that action will occur soon enough or in a sufficiently integrated manner. As Lee (1983) has argued, assessment of environmental impacts of individual projects allows only relatively piecemeal protection of the environment, and this often occurs too late to alter more general commitments to development. What is needed instead is evaluation of policies.

The need for this can be seen in relation to policies on nuclear energy and on agriculture. In both cases, the main thrust of the policy will inevitably have major environmental implications, and environmental action will always be defensive and negative. From an environmental standpoint, it would appear far more appropriate to consider the environmental implications during the development of these policies, rather than at the stage of implementation. This would require the widespread availability of appropriate environmental information.

Environmental Information Systems

Without data, environmental objectives cannot be expressed in a form consonant with economic and social aspects, and they will remain essentially qualitative and vague. Moreover, unless appropriate data are easily available, policy development will inevitably be delayed (or evaluated on the basis of partial information) while the necessary surveys are conducted. Similarly, costly repetition of data collection may occur if information is acquired separately for different purposes.

Herein lies a fundamental and almost universal problem of environmental policy - relevant data are generally lacking and the information which is available is often incomplete, incompatible or inconsistent. The problem is particularly acute at the Community level, because differences in measurement systems between member states increase the degree of incompatibility of the data. Even where specific data gathering exercises are conducted as part of co-ordinated campaigns (e.g. on atmospheric SO_2), marked discrepancies in monitoring techniques may result in hidden inconsistencies in the information.

In recognition of this problem, the Commission has for some years been working on a project to establish an environmental information system in the Community. Initially called (somewhat imprecisely) The Ecological Mapping Project, it has highlighted many of the problems involved in data collection at this scale. Compatibility requires an agreed and generally applicable set of definitions. These in turn must depend upon the uses to which the information is to be put. Since the objective is to have a flexible body of information which can be applied to a wide range of foreseen and unforeseen problems, precise definition of the variables to be measured poses major difficulties.

Data acquisition is costly, and collection of redundant information needs to be avoided. On the other hand, a too narrow specification of the data to be included in the information system will limit the range of policy appraisals that can be carried out. Data collection has to be a compromise between what is ideal and what is practicable.

Because of these problems, and due to inexperience in data compilation and management at such a scale, early attempts to establish the environmental information system were unsuccessful (France and Briggs, 1980). By 1983, however, proposals for a co-ordinated information system on the environment (subsequently called CORINE) had been developed (Briggs, 1982; Commission of the European Communities, 1983) and plans for the first phase of implementation of the system are being drawn up.

ENVIRONMENTAL POLICY AND EMPLOYMENT

One aspect of environmental policy which is receiving increased attention as a result of changing circumstances is its relationship with employment. In the past, the claim has often been made that environmental protection poses a threat to employment by diverting resources from productive sections of the economy, by delaying or deterring innovation, and by raising the costs of production and thereby driving marginal firms out of business.

As noted in the Third Action Programme, however, Community environmental policy is in part based on the premise that environmental action can increase employment by encouraging the design of environmentally sensitive technology, by promoting direct employment in environmental fields (e.g. reclamation, monitoring, management) and by shifting the emphasis in some cases from capital-intensive to more labour-intensive production systems.

Which of these interpretations is valid is difficult to determine. Assessments must take account not only of the immediate, direct effects of environmental policy on employment, but also the longer term and indirect impacts through multiplier effects, changes in trade, product substitution and wage and price adjustments. Several studies have examined these aspects, most notably in the Netherlands, France and Germany (reviewed in OECD, 1984). Results vary. In early studies in the Netherlands, for example, a 1.2 - 1.3 per-cent annual reduction in employment was predicted as a result of environmental policies. On the other hand, two German studies both predicted small but significant increases in employment.

The later of these two studies estimated a net annual increase in employment of 200,000 - 250,000 between 1972 and 1980 through the effect of environmental programmes.

Specific job creation projects in the environmental field can increase the positive effects on employment, but OECD (1984) conclude that the net impact is small, especially compared to other factors. Nevertheless, it is clear that the dire warnings about negative impacts of environmental policy are probably greatly exaggerated and environmental policy will not significantly harm, and may in some cases markedly improve, the employment situation in the European Community.

CONCLUSIONS

Compared to other areas of policy in the European Community, environmental policy has never been a major priority, nor has it commanded large financial support. Although in 1982 some 13 million ECUs were committed to environmental and consumer matters, this represented only about 0.06 percent of the total Community budget for that year. The fact that environmental policy is also a structural policy, cutting across sectoral concerns, has also meant that it has encountered particular problems of co-operation.

Moreover, as has been noted, experience in many aspects of environmental policy at this scale was limited when the policy was established in 1973, and changing external conditions (most notably the economic status of the Community) have caused shifts in the emphasis of environmental policy. Inevitably, therefore, the development of the policy has not been a simple linear process, and several of the main objectives of the First Action Programme remain as yet unfulfilled.

At the same time, the efficacy of policies which have been implemented is difficult to assess. It is apparent that adoption of a Directive does not necessarily imply application of its principles in the member states. Various devices have been employed to mitigate the responsibilities of the member states and to avoid changing national practice, though member states can be (and are) taken to the European Court if they fail to adopt the necessary legislation. Nor has monitoring of the environment before and after policy adoption been undertaken in many instances, so that the impacts of individual policies on the environment cannot be evaluated. Indeed, because of changes in other factors (such as levels of economic activity and national procedures on environmental protection) it is probably impossible in many instances to isolate the effects of Community policy. The success or otherwise of the policy must, therefore, remain largely conjectural.

What is clear, however, is that the pressures on the environment will continue, and in several cases they are likely to increase. The need for a positive and co-ordinated environmental policy within the Community will therefore remain paramount if the adverse effects of other Community and national policies are to be minimised. A major question, however, is still the extent to which individual member states are willing to forego national economic interests for the sake of wider environmental considerations.

Acknowledgement

The author would like to thank MICHEL CORNAERT of the European Community Environment Service for the provision of information and for commenting on an early draft of this chapter.

REFERENCES

An Foras Forbartha (1980) Review 1979/80, An Foras Forbartha, Dublin

Anon (1984) Waste management policy. Preliminary draft prepared by a consultant for the Commission, 21st March 1984

Bach, W., Pankrath, J. and Kellogg, W. (1979) (editors) Man's Impact on Climate, Elsevier, Amsterdam

Briggs, D.J. (1982) The ecological mapping of the European Community, Ekistics, 49: 236-40

Briggs, D.J. and Coleman, R. (in press) Effects of changes in atmospheric CO_2 concentrations on biomass potential and runoff potential in the European Community. Appendix 1 In B. Santer (editor) Socio-economic impacts of Climatic Change, Dornier System GmbH, Friedrichshafen

Brown, L. (1976) British Birds of Prey, Collins, London

Commission of the European Communities (1974) Okologische Folgen der Anwendung moderner Produktions methoden in der Landwirtschaft, Commission of the European Communities Landwirtschaft No. 137, Brussels

Commission of the European Communities (1979) Exchange of information concerning atmospheric pollution by certain sulphur compounds and suspended solids in the European Community, Commission of the European Communities (EUR 6472 EN), Brussels

Commission of the European Communities (1980a) Quality of surface fresh water in the Community (9 vols.). Fourth comprehensive report on the exchange of information on the quality of surface fresh water in the Community (77/795 - EEC), Commission of the European Communities, Brussels

Commission of the European Communities (1980b) Proposal for a Council Directive concerning the assessment of the environmental effects of certain public and private projects, COM (80) 313 final. Commission of the European Communities, Brussels

Commission of the European Communities (1982) The agricultural situation in the Community. 1981 report, Commission of the European Communities, Brussels and Luxembourg

Commission of the European Communities (1983) Communication of the Commission to the Council concerning a methodological approach to an information system on the state of the environment and natural resources in the Community (1984-87), COM(83) final. Commission of the European Communities, Brussels

Commission of the European Communities (1984) Ten years of Community environment policy, Commission of the European Communities, Brussels

Conference of Peripheral Maritime Regions of the EEC (CPMR) (1980) European coastal charter

Cox, R.A. and Penkett, S.A. (1983) Formation of atmospheric acidity. In H. Ott and H. Stangl (editors) Acid deposition: a challenge for Europe. Symposium Proceedings, Karlsruhe 19th-21st September 1983, Commission of the European Communities, Brussels, 58-81

Danz, W. and Henz, H.R. (1981) Integrated development of mountain areas. The alpine region. Regional Policy Series No. 20. Commission of the European Communities, Brussels

Department of the Environment (1983) Digest of environmental protection and water statistics. No. 6, H.M.S.O., London

Environmental Resources Ltd. (1983) Acid rain - review of the phenomenon in the EEC and Europe, report prepared for the Commission of the European Communities. Environmental Resources Ltd., London

Evans, L.S. (1982) Biological effects of acidity in precipitation on vegetation: a review, Environmental and Experimental Biology, 22; 155-69

Foster, S.S.D., Cripps, A.C. and Smith-Carington, A. (1982) Nitrate leaching to groundwater, Philosophical Transactions of the Royal Society, London B296; 477-82

France, J. and Briggs, D.J. (1980) Environmental mapping of the European Community: a review of the proposed method, Journal of the Operational Research Society, 31; 485-95

Haigh, N. (1983) EEC environmental policy and Britain, Environmental Data Services Ltd., London

Hultberg, H. (1983) Effects of acid deposition on aquatic ecosystems. In H. Ott and H. Stangl (editors) Acid deposition: a challenge for Europe. Symposium Proceedings, Karlsruhe, 19th-21st September 1983, Commission of the European Communities, Brussels, 167-85

International Commission for the Protection of the Rhine Against Pollution (1980) Numerical tables of physico-chemical analyses of the waters of the Rhine, International Commission for the Protection of the Rhine Against Pollution, Koblenz

Lee, N. (1983) Environmental impact assessment: a review, Applied Geography, 3; 5-27

MAFF (1981) Atlas of the seas around the British Isles, MAFF, London

Ministère de l'Environnement (1982) L'état de l'environnment, La Documentation Française, Paris

Morling, G. (1981) Effects of acidification on some lakes in western Sweden. Vatten, 1; 25-38

Muniz, I. and Leivestad, H. (1980) Acidification - effects on freshwater fish. In D. Drablos and A. Tollan (editors) Ecological impact of acid precipitation. Proceedings of an International Conference, Norway, 11th-14th March 1980. SNSF, Oslo, 84-92

Nature Conservancy Council (1982) Conservation of species of wild flora and vertebrate fauna threatened in the Community (2 vols.), prepared for the Commission of the European Communities, Nature Conservancy Council, London

OECD (1979) The state of the environment in OECD member countries, Organisation for Economic Co-operation and Development, Paris

OECD (1984) Environment and economics. Issue Papers, International Conference 18th-21st June 1984. Organisation for Economic Co-operation and Development, Paris

OECD (1985) Second OECD report on the state of the environment, Organisation for Economic Co-operation and Development, Paris

Official Journal of the European Communities (1973) Declaration of the Council of the European Communities and of the Representatives of the Governments of the Member States meeting in the Council on the Action Programme of the European Communities on the environment, Official Journal of the European Communities (20.12.73); C 112

Official Journal of the European Communities (1977) Resolution of the Council of the European Communities and the Representatives of the Governments of the Member States meeting in the Council on the continuation and implementation of a European Community policy and action programme on the environment, Official Journal of the European Communities (13.6.77); 20 C 139; 1-46

Official Journal of the European Communities (1982a) Convention on the conservation of European wildlife and natural habitats. Official Journal of the European Communities (10.2.82); 25 L 38; 3-82

Official Journal of the European Communities (1982b) 82/459/EEC Council Decision of 24th June 1982 establishing a reciprocal exchange of information and data from networks and individual stations measuring air pollution within the member states. Official Journal of the European Communities (19.7.82) 25 L 210; 1-7

Official Journal of the European Communities

(1982c) Convention on the conservation of migratory species of wild animals, Official Journal of the European Communities (19.7.82); 25 L 210; 11-22

Official Journal of the European Communities (1983) Council Resolution of the Council of the European Communities and of the Representatives of the Governments of the Member States meeting in the Council on the continuation and implementation of a European Community policy and action programme on the environment (1982 to 1986), Official Journal of the European Communities (17.2.83); 26 C 46; 1-16

Ozenda, P. (1979) Vegetation map of the Council of Europe member states, European Committee for the Conservation of Nature and Natural Resources, Council of Europe, Strasbourg

Raphael, J.C., Margulis, H.L. and Joselaw, M.M. (1975) Residential location, ambient air lead pollution and lead absorption in children. Professional Geographer, 27; 37-42

Rauhut, A. (1980) Survey of industrial emission of cadmium in the European Economic Community, Commission of the European Communities, Brussels

Riffault, H. (1982) (editor) The Europeans and their environment, Commission of the European Communities, Brussels

Roels, H. (1975) Impact of air pollution by lead on heme-biosynthetic pathway in school-age children, Archives of Environmental Health, 31; 310-6

Semb, A. (1978) Sulphur emissions in Europe, Atmospheric Environment, 12; 455-60

SOBEMAP (1981) Quantitative and qualitative inventory of sewage treatment plants in the European Community (11 vols.), prepared for the Commission of the European Communities, SOBEMAP, Brussels

Ulrich, B. (1983) Effects of accumulation of air pollutants in forest ecosystems. In H. Ott and H. Stangl (editors) Acid deposition: a challenge for Europe. Symposium Proceedings Karlsruhe 19th-21st September 1983 Commission of the European Communities, Brussels, 127-46

Wardley-Smith, J. and Dixon, T.R. (1982) An inventory of hydrocarbon spillages in representative areas of the marine environment in member states. Final report. Advisory

Committee on Pollution of the Sea, London

Wardley-Smith, J. and Dixon, T.R. (1983) An inventory of hydrocarbon spillages in the marine environment of member states, Final report to the Commission of the European Communities. Scientific Sub-Committee of the Advisory Committee on Pollution of the Sea, London

Wathern, P., Brown, I.W., Roberts, D.A. and Young, S.N. (1983) Some effects of EEC policy, Vol. 3, Final report for the Commission of the European Communities, University College of Wales, Bangor

Young, C.P. and Gray, E.M. (1978) Nitrate in groundwater. Water Research Centre Technical Report TR69. Water Research Centre, Medmenham

Chapter Five

ENVIRONMENTAL POLICIES IN THE UNITED KINGDOM

Andrew W. Gilg

INTRODUCTION

In 1978, the British Government, in the guise of its publicity agency the Central Office of Information (1978) argued that Environmental Planning in Britain included: land use planning, the development of new towns, policies for inner cities, housing and urban transport policy, the conservation of the countryside, the preservation of historic buildings, the protection of green belts and trees, land reclamation, and the control of pollution. In contrast, a wider and more academic review in 1983 (O'Riordan and Turner, 1983) provided a rather different list which included: environmental economics, planning and environmental protection, economics and ecology, growth and resource depletion, and environmental pollution control. It is the purpose of this chapter to analyse which of these lists most closely reflects the picture of environmental policies in the UK in the 1980s. We begin by exploring how these policies evolved up to 1960.

THE DEVELOPMENT OF ENVIRONMENTAL MANAGEMENT UP TO 1960

Nineteen sixty does not mark a particularly clear watershed, because key dates for environmental policy changes in the UK are the 1850s, late 1940s and mid to late 1970s (Table 5.1). Indeed 1960 - if anything - marks the full flowering of the post war economic recovery, when Britain was told by Harold Macmillan in the 1959 general election that it "had never had it so good". Therefore the main focus of this chapter will be the policies of the late 1940s, their implement-

TABLE 5.1 Key Dates for Changes in Environmental Policy in the UK

1850s	Basic policies to prevent the worst excesses of urbanisation and industrialisation.
1910	First rudimentary planning controls.
1930s	Increasing concern about farmland lost to urban development.
1946-49	Most significant period. Introduction of policies for New Towns, Agriculture, Transport, Land Use Planning, National Parks and Nature Conservation, and in 1949 the concept of environmental policy reaches its zenith.
Late 1960s to early 1970s	The environmental consequences of rapid economic growth are increasingly debated, and controls over pollution gradually introduced. The ideology and practice of planning reaches a second but lower zenith than 1949.
Mid 1970s to late 1970s	The effect of world oil prices and increasing recession are met first by a reluctance to impose existing environmental policies and then by an argument to start dismantling them.
1979	The election of right wing government heralds an attack on environmental policy, but the problems will not go away and new ones emerge (namely the effect of acid rain exported from the UK to Scandinavia). Increasing attempts by the EEC to impose environmental controls on the UK

Note: For a fuller account of the period 1945-82, see Gilg, A.W. (1984).

ation up to the early 1970s, the first questioning of them in the mid 1970s and then the first really major attack that they had to face in the 1980s.

To view these policies in context, it is necessary to go back to the 1850s. The United Kingdom was the first country to experience the full effects of both urbanisation and industrialisation. The 1851 population census showed that for the first time in the world, one country (the UK) had more than half of its people living in towns. The effects were catastrophic in a small crowded island (in 1978 the population density was 230 people per square kilometre) and the outbreak of major epidemics, notably of cholera, forced the government of the day to introduce basic public health standards. Social conditions were also appalling and much of the work of Marx and Engels was inspired by the nineteenth century slums of London and Manchester.

However until 1910 all governments shared the view that the role of the state was only to provide basic environmental policies and thus prevent the worst excesses of free market capitalism (Ideologies D1, D4 and D5 in Table 5.2). Between 1910 and 1930 the changing nature of industry, the desire of people to live in more pleasant surroundings and the introduction of transport facilities allowing greater long-distance travel all came together to encourage the rapid decentralisation of UK cities. The net result was a rapid suburbanisation of many parts of lowland England. The unplanned and uneconomic nature of this sprawl and the large loss of farmland that accompanied it horrified many commentators of the period who argued for the introduction of planning controls on new development (Ideology C3). The onset of the 1939-45 world war amply justified their worst fears, as Britain nearly starved to submission under the German submarine blockade.

After the war the country had not only become used to centrally directed plans, but it had also come to demand them. In 1945 Britain elected a Socialist government committed to the introduction of a 'welfare state'. This not only included state-provision of education and health care but also the creation of planned new towns, the introduction of effective land use planning, the massive support and control of agriculture,

TABLE 5.2 O'Riordan's Environmental Ideologies

ECOCENTRISM	
A Deep environmentalists	B Self reliance soft technologists
1. Lack of faith in modern large-scale scale technology and its associated demands on elitist expertise, central state authority and inherently anti-democratic institutions.	
2. Implication that materialism for its own sake is wrong and that economic growth can be geared to providing for the basic needs for those below subsistence levels.	
3.* Intrinsic importance of nature for the humanity of man.	3. Emphasis on smallness of scale and hence community identity in settlement, work and leisure.
4. Ecological and (other natural) laws dictate human morality.	4. Integration of concepts of work and leisure through a process of personal and communal improvement.
5. Biorights - the right of endangered species or unique landscapes to remain unmolested.	5. Importance of participation in community affairs and of guarantees of the rights of minority interests. Participation seen both as a continuing educational and political function.

TABLE 5.2 (Continued)

TECHNOCENTRISM

C Accomodators

1. Belief that economic growth and resource exploitation can continue assuming:

(a) suitable economic adjustments to taxes, fees etc

(b) improvements in the legal rights to a minimum level of environmental quality

(c) compensation arrangements satisfactory to those who experience adverse environmental and/or social effects

2.+ Acceptance of new project appraisal techniques and decision review arrangements to allow for wider discussion or genuine research for consensus among representative groups of interested parties.

3. Provision of effective environmental management agencies at national and local levels.

D Cornucopians

1. Belief that man can always find a way out of any difficulties either politically, scientifically or technologically.

2. Acceptance that pro-growth goals define the rationality of project appraisal and of policy formulation.

3. Optimistic about the ability of man to improve the lot of the world's people.

4. Faith that scientific and technological expertise provides the basic foundation for advice on matters pertaining to economic growth, public health and safety.

5. Belief that any impediments can be overcome given a will, ingenuity and sufficient resources arising out of wealth.

Note: In the text A3 for example refers to * and C2 to + and so on.

SOURCE: O'Riordan (1981)

the creation of National Parks, the introduction of nature conservation policies and the nationalisation of electricity, coal mining and public transport (Ideologies C1a, C1b, C1c and C3).

A Conservative government was elected in 1951, but many of the policies introduced under Socialist rule in the 1940s were only slightly reduced or modified and the concept of a 'mixed economy' gradually emerged. Indeed the years from 1951 to 1979 can be seen as years of consensus (Ideology C2) when both main political parties (Labour and Conservative) espoused broadly similar policies. During this period environmental policy took the form of guiding, shaping and modifying the mixed economy. The policies were implemented by a mixture of negative controls and positive inducements (mainly grants or subsidies). However, changing circumstances gradually threatened this cosy consensus and led to a major shift in direction in 1979.

One catalyst for the shift in direction was the growing threat of pollution and resource depletion (Ideologies B1 and B3). The first oil crises of the early 1970s produced real evidence to show that unrestrained economic growth was not as inevitable as it had seemed throughout the 1950s and 1960s. The initial government response was to implement further energy conservation policies, but as world recession developed, unemployment in the UK rose from virtually nothing, to nearly 15 percent. With the new exploitation of North Sea reserves, during the 1970s, the UK became first self sufficient in oil, and then a surplus oil producer. The government response gradually changed towards economic growth at the expense of environmental policies. The political response of the public was to elect a right wing Conservative government in both 1979 and 1983 committed to the rolling back of much environmental policy (Ideologies D2, D4 and D5). However, the majority of controls first introduced in the 1940s and modified since then have been retained. Even under the Thatcher regime, new environmental controls (notably over farming operations) have been introduced, although (as will emerge later) these have been criticised for being far too weak and ineffective.

In retrospect, therefore, the period since 1850

has seen a broadening of environmental control in the UK in both theory and practice. This process seemed inevitable and it was broadly accepted until the 1970s when a more divided view emerged. The technocentric continuum described by O'Riordan (Table 5.2) emerged in the 1980s, with the political consensus co-opting environmentalism so that "they can retain control over the transition from cornucopianism to accommodation, thereby repelling any attempts at any more radical solutions to the growth-environmental damage-social justice drama" (O'Riordan, 1981, p.396).

THE UK DECISION MAKING PROCESS

The post-war period up to the early 1970s was an era of consensus politics, under which the Conservatives (the right wing party whose strength is derived from the suburbs and the countryside, and the southern half of the country) had implicitly agreed with Labour (the left wing party whose strength is derived from the older industrial areas in the north, and a rather outmoded concept of worker solidarity) that they would soften their more dogmatic and extreme policies in favour of compromise. In the late 1970s, however, both parties shifted away from the political centre allowing the resurgence of a centre party (the Alliance of SDP and Liberals).

Parliamentary Democracy

The United Kingdom is a parliamentary democracy, in which the government is elected by simple majority of seats contested, and in which a new government has to be elected within five years of the last general election (Mackintosh, 1977). In practice governments (this usually means Prime Ministers) generally decide to call an election after about four years of office. This allows each government about three years in which to enact its main legislative programme before it begins to wind down before a new election. However, there have been times when two general elections have been called in close succession, usually when the first produced only a small majority for the encumbent political party (Table 5.3). Table 5.3 highlights two political "distortions" in the UK - no government since 1945 has gained more than 40 percent of the total electoral vote, and two governments have been elected with a lower

TABLE 5.3 UK Elections since 1945

PROPORTION OF TOTAL ELECTORATE VOTING FOR MAIN PARTIES

Year	Conservative	Labour	Liberal	Government (majority)
1945	29.9	36.0	6.8	Labour (large)
1950	36.5	40.3	2.1	Conservative (small)
1955	38.2	35.6	2.1	Conservative (medium)
1959	39.5	34.5	4.6	Conservative (large)
1964	33.5	34.0	8.6	Labour (tiny)
1966	31.7	36.4	6.5	Labour (large)
1970	33.4	31.0	5.4	Conservative (medium)
1974	29.9	29.3	15.2	Labour (tiny)
1974	26.1	28.6	13.3	Labour (small)
1979	33.3	28.1	10.5	Conservative (medium)
1983+	30.8	20.0	18.4*	Conservative (massive)

*Social Democratic Party (SDP)/Liberal Alliance

+In the 1983 election the Conservatives received 43.5 percent of votes actually cast and gained 397 seats, Labour received 28.3 percent of votes and gained 209 seats, the SDP/Liberal alliance received 26.0 percent of votes but only gained 23 seats.

SOURCE: The Guardian (16th June 1983)

share of the vote than the combined opposition (namely the governments of 1951 and 1974 (first election)).

As noted above, the government is elected on the 'first past the post' principle. Under this sytem, the UK is divided into about 630 constituencies (the number has fluctuated and it was increased to 650 in 1983) with normally between 50,000 and 80,000 electors per constituency. Each constituency elects one Member of Parliament who stands for election as a member of a political party. They are elected even if they receive only one more vote than any of their rivals, and this principle produces the apparent distortions shown in Table 5.3 and mentioned above. The distortions have been made more acute in recent years by the resurgence of centre parties - in 1983 the Social Democratic Party (SDP)/ Liberal alliance received 26.0 percent of the votes but only gained 23 (3.5 percent) of the 650 seats while the Labour party received 28.3 percent of the votes but gained 209 (32 percent) seats. From this basis of "un-proportional representation", it is clear that the UK democracy can produce some very undemocratic results indeed.

Once a government is elected with a majority in parliament, the leader of that political party is usually invited by the Sovereign to become prime minister. The prime minister then has enormous power because he/she can choose who will be in charge of each ministry and because he/she is chairman of the cabinet which makes all major decisions. In the UK there is a hierarchical government structure in which almost all power is devolved from the .top downwards, from the prime minister (Figure 5.1) to the cabinet, to the ministries and then on to their executive agencies. At the same time, pressure groups are always trying to impose their views on the process of decision-making by lobbying at as many points within the hierarchy as they can.

The parliamentary year runs from the autumn of one year (normally October or November) to the summer of the next (normally June or July) and any intended legislation has to be either approved within that time period or lost. In practice, because of the time constraints of Parliamentary

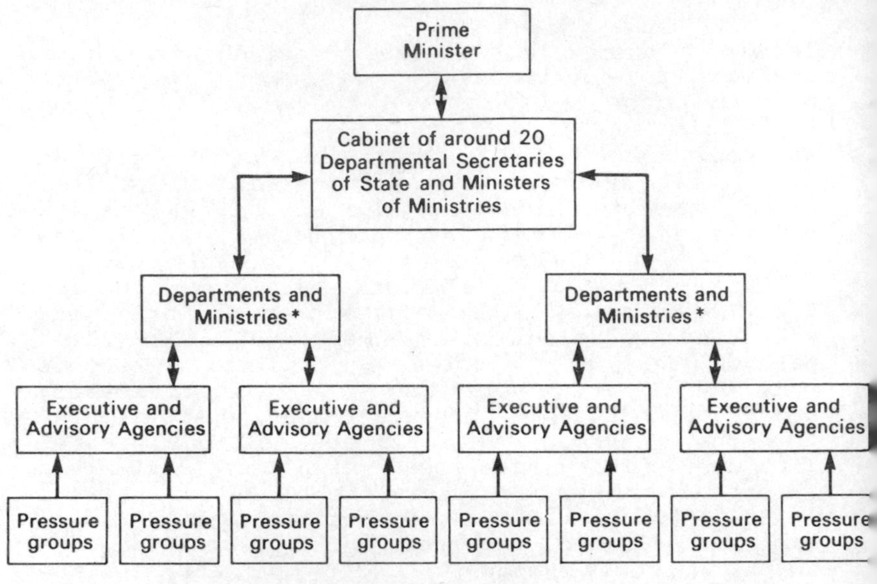

* *At any one time there are about 5 or 6 departments and 15 to 20 Ministries. They are very unequal in size and power.*

↓ Decisions devolved from the top

↑ Pressure to make new or different decisions from below

FIGURE 5.1 Hierarchical structure of government in the United Kingdom

debate and legislative drafting, this means that any one minister or secretary of state for a department can only introduce one major piece of legislation a year. Before he can do this he has to convince his cabinet colleagues that the legislation is worthwhile and that it is worthy of time in the crowded legislative timetable. In terms of environmental legislation this means that major changes only usually occur either every ten years or so, when there is a marked shift in the ideological balance of a government. There is thus a good deal of inertia in the decision making process.

Once a piece of legislation is introduced into parliament as a Bill, it has to undergo a great deal of scrutiny in both the House of Commons (the elected chamber) and the House of Lords (an hereditary and nominated chamber). At this stage the Bill can be modified, and environmental policy particularly can be subject to a good deal of modification (Cox and Lowe, 1983). If the Bill proceeds successfully through all its stages in time, it becomes an Act of Parliament and is then placed on the statute books. However, the Act does not normally come into operation unless dates are specified for certain sections of the Act to come into operation, or until Statutory Instruments are placed before parliament specifying these dates. This process often takes a number of years (see Volumes One to Five of the Countryside Planning Yearbook). For example, 22 of the 109 sections of the Control of Pollution Act (1974) had still not been implemented by 1984 (Cmnd 9149, 1984).

The United Kingdom is not, however, monolithic in its decision making structure. Externally (since accession to the EEC in 1973) the UK government has to accommodate and comply with a wide variety of European decisions - in particular related to agricultural policy. Internally, the UK comprises four constituent countries - England, Wales, Scotland and Northern Ireland (in contrast to Great Britain which comprises England, Wales and Scotland). Of the four, Northern Ireland was until the early 1970s the most independent, with its own elected parliament. As a result of the hostilities there since 1969, most decisions are now taken either by parliament in London or civil servants in Belfast. Scotland has always had its own legal and planning system and the Secretary of State for Scotland makes many decisions for the country. Wales is the least independent of the four countries and although there is a Secretary of State for Wales he has less effective power than his Scottish counterpart and most legislation and statistics embrace both England and Wales, while Scotland has its own legislation and statistical series.

In summary, British parliamentary democracy is a rather slow and cumbersome process which is subject to a variety of checks and balances. Many of the more controversial pieces of legislation are repealed by successive governments and as a result environmental policy seems to oscillate around a central pole. In addition governments .faced with difficult problems often set up inquiries, committees or commissions to consider the problems, in the hope that they will either go away or have to be faced by the next government. Nonetheless, since 1945 all governments have been committed to environmental policies but the degree of commitment has varied across the spectrum of environmental concerns.

THE MAIN ENVIRONMENTAL POLICY AREAS IN THE UK

Many environmental policies in the UK are implicitly or even explicitly designed for either an urban or a rural setting, although some policies bridge this dichotomy in that they are explicitly set up to reconcile development and conservation in either or both. Policies might thus usefully be divided into three broad areas:

(a) the rural land resource base: in which the main issues are the effects on the rural environment of 40 years of policies designed to expand food and timber production.

(b) urban development pressures: in which the main issues centre around the use of land in a small and crowded island like Britain. Any new use has to compete with many other ones (existing and potential) and policies are designed to resolve, and if possible prevent, conflicts between competing land uses. The land use planning system (first set up in 1947) has met varying degrees of success in achieving this aim.

(c) reconciling development and conservation: as the pressures for change in the environment became larger and more pervasive in their effects from the mid 1960s onwards, new policies from those first set up in the late 1940s had to be developed. These have varied from area specific policies like conservation areas to subject specific policies like the Wildlife and Countryside Act 1981 (which deals specifically with the protection of fauna and flora, and with farm management).

Within these three broad areas, O'Riordan (1981, 1982 and 1983) has identified countryside conservation as the main contemporary problem in the rural land resource base area, nuclear power and pollution control as the main contemporary issues in urban development processes and Environmental Impact Assessment and the UK (World) Conservation Strategy as the main contemporary issues in reconciling development and conservation. Overlaying all of these issues, however, he sees three areas of great uncertainty for the rest of the century (O'Riordan, 1982, pp. 409-413):

i. the level of unemployment, and as a related issue,
ii. the amount of voluntary leisure time that will be available, and
iii. the extent to which new urban developments like airports, nuclear and other power stations, and other industrial plant are really needed in a world suffering from chronic overcapacity.

Indeed the only certain feature of contemporary environmental policies is that they are rooted in more uncertainty about the future than were those of the 1950s, 1960s and early 1970s. This is apparent in each of the three main policy areas.

THE RURAL LAND RESOURCE BASE

Background review

Britain is still one of the world's major food importing countries. Although the amount of food imported has been drastically cut in the last decade (Table 5.4), and a much greater percentage of imports comes from the EEC than from further afield, memories of the fod shortages of the second world war are still vivid in the minds of many of todays decision makers. Furthermore, agricultural ministers often point out that food surpluses - where they do occur - are preferable to shortages (as in Poland) so that the costs of surpluses should be seen in this light. The need for self sufficiency is thus a major driving force behind agricultural policy in the United Kingdom. Closely related is the need to maintain a positive balance of payments and money spent on home produced rather than imported food is often seen as money 'saved'. Post war agricultural policy in the UK has therefore been directed towards expansion at almost any cost, and this is manifest not only directly in policy (and grant) support for farming, but also indirectly by explicitly preserving as much

TABLE 5.4 Some key facts about British agriculture

	Average 1971-73	1982	
Cereal area	3,971	4,030	hectares
Full time farm workers	254,000	171,000	persons
Farmers	227,000	203,000	persons
Wheat yields	4.33	6.20	tonnes/ hectares
Wheat self sufficiency	53	106	percent
Barley self sufficiency	94	128	percent
Meat self sufficiency	75	85	percent
Butter self sufficiency	20	64	percent
Cheese self sufficiency	55	71	percent
All food self sufficiency	50	62	percent
Indigenous food self sufficiency	62	76	percent
Income of cropping farm (average)	-	£14,412	
Income of dairy farm (average)	-	£9,782	
Income of mixed farm (average)	-	£4,005	
Market regulation under CAP (total)	£330.2*	£946.7	million
Support for capital works (total)	£108.5*	£185.3	million

*1978-79

SOURCE: Cmnd 8804 (1983)

good agricultural land as possible via the land use planning system (even though only 10 percent of Britain's land surface is developed).

Forestry is also a major user of rural land. However, although the amount of land under timber has doubled from 5 to 10 percent (by area) since 1900, Britain still has to import 90 percent of its timber needs. This is partly because a forestry expansion policy has only existed since 1919 (when the Forestry Commission was founded) and also because the main period of planting was in the 1950s and 1960s and thus much of the timber is still immature and will not be harvestable until the 21st century. However, it is estimated that even then demand will have increased at the same rate as supply so that Britain would still need to import around 90 percent of its timber. Nonetheless, proposed policies to double the forest area have met with much hostility.

Policy analysis

As is clear from the above, the main thrust of both agricultural and forestry policy in the UK has been towards expansion. In agriculture the 1947 Agricultural Act set the expansionist theme (ideologies D1 and D4) when it stated that it aimed to create:

> *a stable and efficient agricultural industry capable of producing such part of the nation's food and other agricultural produce as in the national interest it is desirable to produce in the United Kingdom, and of producing it at minimum prices consistent with proper remuneration and living conditions for farmers and workers in agriculture and an adequate return on capital invested in the industry.*

The policy was implemented via a range of mechanisms. The most important was a system of guaranteed prices under which the government made up any difference between the market price achieved for a product sold and the guaranteed price. When allied to standard quantities or quotas, this policy had the main advantage that consumers benefited from low market prices and governments benefited from a limited liability (because produce actually had to be sold and - from the late 1950s - the introduction of quotas limited the amounts that were eligible for support). Another important mechanism was the system of cash grants (subsidies) available, for example for capital improvements or for each sheep or hill cow kept. Together with guaranteed prices, these mechanisms gave farmers the confidence to invest in more production. They also fostered a strong expansionary climate which was further encouraged by major governmental sponsored research programmes and also by the introduction of marketing boards for many commodities to boost demand for products.

These expansionist policies were only slightly modified when the UK joined the EEC in 1972 because EEC policy objectives and instruments are similar to those in the UK. The main policy instrument of the EEC is the Common Agricultural Policy (CAP) which has three main objectives:

(a) to increase agricultural productivity and earnings,
(b) to stabilise markets, and
(c) to provide adequate supplies at reasonable prices to the consumer.

To achieve these objectives, the CAP uses similar policy instruments to those already used in the UK, namely: market regulation, grants and subsidies, technical advice, research, disease control and farm restructuring.

There are two major differences between CAP policies and those followed by the UK up to 1972, and these have had major impacts on the UK agriculture since 1972. The first is that the system of market regulation is by intervention buying. Under this system the CAP buys up any produce offered to it, at a price level set each year around March. The objective of this intervention buying is to absorb within the EEC surpluses produced in good years, and then sell off the stored produce in bad years. In reality, however, nearly every year has been a good year and so the surpluses have never been sold off (hence "food mountains" accumulate). There are two main reasons for this. The first is that intervention prices have been set too high and so farmers have been encouraged to overproduce. The second reason is that demand for many products (for example butter and milk) has fallen or remained static, and the gap between demand and supply has widened as productivity has continued to rise. The second major difference is that the CAP employs import and tariff barriers, whereas the UK previously adopted a free trade policy. This has allowed CAP prices to remain above world price levels, and it has protected European and UK farmers from the full impact of free market competition. Not surprisingly when cocooned behind massive tariff barriers and cushioned by high support prices from the penalties of over-production, British farmers have responded by embarking on a massive programme of expansion since 1972 (Table 5.4).

Until recently, there was widespread agreement that this expansion was a good thing. Increasingly, however, these policies are being seriously questioned on three grounds (Bowers and Cheshire, 1983). First, as surpluses have built up, initially in the EEC, and now increasingly within the UK, the high cost of the support policy has threatened to bankrupt the EEC every year since the late 1970s. Secondly, the expansion has encouraged many farmers to intensify agricultural production at the expense of countryside landscapes and habitats. The first losses were the traditional landscape of hedgerows (in the arable east), and the ploughing up of chalk and limestone downland. Further expansion has led to the ploughing up or reclamation of moorland and the drainage of wetlands. Thirdly, economists have questioned whether the improvements in farm productivity are as large as they initially appear to be, arguing that what has really happened is the substitution of efficient low input-low output agriculture by inefficient high input-high output agriculture (Norton-Taylor, 1982). The CAP clearly has high economic and environmental costs, but these might still be acceptable if there were food shortages, or if food prices were unacceptably high. However, since neither is true, the policy of agricultural expansion is now being seriously questioned for the first time, although it still remains official government policy within the UK.

As noted earlier, UK forestry policies have to some extent mirrored the expansionist trends within agricultural policies. Forestry policy dates from 1919 when the blockade of the First World War (1914-18) had demonstrated how perilously limited British timber stocks had become. Indeed, at that time, only 5 percent of the land surface of the UK was covered by timber. Accordingly the government set up a Forestry Commission with two main tasks - the creation of a state owned forest and the stimulation of a private timber industry. The first was achieved by land purchase and by an extensive programme of planting which had produced nearly one million hectares of state owned forest by the early 1980s. The second task was achieved by a combination of tax incentives and cash grants designed to encourage landowners to either maintain or plant new forests. These policies have also been successful and they have produced a private forest estate of around 1.2 million hectares by the early 1980s.

Because forestry is not a very profitable use of land in the short term, the only land in the UK where it is commercially viable to plant new forests is the agriculturally marginal land either on sandy lowlands or more usually on the wet uplands in Wales, Scotland and northern England. Not surprisingly, the expansion of new (mainly coniferous) forests into these open moorlands has involved a suite of major changes in landscapes and ecology, and afforestation has been widely opposed by both recreationists and nature conservationists. In common with agriculture, the economics of expansion have also come increasingly into question since the early 1970s and since then forestry policy has been balanced precariously between expansion and steady state (i.e. no change).

In both agriculture and forestry the period of unquestioned expansion seems to be set at an end. It is appropriate, therefore, to reflect on the basis of the policies and to speculate on their likely evolution in the future.

Discussion

Agricultural expansion remains official government policy (Cmnd 7458, 1979) mainly - it is argued - because of the cost and insecurity of foreign supplies. However, the policy has come under increasing attack since 1980. One of the most vitriolic criticisms was mounted by Shoard (1980) who argued that not only were farmers directly subsidised via CAP price support (circa £1,560 million) and capital grants (circa £110 million), but they also received indirect subsidies via tax concessions (circa £800 million), non payment of rates (circa £150 million) and the administration of the Ministry of Agriculture and research (circa £140 million). These total subsidies were in the order of £8,500 per farmer per year in 1980, compared to £1,800 per head for a steel worker. Shoard argued that these subsidies were being used not for the nation's benefit but rather to ravage the countryside through removal of hedgerows, meadows, ancient woodlands and other habitats.

Another critical attack was launched by Norton-Taylor (1982) who argues that farming is not as efficient as it claims to be and that the much heralded improvements in productivity have only been achieved by a massive increase of inputs (many of which are chemically based and derived from fossil fuels). Norton-Taylor concludes that the expansion has led to a chemically over-rich diet which is a direct cause of many modern human health problems (especially heart disease and cancer). He also stresses that fossil fuel based farming cannot continue for ever. Other critics have pointed to the growing cost of agricultural support and the consequent danger that it might bankrupt the CAP (House of Lords 126, 1981). Finally, the MacEwens (MacEwen, 1982a) have demonstrated the loss of open moorland in protected landscapes like Exmoor National park, and in doing so highlighted the folly of one government department (the Department of the Environment) paying out grants to protect the moorland, at the same time as another department (the Ministry of Agriculture) pays out grants to plough up and reclaim the moorland.

The government has only partially responded to these criticisms of agricultural policies. For example, in response to a government sponsored report on moorland loss on Exmoor (Porchester, 1977) the government introduced a Countryside Bill into parliament which - had it been accepted - could have prevented wholesale moorland reclamation for the cost of a one-off compensation payment (Ideology C1(c)). However, the Bill was lost at the 1979 general election and it was replaced by a Wildlife and Countryside Bill which became law in the Wildlife and Countryside Act (1981). This Act gives conservation agencies and planning authorities the power to make management agreements with farmers who have proposed to make damaging alterations to existing habitats (Ideologies C1(b) and C1(c)). However, this power is very expensive to support, and the total budget of the conservation agencies (around £20 million) is very small compared with more than £1,000 million available to the farm development agencies.

It is also argued that the powers created in the Act are only cosmetic, only prevent the worst excesses, and treat the symptoms not the causes. In consequence, Potter (1983) has proposed a radical restructuring of agricultural policy (Ideologies C1, C2 and C3), in which agricultural grant aid is directed towards conservation as well as development. One corollary to this, he argues, is that the balance of support should shift from market regulation to direct grant aid. To back up the new direction he proposes that land use plans and planning controls be introduced over many farming operations or changes of use in the countryside.

Forestry commentators have made similar criticisms and proposals to those outlined for agriculture. However, much of the literature remains committed to expansion, even though as long ago as 1972 a government report (Treasury, 1972) concluded that forestry produced a very low rate of return on a cost-benefit basis. Nonetheless, both the Centre for Agricultural Strategy (1980) and Fairgrieve (1979) argue for an additional 2 million hectares of afforestation, despite the fact that most economists continue to assert that forestry is unprofitable (Miller, 1981). This argument can never be proven, however, because forestry is a long term investment, and most commentators agree that the development of an appreciating asset (if properly controlled) is a good policy. Thus there have been calls for the introduction of planning controls over afforestation (CCP 162, 1984) not only from planning agencies but also from right wing economists (Miller, 1981). Such a move would highlight forestry as what it is - a method of providing a long term asset that can be rich in recreational, landscape and wildlife resources if it is managed as a multi-purpose unit rather than simply as an economic resource (Ideology C1).

URBAN DEVELOPMENT PRESSURES

Background review

The basic arguments in favour of land use planning to control urban development pressures can be traced back to the 1930s and the second world war. During the 1930s many commentators expressed alarm at the rapid expansion of cities like London and Birmingham across good agricultural land, and others pointed out the disparity within Britain between the rapidly growing south and the declining north. The war time bombing in London and the south east merely served to highlight the folly of allowing too much economic growth to congregate in the south east. Within the expanding towns, other commentators pointed to the increasing costs of congestion and conflict between competing land uses. All these arguments provided a foundation for the first real land use planning system in the world, the Town and Country Planning Act of 1947 (Ideologies C1, C2 and C3).

This Act had three main principles, two of which have remained central to land use planning up to the present time, and the other which has been modified. The first and most important of these principles was that no compensation (except for a one-off payment for existing rights) would be paid if planning permission for a new development were refused (Ideology C1(c)). The second and almost equally important principle was that planning would try to divide land uses into non-conflicting land use zones, such as residential areas, commercial areas, industrial areas and public open space (Ideology C1(b)). The third principle, which has been substantially modified, is that most new development would be undertaken by publicly owned organisations (Ideology C3).

This principle was abandoned with the election of a conservative government in 1951 and since then a consensus approach to planning based on the mixed economy has emerged. In this approach it is accepted that virtually all new development will be examined by the planning system and be subject to planning control. It is also accepted that development will derive from a mixture of public and privately derived developments, which planning will try to co-ordinate since "the planning system balances the protection of the natural and the built environment with the pressures of economic and social change. The need for the planning system is unquestioned and its workings have brought great and lasting benefits" (Circular 22/80, 1980) (Ideology C1).

Policy analysis

Planning policy in the UK derives from the 1947 Town and Country Planning Act and although there are major administrative differences between Scotland, and England and Wales, the law is much the same throughout the UK. Some major procedural differences to plan making were introduced in the 1968 Town and Country Planning Act, and these were consolidated with the 1947 Act to produce the current statute under which land use planning derives its power, namely the 1971 Town and Country Planning Act.

Under this 1971 Act, planning is divided broadly into two functions; plan making and development control. Plan making receives all the attention, has most of the literature devoted to it and is the career aspiration of most ambitious planners. In reality, however, its importance has been continually down-graded since 1951 when plans were no longer exclusively implemented by public organisations. Under the present system county councils prepare Structure Plans which are supposed to show the broad patterns of settlement change, industrial and employment development, communications, and landscape conservation regarded as acceptable for the next 10 to 20 years. A more detailed expression is given to these Structure Plans by Local Plans. Unfortunately, Local Plans are prepared by different organisations (the District Councils) and they do not always reflect the Structure Plan for the wider areas as closely as they might. A major problem with both sorts of plan is that it has taken far longer than expected to prepare them. Although most Structure Plans had been completed by 1984, some Local Plans may not be completed before the 21st century.

As a result those charged with making decisions about planning applications to develop or change land use, have had to (and will continue to) operate in many areas in a policy vacuum. A further problem is that development control is undertaken by the District Councils and so it is divorced from those planners charged with the production and review of Structure Plans. Nonetheless, development control is the most significant part of the planning system in the UK because it decides whether or not any proposed development goes ahead. Although the Structure or Local Plan for the area is used as a guide, each application is treated on its merits; permission is not as guaranteed as it is in the majority of countries, like Switzerland or the USA, which have adopted a zoning system. Nonetheless about 80 percent of all applications are granted permission, although the success rate may be so high because many applicants with little chance of success are deterred from applying in the first place.

The development control system involves a series of steps. Every application for development (above a minimum size) is submitted to a local planning authority. After due consultation with interested parties this authority will either grant or refuse permission, or grant permission with conditions. An applicant may appeal to the Department of the Environment over a refusal, or if he feels that the conditions attached to the permission are too onerous. If an appeal is lodged, a Public Inquiry will normally be held by an Inspector (appointed by the Department of the Environment). The Inspector's report will influence the final decision which is made by civil servants, junior or senior ministers, or even the Cabinet and Prime Minister depending on the gravity of the case. Public Inquiries are also held into issues of national or regional importance, and into those that go beyond the normal limits or competence of local planning authorities (such as the development of coal fields, motorways, airports and nuclear power). In this case the procedure has some of the characteristics of an Environmental Impact Assessment.

In summary, the development control system is open and democratic at the local level and small scale, since all decisions are finally taken by locally elected councillors (often heavily advised by planning officials). At the national and regional level, however, bureaucracy and national political considerations begin to take over.

Discussion

A primary aim of land use planning was the protection of rural land from unplanned suburban sprawl. Land use plans in both the Development Plan period (1947 to 1971) and the Structure Plan period (since 1971) have placed a great deal of importance on this aspect of planning, and virtually every plan contained policies for the protection of the open countryside. A key ingredient of these policies was the key settlement concept (Cloke, 1979) under which only about a tenth of existing rural settlements were allowed to grow. Although this concept has been much criticised in recent years (Gilder, 1979), most

Structure Plans contained either policies designed to severely restrain expansion of rural settlements or more commonly variants on the key settlement theme (Cloke, 1983).

The other main protectionist policies were the designation of three types of protected landscape in which planning permission would theoretically be harder to obtain. The first of these relates to green belts, but it has no statutory status in law. Nonetheless since the first provisonal green belt was drawn around London in the 1930s and the publication in 1955 of a circular advising local planning authorities to define green belts, virtually all major British towns and cities have been encircled by such green belts (Elson, 1981). The other two types of protected landscape are National Parks and Areas of Outstanding Natural Beauty (AsONB) both of which derive their statutory protection from the 1949 National Parks and Access to the Countryside Act and the 1947 Town and Country Planning Act. Both have equal landscape importance and planning permissions are normally harder to obtain in them and have more rigorous conditions attached to them when they are obtained. A major problem, however, is that these protected areas (all defined after 1949) contain many existing settlements and developments; there is consequently a continuing conflict between the social and economic needs of these areas, and the need to protect their landscapes from further intensive development and landscape changes.

Despite such inherent problems, policies of landscape protection in Britain seem to have been quite effective. Most studies of planning permission in the countryside have confirmed that the rate of land loss has been signficantly slowed down (Best, 1981), green belts have been preserved (Gregory, 1970; Munton, 1983), urban areas have been contained at a price (Hall, 1973), the open countryside has been preserved from suburban sprawl (even if the key settlements have not always been the ones to grow (Gilg and Blacksell, 1981)), and National Parks and Areas of Outstanding Natural Beauty have been protected from the kind of developments that were threatening their landscapes in the 1930s (Anderson, 1981).

However, preservation of the countryside from urban sprawl has had a price, both internally (rural areas have become a preserve of the middle classes) and externally (the run down of inner cities). One of the main aims of planning in 1947 was to decentralise and reduce congestion in Britain's crowded cities. This aim has been successfully (and some would say too successfully) achieved by a combination of negative and positive policies.

The negative policies were founded on severe restrictions on planning permissions in many parts of Britain's cities and on the prevention of outward urban expansion into green belts. In addition throughout most of the 1950s, 1960s and 1970s, regional policies also served to prevent many employers from expanding in the more successful cities and to steer proposed developments towards less prosperous areas. The positive policies were based on the development of about 20 New Towns beyond the green belts around major cities, and on the expansion of many existing small country towns. In addition, regional policy offered attractive grant aid and subsidies to any firm wishing to move away from the more prosperous regions to less prosperous areas.

These policies have been so successful that many inner cities have become too decentralised and decongested; instead they have become major environmental disaster areas with massive dereliction, acute poverty and high unemployment. In terms of social housing, local councils in the inner city were prevented by the rural bourgeoisie from building new estates in the countryside. Instead they were forced to build large numbers of tower blocks in inner city areas, which are now seen as a regrettable step. In the 1980s, the situation has become so desperate that policies have been reversed, and environmental and planning controls have been almost extinguished in many inner city areas (called Enterprise Zones) in a despairing attempt to revive these run-down areas (Ideology D2 and D5).

In the meantime, the so called 'sun-belt' or 'silicon valley' areas of the UK (found along the motorways, near airports and in the more attractive countryside areas) reaffirm the gap between the environmental "haves" and environmental "have nots". Peter Hall (1974) has concluded that the effect of environmental policies on the growth of cities has been a civilised form of apartheid which has had three main and unfortunate side effects:

(a) a growing separation of home and work place (i.e. suburbanisation) but at the same time a containment of urban sprawl,
(b) a growing division into prosperous pleasant housing for the middle classes, and run down and extremely unpleasant social housing for the working classes, and
(c) a rapid inflation of land values caused by the artificial limiting of land supply by planning controls.

Hall (1973, p.433) concluded that:

> *It certainly was not the intention of the founders (of planning) that people should live cramped lives in homes destined for premature slumdom, far from urban services or jobs; or that city dwellers should live in blank cliffs of flats, far from the ground, without access to play space for their children. Somewhere along the way, a great ideal was lost, a system distorted and the great mass of people betrayed.*

Although these words were written over 10 years ago, there is little doubt that they are as true, if not truer, today - although thankfully there has been a swing back towards low rise and more vernacular forms of social housing. In conclusion planning appears to have been most effective at the local level and over the short term, and least effective at the large scale and over the long term. There is thus a need to alter the organisation of planning so as to give more emphasis to the regional level at the expense of the county level (as is the case in Scotland).

Although the net effect of planning is most clearly expressed in the overall pattern of the 400,000 or so individual decisions taken each year, much attention is also focused on the issues surrounding major developments, not only because of their scale but also because of the widespread impact they have. For example, it was noted earlier that the construction of motorways in the 1960s and 1970s has had a major impact on the location of new industries. Other examples include airports, coalfields, and nuclear power stations.

The 1950s saw the beginning of a massive shift away from public transport for both goods and passengers and throughout the 1960s and 1970s a programme was developed for the construction of around 2400 km of long distance motorway (Ideology D5). No real opposition was encountered at first, but as the effect of motorways became more obvious, and as they began to intrude into protected landscapes (and - perhaps more importantly - into the home environment of articulate middle class professional groups) much more opposition was generated. This, however, exposed one major weakness of the planning system, and of the public inquiry in particular; the fact that protestors could not query the need for the road or its overall concept, they could only query details of its landscaping and minor changes in its route. In spite of this weakness protestors managed to delay the construction of many motorways for many years and to reveal another weakness inherent in the system - the long delays and enormous costs that could be involved (Tyme, 1977).

This problem of delay and debate is highlighted in the example of the third London airport. Soon after a new main airport for London had been developed at Heathrow (in west London), demand began to grow for a new airport. For a while the expansion of Gatwick (to the south of London) and the development of new runways and terminals at Heathrow deflected the demands. Eventually the government was forced to set up a commission to examine a number of possible sites for a new third airport in the late 1960s. In the early 1970s the Government chose a site at Maplin (Foulness) on the Essex coast (east of London), but by the late 1970s the site had become environmentally unacceptable. Consequently in the early 1980s a new inquiry was set up to consider whether the new airport should be built at Stansted to the north of London. This Public Inquiry lasted for nearly two years and it involved 258 working days. By late 1984 no decision had been reached, largely because the issues were so complex that no obvious solution suggests itself. For example, the airport could create up to 500,000 jobs in a rural area and it could have a massive effect on the local environment. Some opponents of the third airport scheme argue that regional airports could and should take the increased air traffic, while others argue that changes in aviation techniques will render the airport unnecessary. Yet others argue that even a fourth airport close to London will soon be needed to cater for expected demand.

These uncertainties extend to the final major development issue, energy sources. During the early 1980's Britain basked in the energy self sufficiency of North Sea oil. Although some optimists predict that reserves are larger than expected, most experts predict a run down in the 1990s. Since the lead time (required for new technology, construction, and delays inherent in the Public Inquiry system) can be anything between 10-20 years for the development of energy sources, decisions concerning the replacement of North Sea oil cannot be postponed far into the future.

The key choice is between the development of coal or nuclear power supplies. Once again the arguments are probably too complex for simple resolution within the Public Inquiry system, which would need to consider, for example,

(a) the problems of predicting energy need, particularly as there is massive overcapacity in electricity producing potential in the UK,
(b) questions about the safety of nuclear energy and its long term effects on the environment,
(c) differential employment prospects, since a modern nuclear power station requires about 600 people, but for the same amount of electricity a coal fired power station needs over 10,000 people, to mine the coal, transport it and then run the power station (Guardian, 11.4.84), and
(d) the effects on the environment, of both coal and nuclear power sources, since both are now being developed in unspoilt rural areas.

The characteristically British response has been one of compromise and concensus where this has been obtainable. For example, after a lengthy Public Inquiry into whether the proposed Belvoir coalfield (in Leicestershire) should be developed or not, the government gave permission for some of the mines but refused permission in the more environmentally sensitive areas. Nationally, and between industries, the spirit of compromise also rules - both coal and nuclear power are being developed in parallel (Ideology C1).

It is not clear from these examples whether British experience reflects true wisdom, inability to decide between the options available or lack of sophisticated policy mechanisms. Certainly, the Public Inquiry system has not been able to cope effectively with major new developments (Outer Circle Policy Unit, 1979). There is probably a case for the introduction of some sort of Environmental Impact Assessment (Ideology C2), although as yet the UK government has resisted demands from the European Community (see Chapter 4) to introduce such a system (O'Riordan et al, 1983). The main reason given is that the government already has enough mechanisms to resolve conflicts between development and conservation. This view is perhaps more optimistic than realistic in the light of experience of reconciling development and conservation.

RECONCILING DEVELOPMENT AND CONSERVATION

Background review

This section examines three areas of management where the issues overlap the executive authority of the agencies outlined in the preceding sections, and where the conflicts are often made more acute by inter-organisation rivalry, sectoral decision-making and lack of multi-purpose planning.

For example, in the field of agricultural development and conservation, the Ministry of Agriculture is charged with the expansion of agricultural production and the attitude of its staff is conditioned by decades of work to further this end. However, another government department - the Department of the Environment - is charged with the protection of the environment and to help it in this task it has two semi-autonomous agencies, the Nature Conservancy Council and the Countryside Commission. From the outset, a compartmentalised and conflicting mode of operation, even within central government, hinders rather than helps environmental management.

Similarly in the field of urban development, energy

<u>policy and air pollution</u>, no national plan for urban development has been published since 1971 (Department of the Environment, 1971) and apart from the 1974 plan for coal (Manners, 1981) and similar individual plans for other energy sources, no overall energy plan has been produced. Instead, individual energy sources are planned by different organisations, such as the National Coal Board, the Central Electricity Generating Board and British Gas. Although there is a Department of Energy, most of the time these individual agencies compete for investment and resources. Furthermore, the industries themselves are internally divided between management and workers; for example plans to modernise the UK coal industry into a few super-efficient mines with the loss of around 20,000 jobs out of around 180,000 were bitterly opposed by the workforce in a strike between March 1984 and March 1985. A major problem arises, however, because future levels of demand and relative costs of different energy sources are difficult to predict. This reinforces the need for a national energy policy based on consensus rather than competition (Spooner, 1981).

A third area where sectoral decision-making is the norm rather than the exception is provided by <u>rural recreation and conservation</u>. Here the growing conflict between increasing use of the countryside for recreation and a diminishing conservation resource (albeit caused largely by agricultural expansion rather than recreational over-use) is largely overseen by the two semi-autonomous agencies of the Department of the Environment. The Nature Conservancy Council deals solely with conservation, whilst the Countryside Commission deals with both conservation and recreation (although it continually changes its mind about which it considers to be most important). This is a problem also faced by the ten National Park Authorities in England and Wales who are charged with both the preservation of the characteristic landscape beauty and the development of facilities for the enjoyment of open-air recreation within the National Parks. At least in this case there is no inter-departmental split of interest.

<u>Policy analysis</u>

In the area of agricultural development and conservation, concern at the effects of unbridled expansion were first expressed in the 1960s when the unintended ecological effects of pesticides were first widely observed (Carson, 1968). However, it was not until the 1970s that the wider disbenefits of agricultural intensification were put into a broader context in Britain with the publication of a Countryside Commission study of agricultural landscape changes (Countryside Commission, 1974). This showed an alarming rate of loss of hedgerows, woodlands, wetlands and other wildlife habitats in the recent past, which continues today. These losses were further emphasised by a Nature Conservation Review which showed how few important conservation sites were actually protected (Nature Conservancy Council, 1976) and a further study of the links between agriculture and conservation in the UK which forecast the widespread demise of many species of places and animals by the year 2000 (Nature Conservancy Council, 1977).

The issues were brought to a political head by two events - agreement by the British government to implement an EEC agreement on conservation; and observed widespread conversion of open moorland to farming in the Exmoor National Park. This latter event, in particular, forced the government to move from a mainly voluntary approach based on persuasion, to a voluntary approach backed up by financial inducements and legal sanctions, in the Wildlife and Countryside Act (1981).

The Act is divided into five parts, of which the two most important deal with wildlife and agricultural development. The wildlife sections are not very controversial and they extend protection to more species. However it is clear that species protection by itself is of little use without appropriate habitat protection. In this respect the Act is much less effective than it might be and thus it has become very controversial (Cox and Lowe, 1983). For example, if a farmer proposes to alter the habitat (i.e. land use) of a Site of Special Scientific Interest (of which there are about 4,000, mainly between one to five hectares each in size) he must notify the Nature Conservancy Council of his intentions (Ideology C2). However, he can only be prevented from harmful destruction by the payment of compensation for notional profits foregone attached to a management agreement, or the land must be purchased (Ideology C1(c)). In areas outside the special sites, and especially in a National Park, if a planning agency or similar organisation objects to the payment of a farm capital grant, they must again offer a management agreement under which <u>they</u> must pay compensation.

The main criticisms of this policy are that it is purely cosmetic, it can only deal with extreme cases (because of the limited budgets of the statutory conservation agencies), it pays compensation for a refusal to permit development (where no other section of society is so favoured) and perhaps most importantly, it continues the politics of confrontation and delays the day when policies can be complementary rather than mutually exclusive (MacEwen, 1982b). In the meantime, the countryside continues to lose habitat and landscape, and the need to conserve what remains increases daily.

In the field of <u>urban development, energy policy and air pollution</u> most of the policies have concentrated on clearing up past excesses rather than developing an agreed policy for the future (Ideology C1). For example, the basic method used to control air pollution from individual firms has been the establishment and implementation of emission standards (Rees, 1977). These are set without reference to any general ambient air standards, by negotiation between individual firms and the government agency involved (the Alkali Inspectorate). Because there are only about 35 inspectors at any one time, and since they rely on persuasion and gentlemen's agreements, there is considerable scope for the regulations to be contravened. Indeed there were only two prosecutions between 1920 and 1966.

This chapter has demonstrated that environmental management policies in Britain have often changed only under the pressure of events and changed circumstances. This theory of 'crisis response' is well illustrated by the principal legislation in air pollution - the 1956 Clean Air Act - which was introduced in the wake of the very serious smog in London in 1952 which killed up to 10,000 people. The main thrust of the Act was the designation of 'smokeless zones' in which inefficient coal burning is banned. However, by 1970 only in London had the percentage of 'black areas' (areas most susceptible to smog) actually designated as 'smokeless zones', risen above 50 percent.

In the main coal burning areas of the industrial cities, the percentages so designated varied from as low as 0.01 percent (in Wales) to only 49.6 percent (in Yorkshire and Humberside).

In spite of this slow rate of take-up, the Clean Air Act has been heralded as a major breakthrough. In London, for example, average winter smoke levels fell from over 300 $\mu g.m^{-3}$ in 1922-23 to around 100 $\mu g.m^{-3}$ in 1970-71. However, this fall may not be due to the policy at all, since oil and gas were anyway replacing coal, and the Act may have merely followed existing trends. Also, other less visible forms of pollution, especially air pollution from car exhausts, have become more important. Finally, closer control in the United Kingdom has merely forced industrialists to export their pollution via higher chimneys, so that it falls as 'acid rain' which kills the forests of Scandinavia and Germany, thus demonstrating that pollution is no respector of international boundaries and has to be dealt with comprehensively.

One British attempt at comprehensive legislation was the 1974 Control of Pollution Act (Ideology C1). However, this too has been implemented in a piecemeal and dilatory manner and by 1st October 1983 only 87 of the Acts' 109 sections were wholly or partly in force. The Royal Commission on Environmental Pollution concluded in 1984 that the claim, made in 1974 by Mrs Thatcher (then in opposition), that the Act represented the most comprehensive attempt for many years to bring pollution under control, remains to be tested (Cmnd 9149, 1984). Other examples of this dilatory approach to pollution include the attitude to straw burning and lead in petrol in the UK; the approach to the former has been one of persuasion followed by reluctant control, and to the latter a reduction by the 1990s rather than the mid 1980s. In both cases, the reluctance to impose controls stems from the powerful farming and car ownership lobbies respectively.

Increasing car ownership has also probably been the most powerful reason for the dramatic increase in countryside recreation since the early 1960s, and as such a major contributor to the growing conflict between <u>rural recreation and conservation</u>. At first it was thought that one solution would be to set up a Countryside Commission and give it powers to provide more sites for rural recreation (Ideology C3). This was the policy followed in the 1968 Countryside Act which allowed the Countryside Commission to set up grant-aided Country Parks and Picnic sites around the major towns, as a recreational contrast to the remoter National Parks set up in the 1950s following the 1949 National Parks Act. However, although over 200 Country Parks were set up in the 1970s the conflicts continued to grow, and in 1974 a government report (Sandford, 1974) argued that where conservation and recreation conflicted so badly that they could not be reconciled, conservation should have precedence. This policy was adopted in 1976 (Circular 4/76, 1976) (Ideology C2).

However, it is still expected that in most cases recreation and conservation will co-exist side by side (Ideology C1) and that multiple-use with a primary land user like agriculture, forestry or water gathering will be possible. Unfortunately, recent experience suggests that without adequate controls or financial inducement, multiple use remains an ideal rather than a realistic proposal. Further criticisms rest on the fact that the policy is overtly class based, in that it favours the conservation of landscapes enjoyed by the middle classes, at the expense of landscapes that may be favoured by the majority. Finally, as in other policy areas, no overall direction in policy is discernible; the general approach seems to be one of muddling through and reacting to events rather than directing them (Ideology D1).

INTERNATIONAL PERSPECTIVE

It has often been argued that the British system of environmental management provides a model for other countries to follow, because of the length of accumulated experience and because the system exercises very close control over most activities. However, it would be most unwise to claim that the British system is a system at all, since it is in reality a very compartmentalised set of boxes in which the intra-relationships within each box are far more important than the inter-relationships between boxes. This lack of concern over inter-relationships is amply demonstrated throughout this chapter, and there is therefore a desperate need for British environmental policy to be both more integrated and more overtly orientated to a long term strategy.

The picture is not one of total gloom, however, and the British system has a number of triumphs to its name. Most notable have been the beneficial effects of development control, green belts and New Towns. As already has been pointed out, however, these benefits have not been experienced by all classes and by all areas. In an earlier period the agricultural policies of deficiency payments and standard quotas contained the checks and balances so conspicuously absent from the CAP.

As for the future, the World Conservation Strategy (International Union for Nature Conservation, 1980) and its British counterpart (Anon, 1983) have argued for a management policy based on sustainable production (Ideologies B1, B2, B3 and B5). However, although these documents have been received cordially in Britain, it is only fair to say that this does not presage any real change of attitudes. Britain remains an essentially Technocentric and Cornucopian society (Table 5.2) and to date all environmental policies fit into either Ideology C or D. It is therefore likely that the British market system will continue to ignore the full social costs and disbenefits of its actions, including the non-provision of real landscape protection and adequate recreation areas, resource over-use and misuse, and environmental pollution (Rees, 1977).

REFERENCES

Anderson, M. (1981) Planning policies and development control in the Sussex Downs, AONB, _Town Planning Review_, 52: 5-25

Anon (1983) _The Conservation and Development Programme for the UK_, Kogan Page, London

Best, R. (1981) _Land use and living space_, Methuen, London

Bowers, J. and Cheshire, P. (1983) _Agriculture the Countryside and Land Use_, Methuen, London

Carson, R.L. (1968) _Silent Spring_, Houghton-Miflin, Boston

CCP 162 (1984) _A better future for the uplands_, Countryside Commission, Cheltenham

Central Office of Information (1978) _Environmental Planning in Britain_, HMSO, London

Centre for Agricultural Strategy (1980) Strategy for the UK forest industry, The Centre, Reading
Circular 4/76 (1976) Report of the National Parks Policy Review Committee, Department of the Environment, HMSO, London
Circular 22/80 (1980) Development Control: Policy and Practice, Department of the Environment, HMSO, London
Cloke, P. (1979) Key settlements in rural areas, Methuen, London
Cloke, P. (1983) An Introduction to Rural Settlement Planning, London, Methuen
Countryside Commission (1974) New agricultural landscapes, The Commission, Cheltenham
Cox, G. and Lowe, P. (1983) A battle not the war: the politics of the Wildlife and Countryside Act, Countryside Planning Yearbook, 4: 48-76
Cmnd 7458 (1979) Farming and the nation, London, HMSO
Cmnd 8804 (1983) Annual Review of Agriculture 1983, HMSO, London
Cmnd 9149 (1984) Royal Commission on Environmental Pollution: Tackling Pollution: Experience and Prospects, HMSO, London
Department of the Environment (1971) Long term population distribution in Great Britain, London, HMSO
Elson, M. (1981) Structure plan policies for pressured rural areas, Countryside Planning Yearbook 2: 49-70
Fairgrieve, R. (1979) A policy for forestry, Conservative Political Centre, London
Gilder, I. (1979) Rural planning policies: An economic appraisal, Pergamon, Oxford
Gilg, A. (1984) Politics and the Countryside: The British Example. In G. Clark, J. Groenendijk and F. Thissen (editors) The Changing Countryside, Geo Books, Norwich, 251-60
Gilg, A. and Blacksell, M. (1981) The Countryside: Planning and Change, Allen and Unwin, London
Gregory, D. (1971) Green Belts and Development Control, Centre for Urban and Regional Studies, Birmingham
Hall, P., Drewett, R., Gracey, H. and Thomas, R. (1973) The Containment of Urban England, Allen and Unwin, 1973, Two volumes
Hall, P. (1974) The containment of urban England, Geographical Journal, 140: 386-418
House of Lords Paper 126 (80-81) (1981) Select

Committee of the House of Lords on the European Communities: The Common Agricultural Policy, HMSO, London

International Union for Nature Conservation (1980) World Conservation Strategy, World Wildlife Fund, London

MacEwen, A. and MacEwen, M. (1982a) National Parks: Conservation or Cosmetics, Allen and Unwin, London

MacEwen, A. and MacEwen, M. (1982b) An unprincipled Act: The Wildlife and Countryside Act 1981, The Planner, 68: 69-71

Mackintosh, J.P. (1977) The Government and Politics of Britain, Hutchinson, London, 4th edition

Manners, G. (1981) Coal in Britain: An uncertain future, Allen and Unwin, London

Miller, R. (1981) State forestry for the axe, Institute of Economic Affairs, London

Munton, R. (1983) London's Green Belt: Containment in Practice, Allen and Unwin, London

Nature Conservancy Council (1976) A nature conservation review, The Council, London

Nature Conservancy Council (1977) Nature Conservation and Agriculture, The Council, London

Norton-Taylor, R. (1982) Whose Land is it Anyway?, Turnstone Press, Wellingborough

O'Riordan, T. (1981) Environmental issues. Progress in Human Geography, 5: 393-407

O'Riordan, T. (1982) Environmental issues. Progress in Human Geography, 6: 409-424

O'Riordan, T. (1983) Environmental issues. Progress in Human Geography, 7: 403-413

O'Riordan, T. et al, (1983) Planning and environmental protection. In T. O'Riordan and R.K. Turner (editors) An Annotated Reader in Environmental Planning and Management, Pergamon, Oxford, 135-210

O'Riordan, T. and Turner, R.K. (1983) An Annotated Reader in Environmental Planning and Management, Pergamon, Oxford

Outer Circle Policy Unit (1979) The Big Public Inquiry, The Unit, London

Porchester, Lord (1977) A Study of Exmoor: A report to the Secretary of State for the Environment and the Ministry of Agriculture, HMSO, London

Potter, C. (1983) Investing in rural harmony: An alternative package of agricultural subsidies and incentives for England and Wales, World Wildlife Fund, London, 45pp

Rees, J. (1977) The economics of environmental management, Geography, 62: 311-324

United Kingdom

Sandford, Lord (1974) Report of the National Parks Review Committee to the Department of the Environment, HMSO, London

Shoard, M. (1980) The Theft of the Countryside, Maurice Temple Smith, London

Spooner, D.J. (1981) The geography of coal's second coming, Geography, 66: 29-41

Treasury, Her Majesty's (1972) Forestry in Great Britain: An interdepartmental Cost/Benefit Study, HMSO, London

Tyme, J. (1977) Motorways versus Democracy, Macmillan, London

Chapter Six

ENVIRONMENTAL POLICIES IN AUSTRALIA - CLIMBING THE DOWN ESCALATOR

John Formby

> *Now, here, you see, it takes all the running you can do, to stay in the same place. If you want to get somewhere else, you must run twice as fast as that!*
> *(Lewis Carrol, Through the Looking Glass)*

INTRODUCTION

A casual observer, noting Australia's large size and comparatively low population, might conclude that its environmental problems are likely to be few. In reality, however, they are notable for their great variety. The reasons for this include Australia's possession and exploitation of a large range of natural resources, both mineral and biological; its wide variety of environments, many of them fragile; and its high level of urbanisation, with the attendant problems of crowding and pollution along the more fertile coastal fringes.

Because of the variety of significant environmental issues and their attendant policy responses, to attempt to deal with them all within one chapter would inevitably lend to superficiality. Neither is it intended simply to review each major environmental policy area in turn (for such a review see Gilpin, 1980). For the purposes of an international comparison, it would seem more useful to place Australian environmental policy in the wider context of the influences which have determined its nature and effectiveness.

A major purpose of this volume, as well as providing a global overview of the progress of environmental policy, must be to allow countries to learn from the environmental policy experience of others. However, environmental policies are not just techniques which can simply be transferred with similar success from one country to another. They are courses of action pursued by government and determined by political pressures and compromises, institutional peculiarities, economic circumstances, governmental objectives and priorities, and the nature of other, overlapping policies. As the international experience with EIA has shown, policies based on similar underlying concepts develop quite different characteristics in different countries (see O'Riordan and Sewell, 1981).

To learn from the environmental policy experience of other nations, therefore, it is necessary to understand the way in which environmental policies have grown from the economic, social, political and institutional influences which apply in each case. The approach in this chapter will be to examine such influences in the Australian case, and illustrate them with examples from a range of environmental policy issues. Here we will note some of these influences, and examine them more fully in the remainder of the chapter.

Australia in Context

Australia's historical inheritance includes a record of predominantly utilitarian and exploitive attitudes towards the environment and a high level of dependence on natural resource development, initially in pastoral and agricultural activities and since the late 1960s increasingly in mineral resources. There has been considerable land degradation, due to the combination of generally poor soils, a largely arid and uncertain climate, excessive land clearance and at times poor management practices and inappropriate government policies. Somewhat paradoxically, a high level of urbanisation has resulted, in part, from high levels of protection for manufacturing aimed at lessening dependence on primary production and the uncertainties of international markets.

Australia has also inherited political institutions based largely on the Westminster (UK) model (see Chapter 5), but with the very significant superimposition of a federal system embodying both divison and overlap of responsibilities for environmental and resource management between the Commonwealth and State governments. Governments, rather than the courts, have played a dominant role in determining environmental and resource allocation questions, and in supporting and providing the physical infrastructure for resource and industrial development. The prevailing values of the past are reflected in a multiplicity of single-purpose development-oriented government agencies, legislation and policies, many of which are slow to change.

Of the major parties, the Liberal and National-Country Parties, which have normally formed a (LNCP) coalition in government, have pursued essentially conservative policies. The Australian Labour Party (ALP) while embodying a substantial left-wing faction, when in office has - with the notable exception of the 1972-75 Whitlam government - largely implemented moderate policies and introduced change only gradually. Such policy orientations reflect the values of a materialistic society and a political climate which is generally conservative.

HISTORY, RURAL DEVELOPMENT AND LAND DEGRADATION

> *Australians have a curious relationship with the land which sustains them. Not for most, including most farmers and graziers, could it be said, as Aborigines say "the land is my mother and my father"; the image, rather, is of a mean and capricious step-parent who must be battled all the way. The land and the elements have been an enemy which must be fought and gambled against (Canberra Times, 9th April 1983).*

To most early immigrants the harsh Australian landscape and strange animals and vegetation must have seemed alien and hostile. For many, Australia was a place to get rich and get out. Such attitudes were reinforced by the prevailing ethos of the gold rushes of the 1860s. Unlike the United States (Chapter 2), Australia did not break its ties with Britain and for many generations Britain was still called 'home'. A misguided mixture of nostalgia and desire to improve led to the importation of unsutiable exotic flora and fauna, many of which (most notably the rabbit) have caused enormous environmental damage and financial loss.

The great empty spaces of the inland and the tropical north inevitably generated the view that Australia needed to be developed and populated. Growth - in almost any form - came to be regarded as highly desirable, with little regard to any adverse consequences or opportunity costs. Such attitudes, although overlain by more sophisticated views, are still firmly entrenched in many institutions and in the value systems of many Australians.

Among the effects of white settlement on the environment was wholesale clearing of tree cover to improve pasture and for commercial and other purposes. Timber cover must have seemed so extensive as to be almost inexhaustible. Bolton notes that "Commissioner Fry of the New South Wales Lands Department informed an official inquiry in 1847 that the Big Scrub in the Richmond River cedar country could not be cleared for five or six centuries. Within thirty years selectors were farming the same country, stripped of its timber" (Bolton, 1981, p.40).

The history of extensive land clearance, the application of unsuitable European farming methods and a legacy of poor management practices have been major contributors to the extensive land degradation in Australia. A recent report (Woods, 1983, p.67) concluded that 51 percent of rural land in Australia needs treatment for land degradation, more than half of which needs treatment by works as well as better land management, and that a substantial proportion of rural land is continuing to lose its productive potential.

Land degradation has also occurred as an outcome of government policies aimed at other objectives. Blyth and Kirby (1984) discuss a number of these. They argue that the high proportion of leasehold tenure in Australia, combined with limited periods of tenure or uncertainty as to renewal, price controls on the sale of leases and restrictions on the size of holdings, has led to exploitive land use practices. Government subsidies have encouraged fertiliser use on lands unsuited to cultivation, or in quantities damaging to soil structure. Extreme underpricing of irrigation water has resulted in overuse and extensive salinity problems. Land clearance was encouraged until 1983 by the allowance of its full costs as a tax deduction. Drought assistance such as fodder subsidies has aided retention of livestock during drought. Government intervention in agricultural commodity pricing has led to increased cropping of marginal lands.

On the credit side, government extension services have largely overcome the information gap which was a major problem in the 1940s (Blyth and Kirby, 1984, p.14). Land use and land clearing regulations aimed at reducing land degradation have been introduced by some States, and many soil conservation activities are allowable as tax deductions. However, the main difficulties lie with the range of policies listed above, adopted for purposes such as expansion of production, stabilisation of prices, and land settlement and development. Changing circumstances have made such objectives decreasingly valid, and the benefits of the associated policies need to be reviewed against their social costs (including their contribution to land degradation). Most of these policies, however, incorporate financial benefits for the pastoral and agricultural industries, and rural interests remain a strong and vocal political force.

RESOURCE DEVELOPMENT, FEDERALISM AND ENVIRONMENTAL POLICY: AN OVERVIEW

The nature of Australian environmental policy has been heavily influenced by high levels of natural resource development, a Federal system of government, and the relationships between the two. Essential features of the situation are an uneven distribution of natural resources between the States, and a Constitution which leaves most direct powers over resources and environment to the States, but gives the Commonwealth a number of other powers which can be applied to implement environmental policy.

High levels of resource development have resulted in considerable pressures on the natural environment. The list of major environmental controversies in Australia is dominated by issues concerning the effects of particular resource developments on the natural environment. Environmental pressures have been increased by strong pro-development attitudes. These have been reinforced by the prevailing view (at least up to the 1970s) that resource developers needed to be attracted by the provision of incentives, and that they would be deterred by the imposition of special taxes or strict environmental conditions.

Commonwealth and State

The uneven distribution of resources, together with the different responsibilities, constituencies, objectives and powers of States and Commonwealth, has led to State/Commonwealth disagreements over

(a) the distribution of the costs and benefits of resource developments,
(b) the environmental management of developments, and
(c) at times debate over whether or not, on environmental grounds, such projects should proceed.

The overlap of Constitutional powers has in a number of instances allowed the Commonwealth to intervene successfully, although in others it has chosen not to do so.

The extent to which the Commonwealth government is prepared to intervene depends to some extent on the party in power: the ALP has been more interventionist in environmental issues than the LNCP. However, Commonwealth governments in general are likely to place greater weight on environmental values in resource development issues than are the State governments concerned. This is partly because, where such issues have become nationally controversial, there is likely to be an actual or perceived differential between the distribution of the economic benefits and the environmental costs of the resource development concerned. The economic benefits of such a development may accrue, or be perceived as accruing, mainly to the State in which it takes place, while the environmental costs may be of concern to many in the rest of Australia. Those outside the State concerned are therefore likely to place a greater weight on the environmental costs than those within it.

However, there are also regional differences in the weighting given to environmental values. Industrialisation in Australia is located mainly in the more heavily populated States of New South

Wales and Victoria. These States are more likely to be tolerant of environmental concerns than Queensland, Western Australia and the Northern Territory, which are more dependent on resource development, or the resource-poor States of Tasmania and South Australia where development is at a premium. Such differences are reinforced by the view, fostered by some prominent politicians in the resource-developing States, that they are making a disproportionate contribution to the welfare of the nation as a whole - for example, by a greater contribution to export earnings and Commonwealth taxation revenue, and by paying higher prices for manufactured goods as a result of tariff barriers. Such views, however suspect their justification, reinforce State opposition to Commonwealth intervention in resource development questions.

Given that the Constitution leaves most direct powers concerning the environment to the States, and given their differing resource endowments and economic circumstances, it is often misleading to speak of Australian environmental policy. Rather, there are the policies of six State governments (all with similarities but also with considerable differences), those of the Northern Territory (with its recently increased degree of self-government), and the overlapping policies of the Commonwealth government itself. The result has been a multiplicity of government institutions concerned with the environment as each State, and the Commonwealth, has developed its own environmental and related legislation and administrative structures, together with joint State/ Commonwealth organisations aimed at achieving co-operation and co-ordination. Policy problems arise where uniform standards are considered desirable, where State and Commonwealth powers overlap, or where resources cross State boundaries. An example of the latter is Australia's major river (the Murray-Darling), where State governments for many years have failed to give the River Murray Commission sufficient authority, particularly in relation to water quality.

Mineral Resources

Competition between States for mineral resource development and for resource-based industrial development - notably aluminium refining based on cheap power from coal in NSW and Queensland, gas in WA and hydro-electric power in Tasmania - seems likely to have contributed to a lowering of the environmental standards imposed on developers, and to sales of energy at excessively low prices. Intensive regional resource-based development - such as the coal-based growth in the Hunter and Latrobe Valleys in NSW and Victoria respectively - has led to social as well as physical environmental problems. These problems relate to failings in the provision of physical infrastructure and social services to meet the needs of growth, complicated by the division in responsibilities and powers between Federal, State and local government. Such developments also exposed the problems of the overalapping and cumulative social and environmental effects of a number of closely spaced projects, problems not well handled by the requirement for environmental impact assessment of individual projects.

From the early 1970s, reflecting the growing demand for Australian mineral resources, governments became more concerned with increasing the Australian share of benefits from mineral development. Here the Commonwealth government, particularly the Whitlam Labour government in 1972-75, took the lead. The Commonwealth government's powers over exports were used as a means of increasing the prices received for them, and at times as a means of imposing environmental standards on mining operations or apportioning the market among Australian producers. Restrictions on foreign ownership and control were increased, partly to increase the proportion of profits retained in Australia and partly as a response to economic nationalism; and the level of taxes and charges on the mining industry was raised by both State and Federal governments. State attitudes to the Commonwealth initiatives were mixed, depending very much on their gains and losses from the new arrangements (for more extensive accounts, see Stevenson, 1977; Harris, 1984).

There has been considerable concern that rapid development of the minerals sector would damage manufacturing industry, and require major structural readjustments with their associated social costs. Scenarios for the likely course of events have varied considerably, including some predictions of major labour shortages and others of a massive increase in unemployment. A range of policy responses has been proposed (see Dixon, 1978; Blandy, 1981).

Neither position has yet emerged. The rate of growth of mineral resource development has not been as rapid as many expected, and it has been only one of a complex set of factors involved in the high rate of unemployment in Australia since the mid-1970s (Sheehan, 1980; Hughes, 1980). Nevertheless, the policy responses to increasing demand for Australia's mineral resources have had, and will have, major implications for the social and physical environment, affecting the nature, magnitude and distribution of impacts.

Policy and Decision Making

As the preceding discussion illustrates, there is no clear dividing line between environmental policies (defined to include the social as well as the physical environment) and other policies. Discussion of resource policy which begins with the effects on the natural environment of individual proposals quickly extends into consideration of their social costs and benefits and the cumulative effects of adjacent projects. Resource development policy in a more general sense involves questions of the distribution of economic and environmental costs and benefits between regions, States and the rest of Australia; between developers and the community; between Australia and overseas; and between present and future generations. This requires consideration of the appropriate rates of development of different mineral resources, the effects on employment and on other sectors of the economy, and the social costs of restructuring. These aspects, and others, imply multiple policy choices with a variety of social and environmental effects.

Despite the important environmental consequences which flow from such policy choices, and the differing nature and distribution of the environmental effects of different policy configurations, there has been little environmental input at the policy level concerned with strategies of resource development and economic management and the relationships between them. Increased consideration of environmental effects has been mainly confined to specific projects, where there has been some success in influencing the environmental conditions under which individual projects proceed, and in some cases in preventing environmentally damaging proposals.

There are many reasons for the comparative failure to consider the environmental dimension at the policy level. Environmental groups have tended to direct the bulk of their limited resources towards the most urgent issues, which are usually specific environmentally damaging proposals. Such issues capture and focus public attention. Broad policy issues tend to be more complex and interrelated, and they require continuous effort over a long period to bring about change. Results are often achieved only in a piecemeal and incremental way. Policy-making occurs in a labyrinthine bureaucratic setting, to which public access and input is limited.

Environmental pressure groups are generally not in as good a position as business interests to influence the policy process through contacts with policymakers. Neither have they sufficiently developed the specialised expertise in lobbying necessary to do so. Matthews (1976, p.340) showed the extremely heavy representation of business and primary producers' associations on advisory committees to the Commonwealth government, as compared with environmental groups (127 as against 2) and of producer groups as compared with non-producer groups (203 against 40). In a study of national elites during the Whitlam Labour government's period in office, Higley et al, (1979, esp. Tables 7.9 to 7.11 therein) showed the high proportion of business leaders in the central elite and the high proportion of business leader's contacts with both LNCP and Labour Party central elite sectors.

As a means of increasing public participation and environmental input into decision-making, EIA in Australia has been only moderately successful. Implementation of the requirement has been piecemeal and the restrictive rules on legal standing in Australia have generally prevented enforcement of EIA requirements through the courts. Most of the EIA which has been carried out has concerned projects, not policies.

Government environmental agencies have not usually been in a position to provide strong inputs at the policy level. They have been faced by an array of well-established and traditionally development-oriented government departments. Environmental agencies are in most cases low in the departmental and Ministerial hierarchies, and government support for their activities is often uncertain.

None of the major political parties has a strong environmental record, although that of the Labour Party has been considerably better than the others in recent years. In this the political parties largely reflect the values and political realities of the surrounding society, although it may be that the political parties and public institutions have fallen somewhat behind changing public opinion. Certainly, one of the prominent aspects of environmental issues in Australia has been the resistance to change evident in institutions, especially when they are under pressure to take increased account of the environmental dimension in their procedures and decisions.

FEDERALISM AND ENVIRONMENT - SOME CASES

Five resource and environmental controversies, above all the others, have engaged the national interest and heightened environmental consciousness in Australia. These have been concerned about the effects of possible oil drilling and other pressures on the Great Barrier Reef; the mineral sand mining on Fraser Island, off the Queensland coast; the flooding of Lake Pedder and the proposed Gordon-below-Franklin dam, both for hydro-electric schemes in Tasmania's South-West wilderness area; and uranium mining and export.

Four of these issues generated major Commonwealth government-instigated public inquiries; the four discussed below involved major Commonwealth/State jurisdictional and policy disputes (in the case of uranium the richest deposits are in the Northern Territory where Commonwealth law was pre-eminent), and three required High Court decisions to define the extent of Commonwealth government powers.

The Great Barrier Reef

Conservation of the Reef first became a national issue in 1967, with a proposal to mine part of it for limestone. Interest group and public opposition to the proposal prevailed, but concern over the future of the Reef was given new impetus by the Santa Barbara oil blow-out, off California, in early 1969. Public attention was drawn to the fact that almost all the Reef was covered by oil exploration permits. Following a sustained public campaign (Wright, 1977, gives a history of the issue to 1976), during which trade unions placed a complete ban on Reef drilling, joint Commonwealth/State Royal Commissions were appointed, after initial opposition from Queensland. Two of the three Commissioners considered that oil drilling could be permitted in limited parts of the Reef region away from reefs or islands. The Commonwealth Whitlam Labour government nevertheless decided, in 1975, that no drilling should take place until further scientific evidence was available about the long-term effects of oil pollution. It also introduced the Great Barrier Reef Marine Park Act (1975), which was supported by all political parties.

However, the Queensland government continued to support the case for oil drilling and to oppose the declaration of sections of the Marine Park under the Act. Within the Fraser LCNP government, which had taken Federal office in November 1975, there was a significant element of support for the Queensland position. By 1979 - almost four years after passage of the Act - no section of the Marine Park had yet been declared. Leaked ministerial correspondence, revealed in Federal Parliament by the Labour opposition, showed that the Federal Minister for Minerals and Energy (Mr. Newman) had sought to delay declaration of the Capricornia section of the Marine Park until proposals for renewals for oil exploration permits in the area could be processed (National Times, 9th June 1979). The embarrassment which this incident caused the government appears to have influenced its announcement, shortly afterwards, of an indefinite moratorium on drilling for oil on the Reef.

In 1975 the Whitlam government had passed the Seas and Submerged Lands Act (1973) which gave the Commonwealth government sovereignty over the territorial sea and continental shelf. The validity of the Act was challenged by the States but upheld by the High Court (New South Wales v. Commonwealth (Offshore Sovereignty Case) 1975). The High Court decision was based centrally on the external affairs power of the Commonwealth government under the Constitution (s. 51(29)). The decision gave the Commonwealth government predominant power over the Reef, and it meant that the Great Barrier Reef Marine Park Act (1975) would over-ride any inconsistent State legislation. This power enabled the Commonwealth government in 1981 to unilaterally declare the Cairns section of the Marine Park, after two years of negotiations in which the Queensland government had failed to reach agreement.

No further sections of the Marine Park were declared until after the Hawke Labour government took office. In September 1983 regulations prohibiting oil drilling in the Reef region came into force under the Great Barrier Reef Marine Park Act (1975). In October 1983 almost all the remainder of the Reef was declared as Marine Park. Zoning plans are being prepared for each section, but this task will take several years.

Fraser Island

Australia's commercial deposits of mineral sands unfortunately tend to occur in coastal locations with significant conservation value, particularly along the more closely populated eastern coastline. As a result of a series of environmental disputes, much stronger controls have been placed on the industry over the last decade, particularly in New South Wales.

Fraser Island is the largest sand island in the world. It is heavily forested, with many beautiful and rare perched dune lakes. Opposition to sand mining on the island had been active since 1971, but it was not until 1975 that the Whitlam government (after considerable internal dissension over the issue) instituted a public environmental inquiry into the matter. This was the first such inquiry held under the provisions of the newly enacted Environment Protection (Impact of Proposals) Act (1974-75). (Roddewig, 1978, gives a detailed account of the politics of the issue).

The constitutional significance of the issue arose following a legal challenge by the sand mining lessees over the right of the Commonwealth Minister for Minerals and Energy to take the findings of the inquiry into account when deciding whether or not to grant an export licence. The High Court in effect confirmed the right of the Commonwealth

Parliament to exercise its constitutional power over overseas trade and commerce having regard to any matter, not just considerations of trading policy (Murphyores Inc. Pty Ltd. v. Commonwealth).

In 1976 the Fraser government announced an end to mineral export approvals from all except a small area of the island.

Tasmanian Dams

Tasmania has long sought to attract heavy industry by supplying cheap hydro-electric power. This policy has been widely questioned in terms of the alternative forms of investment which might be made to increase employment and economic development. The Tasmanian Hydro-Electric Commission has over the years been the archetypal single-purpose, development-oriented government agency. It has been over-optimistic in its forecasts of electricity demand, and it over-estimated the costs of thermal power generation as an alternative to hydro-electric power from the Gordon-below-Franklin Scheme (Saddler et al, 1980).

Conservation groups have fought a long and persistent campaign over South-West Tasmania, one of the world's few remaining large temperate wilderness areas. (For a review of some of the complex politics of the issue, see Davis, 1980). Opposition to the dam has had strong support from mainland Australia, but not from the majority of Tasmanians. For example, a Morgan Gallup poll in January 1983 found 48 percent of Australians were opposed to the Gordon-below-Franklin dam, 25 percent in favour and 27 percent had no opinion. The corresponding figures for Tasmania, however, were 36, 48 and 16 percent respectively (Financial Review, 10th February 1983).

The original Lake Pedder, with its extensive white quartzite beach, was a site of great natural beauty. Despite offers of financial compensation by the Whitlam government in 1973 following the recommendations of the Lake Pedder Committee of Inquiry, the Tasmanian government refused to halt flooding of the Lake for the Gordon River Power Development Stage One.

It appeared that history would repeat itself in the 1980s with the proposed Gordon-below-Franklin dam, following the Fraser government's refusal to intervene in the issue. However, on gaining Federal office, the Hawke Labour government implemented an election promise to stop the dam. The resultant legislation was challenged by the Tasmanian government in the High Court in July 1983. A four-three majority of the Court upheld the legislation on three constitutional grounds. These were:

(a) the external affairs power (s.51(29)), based on which the Commonwealth had passed laws to implement its ratification of the UNESCO Convention for the Protection of the World Cultural and Natural Heritage, under which the South-West Tasmanian wilderness has been declared a world heritage area,
(b) the 'corporations power' (s.51(20)), under which the Commonwealth had directed the Hydro-Electric Commission not to proceed with the dam, and
(c) the 'race' power (s.51(26)), to make laws concerning 'the people of any race for whom it is deemed necessary to make special laws', based on which the Commonwealth said it was protecting archaeological sites of special significance to Aborigines.

The High Court decision was highly significant in extending the potential application of Commonwealth powers, not just in relation to environment. For example, by entering into a genuine international treaty the Commonwealth can legislate to implement the treaty, even if it does not otherwise have that power. The Commonwealth may make laws about foreign or trading corporations, even matters which are otherwise outside Commonwealth powers.

The extent to which the Commonwealth government makes use of its expanded powers is another matter. The federal balance is a political as well as a constitutional construct, and disturbances to that balance by the increased use of Commonwealth powers can incur political costs. This has been the case in Tasmania, where Federal intervention has helped to consolidate the Liberal Party in power after many years of Labour government. In a current (late 1984) issue concerning the bulldozing of a road through the Daintree rainforest in Queensland, the Commonwealth government has refused to intervene on the grounds that it does not have the power to do so, although there is substantial legal opinion to the contrary (Age, 16th August 1984). The government has said it will not nominate the area for World Heritage listing without the consent of the Queensland government. There is apparently concern that in the forthcoming Federal election, the Queensland Premier would use unilateral nomination against the Hawke government and thus affect its chances in marginal seats in North Queensland (Age, 12th September 1984).

The preceding cases illustrate some aspects of Commonwealth and State environmental powers, the differing Commonwealth and State attitudes to environmental questions, and the results of Commonwealth/State conflicts on some issues of major public interest. The cases described have been significant landmarks in Australian environmental decision-making. In many ways, however, they are atypical. Most environmental issues are decided within the States, without Commonwealth intervention. Many decisions with important environmental consequences do not attract such strong public attention, and few environmental issues come before the courts. The proportion of victories for environmentalists has been considerably lower than the above sample would suggest.

To illustrate some of the problems of increasing the weight given to environmenal considerations at a more routine level of decision-making, we must turn to the experience with the EIA requirement.

ENVIRONMENTAL IMPACT ASSESSMENT AND SOME INSTITUTIONAL CONSTRAINTS

Four institutional features, among others, have helped to decrease the effectiveness of the EIA requirement in Australia, and to provide other problems for those seeking to improve the environmental content of decision-making. They are the framing of EIA requirements so that their implementation is subject to political discretion; the restrictions on legal standing; secrecy in government; and the problems of relating EIA requirements to pre-existing statutory land-use planning procedures.

Environmental Impact Assessment
The Australian experience with EIA is described in Formby (1981), and only salient features are noted here. Under the Commonwealth Environmental Protection (Impact of Proposals) Act (1974-75), for the seven years 1975-76 to 1981-82, a total of only 62 EISs were required (Anderson, 1982) - a low figure given the range of Commonwealth government responsibilities. All six States have some form of EIA requirement, but only three have enacted EIA legislation. With the exception of New South Wales (NSW) the various State EIA requirements overall are weak, embody a variety of failings and are almost totally unenforceable in the courts. Some States require EISs only infrequently, the quality of EISs is often poor, and many clearly have little influence on decision-making.

Only NSW, Victoria and the Commonwealth make provision for public inquiries in their EIA procedures. The Commonwealth has only held two public environmental inquiries under the Act. The Commonwealth, NSW and South Australian procedures provide for publication of EISs. Those of Queensland do not, and in Victoria, Western Australia and Tasmania public review is optional, although normally provided. In all States except Queensland there is a procedural provision for administrative review of an EIS by a body other than the government department responsible for making or approving the proposal. However, in most cases the reviewing authority (usually the minister in charge of the department administering the EIA procedures) has no power after carrying out such a review, except to give advice.

Discretionary Environmental Impact Assessment
A feature of both Commonwealth and State EIA requirements is the large extent to which their operation is subject to political discretion. This is obviously the case where EIA requirements are not embodied in legislation. Where there is legislation, except in the case of NSW, it is expressed so that its implementation cannot be enforced in the courts, largely by making the exercise of the various steps of implementation a matter for ministerial or administrative decision. It was undoubtedly the deliberate intention of the governments responsible for introducing the

various EIA requirements to retain political control of the process. However, this has detracted from the effectiveness of the EIA requirement.

Arguments in favour of the present system are that it avoids the high costs and long delays that may accompany legal action, and that decisions about the implementation of EIA procedures should be made by elected governments rather than in the courts. As to the first point, legal delays need not be excessive: the NSW Land and Environmental Court has 'in almost every case' disposed of matters involving major development proposals in less than three months (Cripps, 1973, p.17). With regard to the second point, while agreeing that the political decision-makers should have the ultimate responsibility (having considered the environmental consequences) for deciding whether or not a proposal should proceed, there is still a strong case for allowing legal enforcement of the preceding stages of the EIA procedural requirements. This would ensure that an EIS is prepared when warranted; that its content is adequate; that it is produced before the decision to proceed is made; that sufficient time is allowed for public comment; and so on. At present environmental interests have little recourse, except for public pressure, where there is avoidance of EIA procedural requirements.

Legal Standing

Even where administrative action is unequivocally required under EIA or other legislation, it is very unlikely that environmental groups will be given standing by the courts to attempt to enforce compliance. The limits on standing in Australia were demonstrated in Australian Conservation Foundation Inc v. The Commonwealth of Australia. In this case the Foundation challenged the validity of Commonwealth approval of a proposal to establish a tourist resort in Central Queensland, on the basis that the government had failed to comply with the Environmental Protection (Impact of Proposals) Act (1974/75). However, the High Court found that the Foundation did not have standing. According to Justice Gibbs, in an interpretation which had been accepted in subsequent cases, standing requires "having a special interest in the subject matter of the action".

The Foundation's conservation-oriented objectives and its large membership of environmentally-concerned Australians, however, were not considered to constitute such an interest. An interest (again quoting Justice Gibbs):

> *...does not mean a mere intellectual or emotional concern. A person is not interested within the meaning of the rule, unless he is likely to gain some advantage, other than the satisfaction of righting a wrong, upholding a principle or winning a contest, if his action succeeds or to suffer some disadvantage, other than a sense of grievance or a debt for costs, if his action fails. A belief, however strongly felt, that the law generally, or a particular law, should be observed, or that conduct of a particular kind should be prevented does not suffice to give its possessor locus standi.*

Clearly the restrictions on standing are of considerable importance for environmental policy generally as well as for EIA. Individuals and groups at present do not have the same legal protection for their environmental interests as for their economic interests, a situation which does not reflect changing community values. Consequently the effective pressure on politicians to improve environmental policy is greatly reduced.

Public Access to Information

The high level of political discretion embodied in the EIA legislation, the limitations on standing and the strong conventions of secrecy in government are all in some sense related to the Westminster-derived conventions of government in Australia. In relation to restraints on public access to information, three Westminster conventions are particularly relevant. These are:

(a) individual ministerial responsibility: ministers are responsible to parliament for activities of their departments,

(b) cabinet solidarity and secrecy: ministers must support and take equal responsibility for cabinet decisions, whatever their personal view of such decisions may be, and

(c) public service neutrality and anonymity: public servants must give full loyalty and impartial advice to any government, regardless of their own political beliefs, and their own views should not be seen to clash with those of the government.

The overall effect of these conventions is to consign large areas of information to secrecy, and to provide a convenient excuse for a general reluctance to provide information to the public. Obviously it is important for environmental and other public interest groups to be informed about the environmental and other consequences of proposals and policies before decisions are made. The question is whether the benefits of better public access to information outweigh any losses in terms of the effective operation of government under the Westminster conventions.

The first point to be made is that the conventions - as stated above - have been greatly modified in practice. The links of accountability of bureaucrats to ministers, and ministers to parliament, are weaker than the conventions suggest, and the bureaucracy has considerable independent power. The Royal Commission on Australian Government Administration (1976, p.39) concluded that the public service is able "to function to some degree as a self-contained elite group exercising significant power generally in the interests of the *status quo* but without being effectively accountable for its exercise". The need to open the public service to a greater degree of public scrutiny has considerable support in Australia. But the *Commonwealth Freedom of Information Act* (1982), which was ten years in the making after strong resistance from sections of the public service and government, retains many broadly stated restrictions and exemptions on the provision of information. It represents only a cautious step towards greater freedom of information.

Environmental Impact Assessment and Land Use Controls

Neither land use planning and development controls nor EIA alone appear to be adequate to deal with the environmental pressures of economic development. Without the framework provided by land use planning, the task of environmental assessment of major projects would become open-ended, and it would be necessary to make assumptions and predictions about other future land uses as part of the assessment. Different assumptions made by different EISs would quickly lead to uncertainty and confusion. On the other hand, land use planning and control cannot provide a review of the environmental and other costs of a specific proposal as an adequate basis for deciding whether or not the project should proceed.

EIA and planning controls should be complementary. Nevertheless there has been considerable complaint about the problems of relating the two: unless they are formally integrated in some way, for example, a developer has to conform to two separate sets of requirements. In the writer's view, the difficulties involved have been exaggerated. Much of the resistance to EIA has arisen because it cuts across the established way of doing things adopted by many organisations and professions, including town planning.

Nevertheless, it is advantageous if EIA and land use planning and control requirements can be integrated in the legislation. The NSW Environmental Planning and Assessment Act (1979) is an attempt to bring about such an integration. At the same time it sets aside the established rules of standing, by providing (s.123) that any person can bring proceedings to remedy or restrain a breach of the Act. This, of course, does not apply to the extensive range of other NSW environmental legislation.

The Act provides for 'environmental planning instruments' to be prepared at three levels: State Environmental Policies, Regional Environmental Plans, and Local Environmental Plans. Under these instruments certain developments or activities may require consent (under Part IV of the Act) before being carried out. The consent authority is usually the local council, but it may be a higher level of government. These provisions are basically the familiar process of development control (as used in Britain - see Chapter 5). But the Act also introduces EIA into the development control process, but stipulating that all proposals which require development consent must be accompanied by information on likely environmental impacts (s.77(3)(c)), and that for certain 'designated developments' which require development consent, the preparation of an EIS is mandatory.

Under Part V of the Act, for proposals where development consent under a planning instrument is not required, but which are likely to affect the environment 'significantly', the 'determining authority' must obtain and consider an EIS (s.112(1)). There are thus two distinct ways in which proposals may become subject to EIA. The intent of the Part V provision is to ensure appropriate EIA for proposals which do not require consent under the planning control provisions of Part IV of the Act. However, without entering into a detailed review (for which see Barker, 1981; Farrier, 1984), the provisions of the Act create a number of problems. These arise in part because the requirements for EIA under Part IV are potentially narrower than under Part V - Part IV lists specific categories of designated developments on which EIS is required, whereas Part V requires EIA for any proposals likely to affect the environment significantly.

There has therefore been some litigation on the basis that, if a development can be brought under Part IV, but it is not a designated development, then an EIS is not required - even though (under Part V) the development may have affected the environment significantly and it therefore required an EIS. Further, the question of which developments require consent under Part IV depends on the specific environmental planning instrument in question. The effect of these and other provisions is that:

> *At best this means that not all proposals having a significant effect on the environment will be the subject of an environmental impact statement. At worst it can mean that exactly the same kind of proposals can be subjected to fundamentally different environmental assessment requirements depending upon precisely where it is to take place (Farrier, 1984, p.167).*

Despite these problems, however, the Act overall is a considerable advance on other State provisions for EIA.

THE HUNTER REGION - RESOURCE DEVELOPMENT, POLICY AND ENVIRONMENT

The Hunter Region in many ways presents an exaggerated microcosm of the environmental policy problems of Australia as a whole. At the same time, it is a well defined Region with a distinctive character.

Because of its illustrative nature, the case is dealt with in somewhat more detail than the others reviewed in this Chapter. The Region demonstrates the environmental and social problems as well as the benefits which accelerated resource development brings. It also highlights the difficulties which pre-existing institutions have in coping successfully with such change, and the way in which environmental policy and management activities tend to occur as belated responses to economic and resource development decisions and actions, rather than as part of the original decision-making process. The Region also illustrates some problems in obtaining effective and meaningful public participation in government decisions. Such problems are exacerbated because, under a three-tier system of government, regional interests are not always effectively represented.

The Hunter Region lies about 100km north of Sydney, New South Wales. Its main city and port - Newcastle - is an important industrial centre, and the Region has an established rural sector, with a significant wine-growing industry. The Region's outstanding feature, however, is its very large reserves of black coal.

The rapid oil price rises from the mid 1970s brought about a renewed demand for coal for export. At the same time domestic consumption of coal increased as the NSW government implemented a policy of building up power-generating capacity in the Region in order to attract energy-intensive industry. By the 1980s over $A10,000 million in investment was planned or under construction in the Region (Perkins, 1984, Table 12 therein). This included more than twenty new or extended open-cut coal mines, two large new power stations, and two new or greatly expanded aluminium smelters.

These developments, together with a range of associated projects such as dams, coal loaders and rail upgrading, placed great pressure on the social and physical environment of the Region. Development pressures reached a peak in 1980-82, but there has since been a marked slowing down in the pace of development following declining forecasts of coal demand.

The sheer volume of existing and proposed open-cut mining activities, together with other major contributions, are transforming the landscape of the Hunter Region. Much of the mining will be on marginal and degraded farmland, which will subsequently be rehabilitated. Nevertheless, the large number of open cut mining operations (some proposed to be up to three kilometres long and 300 metres deep), together with coal dumps, power stations, dams, conveyors and other ancillary activities, will have extensive and increasing visual and physical impacts. There are problems with dust and noise from mining operations and heavy vehicle traffic, and there is mounting concern about air pollution from a variety of other sources, including six power stations, two aluminium refineries, and various heavy industries in Newcastle.

Accelerated development in the Region has had serious social effects. There have been major shortages in physical infrastructure (such as housing, water supply, sewerage and transport) and in the provision of community services. The incidence of the costs and benefits of development has been uneven. Existing residents have been subjected to higher rents or to rate increases levied to help pay for the additional infrastructure required to meet the influx of population.

Decision-making Under Pressure

The machinery of government in NSW has often been both slow to react to the problems of the Region arising from accelerated development and inadequate in planning for an co-ordinating development and change. Under the pressures of accelerated development, the formal institutions and routines for planning were to a considerable extent by-passed by more informal and non-routine procedures and ad hoc decisions and responses. Decision-making became increasingly piecemeal and non-comprehensive.

There were several reasons for this. Because of the significant externalities and non-incremental infrastructure requirements of many large projects, as well as their economic significance, non-routine processes of bargaining were involved between government and developers to determine the terms and conditions under which developments would proceed. Such processes often effectively short-circuited or pre-empted established procedures. The complex and overlapping ramifications of the range of developments under way in the Region placed great strains on the established routines and capabilities of government organisations. They also required unprecedented degrees of co-ordination between the organisations for which the pre-existing structure of predominantly single-purpose government agencies was not well suited. The main formal instrument for planning and development control, the Environmental Planning and Assessment Act (1979), did not prove to be a sufficiently effective means of planning and co-ordinating development under conditions of rapid change (for reasons to be discussed later).

Such institutional deficiencies, together with the problems generated by accelerated development, led to slow or inadequate initial responses. These in turn, created pressures for rapid, crisis-generated decisions. There was also concern that if quick decisions were not made to attract and secure agreements for major industrial developments important opportunities might be foregone.

Economic Strategy

Following its election in 1976, the Wran Labour government in NSW sought a means of reversing the State's high unemployment and declining industrial activity, which were at that time particularly marked in the Hunter Region. The government recognised the potential importance of the coal reserves in the Region as a source of economic growth in a period of rising oil prices. However, it saw also that coal mining for export would not in itself make great inroads into unemployment. The State government therefore began an active campaign, using the Industrial Investment Unit in the Premier's Department, to attract energy-intensive industries to the Region, coupled with a programme of greatly expanding the Region's electricity generating capacity (Australian Financial Review 1-3 September, 1981).

This was not a particularly original course of

action, since several States were competing against each other to obtain aluminium smelters. Nor, following the construction period, would the longer-term employment needs of such industry be high in relation to the size of the capital investment.

The strategy was adopted without any systematic review of optional development paths for the Region. Given the size of its coal reserves, there is bound to be a strong component of heavy industrial development in any economic strategy for the Region. But this would not preclude a variety of patterns of development with differing emphases - for example, one which placed somewhat less weight on obtaining a few large, energy-intensive projects together with stronger promotion of other, more employment-intensive industries, a range of which are already established in the Region.

Further, there was no comprehensive assessment of the likely social and environmental effects of the upsurge of development on the Region, much less any comparisons with the effects of alternative patterns of development. There has also been concern that, in its eagerness to secure development, the NSW government is subsidising developers by supplying power at excessively cheap prices (Dick, 1981, pp.11,12), but not requiring them to meet the full infrastructure costs of their projects, or by not applying sufficiently stringent environmental controls. There are, of course, opposing views on such matters (for example Ritchie, 1983). But where negotiations and decision-making concerning major proposals are carried out in haste and in secret (the electricity prices agreed with the aluminium refineries were not made public), there is less likely to be a full and balanced evaluation of all the costs and benefits of such proposals, including their external social and environmental costs.

<u>Deficiencies in Infrastructure Provisions</u>
The State government was slow in acting to overcome the financial and logistical obstacles to providing the physical and social infrastructure required by the new development. As the pace of growth increased in the late 1970s, its accompanying social, environmental and infrastructure problems became more apparent. Conflicts arose between levels of government, as local councils in areas where development was most intense met with finan-

cial difficulties in attempting to provide the infrastructure needs of their rapidly growing populations. At the same time there was growing protest within the Region, based on concern about such matters and at the lack of local involvement in the decision-making processes affecting the Region. These concerns were expressed in the publication _'Who Asked Us? Coal, Power Aluminium - The Hunter Region's only Future?'_ published by a coalition of Regional community groups (Newcastle Ecology Centre, 1980).

During the late 1970s the NSW government established several bodies to examine the infrastructure needs of the Region (Parker, 1982, pp. 120-139). Although the reports of these bodies drew attention to the inadequacies of existing infrastructure to meet the needs of growth, and to the special financial assistance which local government would require, the government failed to take effective action until infrastructure shortages and their associated social problems led to sustained public protest.

The government then made a number of crisis-generated responses. These included the appointment in 1980 of a Regional Infrastructure Co-ordinator within the Premier's Department, and of the Hunter Region Parliamentary Panel (made up of the seven members of State Parliament from the Region).

Community and local government protest continued in 1981. This centred on the arguments that infrastructure costs were being borne by the Region's community, and that the incidence of such costs fell more heavily on existing residents and disadvantaged groups than on the incoming workforce. Particular concern was caused by the announcement by the State government in June 1981 that no funds would be available for the early augmentation of the water supply and sewerage projects in Singleton and Muswellbrook, towns where the population growth was most rapid. After investigations by a range of government bodies, a new programme was announced to accelerate the provision of grants towards water supply and sewage headworks (Parker, 1982, pp. 132-137). It was not until September 1982 that the NSW government announced formal guidelines for infrastructure funding requirements for major new industrial developments

(NSW Premier's Department, 1982).

In this and other instances the government's dominant mode of operation was to react to specific crises after each arose, rather than to anticipate and pre-empt problems.

The Role of Statutory Planning

It might have been expected that the main formal instrument for planning in NSW, the Environmental Planning and Assessment Act (1979), would have played a greater role in ensuring that planning and decision-making for the Region was more comprehensive, anticipatory and co-ordinated. The Act's objectives include 'the proper management, development and conservation of natural and manmade resources' and the provision and co-ordination of physical infrastructure and community service (Ss. 5(a)(4) and (5)). But the Act has not proved to be a sufficient means of meeting such objectives in a situation of rapid change.

The EIA requirements for specific projects under the Act have some weaknesses (as noted earlier), but the main problems have occurred at the Regional planning level. According to Dick (1981, p.16), the Hunter Regional Environmental Plan, prepared in accordance with the Act (NSW Department of Environment and Planning, 1982), is:

> *Concerned mainly with spatial matters - the location of economic activity. It virtually ignores the critical matter of timing: there is no timetable for development and no scheduling of projects to avoid supply bottlenecks. In particular there seems to have been no manpower planning.*

In the Planning Report which accompanies the Plan there is no evaluation of clearly defined alternative courses of development for the Region. The planning method for the Upper Hunter appears to have taken the predicted broad effects of future developments as given, and then used these as a basis for policies to manage the effects of growth and change (NSW Department of Environment and Planning, 1982, p.97). The planning method for the Lower Hunter concerned itself largely with alternative spatial arrangements for urban growth (p.98). The Plan itself consists of a series of very broad 'motherhood' policy statements, together with strategies which are often not much more specific.

Despite its efforts to present a broader policy framework, the Plan is still heavily based on traditional concepts of land use planning, and this is reflected in the nature of its policies and strategies. The Plan has provided a useful basic point of reference in managing the Region. But the inherent limitations and problems of the statutory planning process, together with the length of time required for public consultation and preparation of statutory plans, detract from its suitability as a central vehicle for economic, social and physical planning under conditions of rapid change.

This point was recognised by those responsible for the Plan, when they noted that it is only part of a 'package of plans' for the Region (NSW Department of Environment and Planning, 1982, p.88) - the other plans being those of the various government authorities responsible for different aspects of social, economic or physical planning. However, the 'package of plans' demonstrably did not add up to a sufficient means of managing economic growth and change and its effects in the Region. (Other critiques of government planning for the Region include Garlick, 1984 (economic policy); Boer, 1984 (environmental planning); Perkins, 1984 (manpower policy); and Day, 1984 (water policy).)

Regionalisation

It is arguable that the problems of the Hunter Region have been increased because, while decisions were being made and developments taking place which affected the Region as a whole, there is no corresponding Regional level of government. Major decisions concerning the Region are made by the NSW government, and in such decisions the interests of the State as a whole are likely to dominate those of the Region. A NSW government Inquiry (Review of New South Wales Government Administration, 1977 and 1980) noted that the centralised planning and decision-making structure of NSW government agencies is not always adequate for coping with regional problems (1977, p.79), and it recommended a range of decentralisation measures.

The State government has made some moves in this direction, and there are now various Regional government and non-government bodies (for example the Hunter Development Board, Hunter Planning Committee, the Hunter Regional Community Forum, the Summit Conference Steering Committee and the Regional Association of Councils. Davis (1984) gives basic information about a range of such organisations). But the functions of such bodies are fragmented and they are limited to advisory roles. There is no overall regional body with powers to carry out and co-ordinate economic, social and environmental planning.

In the Latrobe Valley (Victoria) development is based on brown coal deposits, and there are many similarities to the Hunter Region. The Victoria State government has established the Latrobe Regional Commission (<u>under the Latrobe Regional Commission Act (1973</u>) with a range of functions including the acquisition, sub-division and sale of land, the preparation and implementation of regional strategy plans, and the preparation of co-ordinated plans of works for the Region and infrastructure plans for specific developments.

In considering regionalisation, a distinction must be drawn between formal political regionalisation - some form of elected regional government - and administrative regionalisation. In Australia the likelihood of the former is very small. But in the Hunter Region, given the deficiencies in government decision-making and co-ordination which have occurred, and the Region's distinctive identity, there is a strong case for the establishment of a Regional body analogous to the Latrobe Regional Commission.

<u>Policy and Environment in the Hunter Region</u>
Under the pressures of accelerated development in the Hunter Region, planning and decision-making by the bureaucractic machinery of government - the line departments, the institutions of statutory planning - was often slow, inadequate, and poorly co-ordinated. At the same time the central decision-makers of State government (focussed around the Premier, Cabinet and Premier's Department) pursued a strongly interventionist, but frequently reactive and ad hoc approach.

One commentator (Australian Financial Review,

3rd September 1981, p.16) has described the Wran government's style:

> *...the most enduring impression is not one of a well-drilled army of inter-departmental committees solving the problems of overlapping jurisdictions and reordering departmental priorities in a co-ordinated effort.*
>
> *It is the contrary vision of a strong, executive-style Cabinet government, negotiating directly with private industry, and utilising a coterie of highly specialised think-tanks and offshoots to impose its will and timetable on a vast governmental apparatus of variable enterprise and energy.*

Such a description, however, fails to state the deficiencies embodied in this style of government. To some extent the ad hoc measures and decisions which bypassed established routines were reasonable responses to the need to meet pressing problems and expedite lagging institutional decision-making. But there was also insufficient recognition by government of the disadvantages of such an approach. In the present context it should not be necessary to labour the dangers of taking major policy decisions without adequate review of their full range of social and environmental, as well as economic consequences, together with those of alternative course of action.

Also, to the extent that formal institutional procedures are short-circuited, the provisions for public participation and government accountability which they embody are rendered ineffective. Another difficulty with crisis-generated arrangements is that once the crisis has subsided, they may be inappropriate or even counter-productive. The strategy of supplementing existing institutions by ad hoc arrangements instead of modifying the institutions themselves, may lead to the latter emerging from the crisis in a weaker state than before.

The central lesson, for present purposes, of the case of the Hunter Region is the difficulty of introducing environmental considerations at the policy level, given the characteristics of actual governmental decision-making processes as described. Such difficulty increases in a situation of rapid change, where the need for environmental policy inputs is likely to be at its greatest.

PROGRESS IN ENVIRONMENTAL POLICY

From an environmentalist's viewpoint, is there a continuing improvement in the quality of Australian environmental policy? Certainly, since the 1960s there have been great changes in public attitudes, environmental management agencies of various kinds have been established in all States and the idea that the environmental effects of proposals should be considered in decision-making is widely acknowledged by politicians and bureaucrats. But the extent to which this concept is actually put into practice is quite variable, and has been confined largely to the project rather than the policy level. Even here, the environmental dimension of decision-making is still often confined, in reality, to examining means of reducing the project's adverse environmental impacts, rather than any serious consideration being given to whether or not the project should proceed.

There has also been considerable slowdown in the rate of development of environmental policy and management since the heady days of the Whitlam government, when new policy initiatives were frequent and environmental management was a growth area. In part this is because some of the most glaring environmental policy needs have been met. But also, with the economic recession since the early 1970s government priorities have changed; environmental considerations are now less likely to be allowed to impede development.

The Fraser LNCP government, which replaced the Whitlam government in 1975, was markedly less sympathetic to environmental concerns. Under its New Federalism policies, it supported a smaller role for the Commonwealth government in favour of the States in a range of matters including environmental policy.

The Hawke Labour government, which won Federal office in March 1983, prevented the Gordon-below-Franklin dam in Tasmania, but it subsequently has not applied the powers confirmed by the High

Court in that instance to the Daintree rainforest issue in Queensland. On some environmental issues the Hawke government has retreated from previous Labour Party positions. Two such cases illustrate the point.

Uranium Policy

The question of uranium mining and export has been a subject of major controversy in Australia for more than a decade (Formby, 1981, 1984). The 1982 ALP National Conference adopted a policy than uranium mining and export would be phased out, with the possible exception of developments such as the huge Roxby Downs deposit in South Australia, where uranium would be mined 'incidentally' to other minerals (Australian Labour Party, 1982, paras 55-66). However, in November 1983, the labour parliamentary Caucus voted in favour of developing Roxby Downs and of allowing the two existing mines (Ranger and Nabarlek) to continue. This decision was endorsed by a narrow margin at the 1984 ALP National Conference.

To a considerable degree these decisions reflect Mr. Hawke's support for uranium mining and export. But they are also part of a longer-term retreat from the anti-uranium position adopted by the Labour Party at the 1977 National Conference. As one correspondent described it, "the left and others in the party against uranium mining are running up an escalator that is running down" (Age, 8th November 1983).

Aboriginal Land Rights

Mining companies in Australia have been strongly opposed to the principle that Aborigines should be able to veto mining on their own land. This principle, however, is incorporated in the Labour Party's Platform at the 1984 National Conference, and it is expected to be included in uniform national Aboriginal land rights legislation being prepared by the Commonwealth government.

In the run-up to the December 1984 Federal election, Mr. Hawke said that the Federal government would not interfere with the Western Australian government's decision not to allow a veto over mining on Aboriginal land. He also said that "the general position of the Government is that we don't believe that the right of veto is an integral part of having effective, fair and efficient land rights legislation" (Sydney Morning Herald, 24th October 1984), and that the proposed national legislation might not be framed so as to over-ride separate State legislation.

The National Conservation Strategy

Australian environmental policy has had a tendency to be weak in implementation. Legislation has been passed or initiatives taken which appear to show much promise, but there is a subsequent decline of commitment in the implemenation process. To some degree this is due to institutional features such as the restrictions of legal standing (discussed in relation to EIA), and to the general propensity of institutions to resist change. Also, governments are prone to take symbolic action in response to public pressure but to back away from the hard decisions which implementation brings. (An example of this process is the history of the Victorian Environment Protection Authority, recounted in Gilpin (1980) and Russ and Tanner (1978).)

The National Conservation Strategy, proposed by a widely-based Conference in June 1983, appears to be in danger of following a similar path. The Fraser government announced, in May 1980, that it had adopted the principles of the World Conservation Strategy and - with the agreement of the States - it proposed to develop a National Conservation Strategy. The National Strategy, framed by representatives of business and government as well as the environmental movement, contains both principles and action recommendations (Department of Home Affairs and Environment, 1983). But it does not embody a detailed programme for implementing such actions. A Consultative Committee recommended by the Conference did not meet until eight months later. Some States have taken limited action, but there is no strong organisation at the national level to publicise the Strategy and to promote its implementation (Wilcox, 1984).

The Commonwealth Government's Role

Experience, even in recent years, has shown that the States are not always adequate guardians of the environment, and that a strong Commonwealth government overview role in environmental policy is desirable in the national interest. Commonwealth government action can help to bring about improved State policies (The Commonwealth EIA legislation had such an effect on State EIA requirements), to prevent parochial decisions (as in the Great Barrier Reef, Fraser Island and Gordon-below-Franklin cases), and to promote national action (on issues such as the National Conservation Strategy).

The main barriers to expanded Commonwealth activity in the environmental field are not Constitutional but political. Encroachment by the Commonwealth on areas where the States have traditionally exercised power brings protests about 'States' rights - still a powerful political weapon in the outer States which have historically been suspicious of the economic and political power of the more heavily populated States of New South Wales and Victoria.

Unfortunately the present Commonwealth government has so far not shown great enthusiasm for environmental policy initiatives. On the Daintree and Aboriginal land rights issues it has backed away from conflicts with the States.

PROSPECTS FOR CHANGE

As these examples indicate, only a slow rate of improvement in environmental policy is likely. This is to be expected in a country where economic performance is less than satisfactory, which is highly dependent on the development and export of natural resources, which is fundamentally conservative in political orientation, and where materialism and the development ethic are still strong. Nevertheless, the environmental movement remains vigorous, and it has had some notable successes. There is increasing recognition of the desirability of examining thoroughly the economic, social and physical environmental effects of policy options, but there are few good examples of this being done (one is the Reports of the Ranger Uranium Environmental Inquiry (1976, 1977)).

It may be argued that the scarcity of such examples is due to the difficulty of imposing more comprehensive planning and review procedures on the incremental, fragmented and bureaucratic-political processes of government, and that various 'interventionist' strategies - such as those proposed by Rondinelli (1976) - provide a more practical response. But while such strategies have their uses, they are unlikely to provide an adequate substitute for more comprehensive review in ensuring that environmental and social consequences are fully considered. This is illustrated by the results of the New South Wales experience in policy-making for the Hunter Region, which to a considerable extent amounted to an exercise in interventionist strategy.

The main obstacle to more comprehensive, environmentally conscious planning is the lack of political will to impose it. This, in turn, reflects the dominant values and the distribution of political, institutional and economic power in Australia.

REFERENCES

Anderson, E.M. (1982) Personal communication, Commonwealth Department of Home Affairs and Environment, Canberra

Australian Conservation Foundation Inc. v. The Commonwealth of Australia (1980) 28 Australian Law Journal Reports 176

Australian Labour Party (1982) Australian Labour Party Constitution Platform and Rules, Australian Labour Party, Barton, Australian Capital Territory

Barker, M. (1981) The policy behind the E.P.A. Act : A legal analysis, Paper presented to Australian Conservation Foundation Seminar on the New South Wales Environmental Planning and Assessment Act 1979, Canberra, July 1981. Faculty of Law, Australian National University, Canberra

Blandy, R. (1981) Labour problems of the minerals boom, Department of Economics, Flinders University, Adelaide, South Australia

Blyth, M.J. and Kirby, M.G. (1984) The impact of government policy on land degradation in the rural sector, In T.J. Jakeman, D.G. Day and A.K. Dragun (editors), Policy Approaches to Environmental Control, Centre for Resource and Environmental Studies, Australian National University, Canberra

Boer, B. (1984) Environmental assessment of major resource projects: The Hunter Valley experience, In Papers of the Australian Mining Industry Council Workshop on Industry and

University of Adelaide. Australian Mining Industry Council, Canberra, pp. 97-117

Bolton, G. (1981) Spoils and Spoilers, George Allen and Unwin, North Sydney

Cripps, J.S. (1983) Planning appeals and review systems in New South Wales, Speech to Royal Australian Planning Institute (ACT Division) Seminar 'The Planning Appeals System and Canberra', Australian Academy of Science, May

Davis, T. (1984) Social Planning Organisations in the Hunter Region, New South Wales Government Printer, Sydney

Davis, B. (1980) The struggle for South-West Tasmania, In R. Scott (editor), Interest Groups and Public Policy, Macmillan, South Melbourne, 152-169

Day, D.G. (1984) Water and Coal: Industry, Environment and Institutions in the Hunter Valley, NSW, CRES Monograph, Centre for Resource and Environmental Studies, Australian National University, Canberra

Dick, H.W. (1981) The Hunter Valley: Development or Indigestion, Current Affairs Bulletin, 58: 4-17

Dixon, G. (1978) Resources and the national economy in the 1980s, In P. Hastings and A. Farran (editors), Australia's Resources Future, Nelson, West Melbourne, 185-212

Farrier, D. (1984) Environmental assessment in New South Wales. Environmental and Planning Law Journal, June; 151-172

Formby, J. (1981) The Australian experience. In T. O'Riordan and W.R.D. Sewell (editors), Project Appraisal and Policy Review, Wiley, New York, 187-225

Formby, J. (1984) The Determinants of Public Policy: With Reference to Environmental Impact Assessment Policy in Australia, Ph.D. thesis, Centre for Resource and Environmental Studies, Australian National University, Canberra

Garlick, S. (1984) A need for policy reassessment: a case study of the Hunter Region. Guest lecture, urban and regional development theory, Department of Town and Country Planning, University of Sydney. Hunter Valley Research Foundation, Newcastle, New South Wales

Gilpin, A. (1980) Environment Policy in Australia, University of Queensland Press, St. Lucia, Queensland

Harris, S.F. (1984) State and Federal objective

and policies towards resource development and use, CRES Working paper 1984/10, Centre for Resource and Environmental Studies, Australian National University, Canberra

Higley, J., Deacon, D. and Smart, D. (1979) Elites in Australia, Routledge & Kegan Paul, London

Hughes, B. (1980) Exit Full Employment, Angus and Robertson, Sydney

Newcastle Ecology Centre (1980) Who Asked Us? Coal, Power and Aluminium - the Hunter Region's Only Future? Newcastle Ecology Centre, Newcastle, New South Wales

New South Wales v. Commonwealth (Offshore Sovereignty Case) (1975) 8 Australian Law Reports 1; 50 Australian Law Journal Reports 218

New South Wales Department of Environment and Planning (1982) Hunter Region: Regional Environmental Plan No. 1, Department of Environment and Planning, Sydney

New South Wales Premier's Department (1982) Infrastructure financing policy statement and explanatory papers, December, New South Wales Premier's Department, Sydney

Matthews, T. (1976) Interest group access to the Australian Government bureaucracy. In Royal Commission on Australian Government Administration, Appendix Volume Two, Australian Government Publishing Service, Canberra, 332-365

Murphyores Inc. Pty Ltd. v. Commonwealth (1976) 9 Australian Law Reports 199; 50 Australian Law Journal Reports 570

O'Riordan, T. and Sewell, W.R.D. (editors) (1981) Project Appraisal and Policy Review, Wiley, New York

Parker, P. (1982) Market Town to Mining Town: Resource Development, Infrastructure Costs and Local Government in Singleton, Australia, Master's thesis, Centre for Resource and Environmental Studies, Australian National University, Canberra

Perkins, F. (1984) Manpower and Resource Development: the Case of the Hunter Region, NSW. Centre for Resource and Environmental Studies, Australian National University

Review of New South Wales Government Administration (1977) Directions for Change: Interim Report, New South Wales Government Printer, Sydney

Review of New South Wales Government Administration (1980) Towards Regionalisation, Access and Community Participation. Report of the Task

Force on Regionalisation of Government Administration and Community Participation. New South Wales Government Printer, Sydney

Ritchie, B. (1983) Where the coal boom went wrong. In Reviewing the Coal Boom, papers delivered at the seventh annual public discussion on coal mining development in the Singleton Shire. Singleton Shire Council, Singleton, New South Wales, 15-27

Roddewig, R.J. (1978) Green Bans, Hale and Iremonger, Sydney

Rondinelli, D.A. (1976) Public planning and political strategy. Long Range Planning, 9; 75-82

Royal Commission on Australian Government Administration (1976) Report, Australian Government Publishing Service, Canberra

Saddler, H., Bennett, J., Reynolds, I. and Smith, B. (1980) Public Choice in Tasmania: Aspects of the lower Gordon River Hydro-Electric Development Proposal, Centre for Resource and Environmental Studies, Australian National University, Canberra

Sheehan, P. (1980) Crisis in Abundance, Penguin, Ringwood, Victoria

Stevenson, G. (1977) Mineral Resources and Australian Federalism, Centre for Research on Federal Financial Relations, Australian National University, Canberra

Woods, L.E. (1983) Land Degradation in Australia, Australian Government Publishing Service, Canberra

Wright, J. (1977) The Coral Battleground, Nelson, West Melbourne

Chapter Seven

ENVIRONMENTAL POLICIES IN INDIA

S.L. Kayastha

INTRODUCTION

India shares with other countries a growing concern over environmental deterioration. As science and technology evolve, the pace of resource exploitation grows greater and deeper causing the so-called 'Environment-Development Crisis'. Scientists and citizens alike are worried about it. Governments are also patently aware of the problem. Ultimately, it is a question of survival. But without environmental studies and analysis, and the formulation and implementation of suitable environmental management policies, the crisis cannot be averted. Time is of the essence. This calls in the first place for an appraisal of environmental attitudes and policies.

NATIONAL POLICY ON ENVIRONMENT: A PERSPECTIVE

The physical, human and cultural environment of India has a wealth of incomparable variety. India has - in the Himalayas - the loftiest mountain range in the world. It also has low hills and plateaux; dense evergreen forests and scrub jungles; large perennial rivers and numerous streams; broad fertile plains, deltas and estuarine systems; arid tracts and deserts; and coastal plains. Physical variety is complemented by climatic variety. The seasonal monsoons distribute their favours capriciously so that there are regions of very heavy to moderate rainfall and there are also rainless tracts. Higher latitudes are subject to extremes of temperature, while lower latitudes have a more uniform climate. Climate is also affected by elevation and proximity to sea. The character and distribution of fauna varies with physical, climatic and floral features of the country (Hora, 1937).

Yet, amongst this diversity, there is a degree of uniformity. Spate (1967) aptly observes that underlying the life in India is one great common factor; the rhythm of life. Being an agricultural country, this gives an ordered pattern to the life and work of the Indian people.

Continuity and Change

Traditions, mythology, religious books and other sources reveal that flora and fauna were more extensive and varied in the past than they are today. Environmental conditions favoured the growth of natural vegetation which grew luxuriantly during the Vedic period (2500 B.C. to 1500 B.C.). Most of the Indus basin was covered with dense forests which were cleared by the Aryans in their eastward and southward expansion for settlement and in reclaiming land for agriculture (Saxena, 1976). Several names of forests are mentioned by Paṇini (600 B.C.), as were a large number of flourishing centres of population (Agarwal, 1953).

It is commonly believed that Puranas covered a period in the life of Indian people extending over 1000 years (up to about 950 A.D.). Ali (1965) observes that the whole of the Upper Gangetic Basin was mostly covered with woodlands and forests. It is believed that Paleolithic man was a hunter and food gatherer. During the Mesolithic age, with the acquisition of certain tools, he developed an aggressive attitude towards his environment. Neolithic man cleared natural vegetation and practised agriculture. In India in the Proto-historic period the earliest remains of settled culture are of little agricultural villages in Baluchistan and Lower Sind. These date back from perhaps the end of the 4th millenium B.C. (Basham, 1954).

Physical conditions express themselves in plant cover, which in turn greatly influences the animal populations. Even though Newbigin (1968) remarks that the Himalayas block off India from the rest of Asia, she also admits (on faunal evidence) that India south of the Himalayas - as well as Africa south of the Sahara - have received at least the majority of animals living within them from a northern source. The isolation of India is only relative.

It is not easy to reconstruct palaeo-environments, especially in the absence of core data about soils, flora and fauna. Anthropological materials in the form of tool types (such as choppers, hand-axes and cleavers) are found with some perceptible differences in all the regions (Ghosh, 1981) and these throw some light on past environments. But there are large gaps in any systematic attempt to trace lucidly the early environmental conditions and history of resource use. A systematic account of climate and other natural resources has only been available since the British Period in India. The general growth of civilisation, population and settlement has been a catalyst for greater exploitation of resources but this has occurred without any clear understanding of the sum of wealth, acceptable tolerance levels and changing environmental conditions. There was in India "a remarkable continuity in the approach to balanced consumption and conservation of natural resources including forests and wild life" (Pal, 1981).

The importance of maintaining ecological balance to sustain life has been known in the country from 3000 B.C. or so. Emperor Ashoka laid down specific guidelines for the conservation of wild-life. It has been known from Vedic times that nature and mankind form an inseparable part of the life support system (Khoshoo, 1983). However, the increasing pressure of population, agriculture, livestock, settlement and industry, has brought varying degrees of environmental deterioration. During the Moghal period resources were exploited with scant regard to their conservation.

It is significant that after Independence in 1947 the constitution makers and national leaders had the wisdom to emphasise the protection and improvement of the environment. Consequently, India is one of the few countries of the world whose constitution lays adequate stress on the need for protection and careful use of natural resources. Article 48(A) states that "the State shall endeavour to protect and improve the environment and to safeguard the forests and wild life of the country". Article 51(A)g imposes a duty on the citizens to protect and improve the natural environment - including forests, lakes, rivers, wildlife and to have compassion for all living creatures. The Directive Principles also recognise the importance of maintaining the natural heritage as part of the total environment.

Recent Developments

The country has a firm foundation (in the Constitution) on which to plan policies, laws and regulations designed to deal with complex and large-scale environmental problems. The first concrete step in pursuance of the constitutional provision and to deter the accelerating pace of environmental damage was taken in April 1972. This was the establishment of the National Committee on Environmental Planning and Co-ordination (NCEPC) to provide a focal point in government decision-making, where environmental considerations of policy and management could receive close attention in an integrated manner. In addition, two committees were set up to aid in this task; the Environment Research Committee (ERC) and the National Committee for Man and Biosphere Programme (MAB).

Mrs. Indira Gandhi, the Prime Minister of India, showed a keen interest in the task of protection, awareness, policy and management of the environment. In her inaugural address to the NCEPC in 1972, she remarked that:

> *the ecological problems with which we are now concerned embrace diverse aspects ranging from the economic, social, psychological problems of human settlements, to management and use of natural resources and conservation of natural habitats (Gandhi, 1984).*

Earlier (in 1972) she had expressed concern on environmental issues in the U.N. Conference on the Human Environment in Stockholm. She maintained a strong interest in the links between environment and development, in the need for environmental protection, in the provision for environmental conservation and management for sustainable development in the Indian Constitution, and in policies for economic growth. These commitments resulted in the setting up in February 1980 of a high level committee headed by the Deputy Chairman of the Planning Commission. On the recommendations of this Committee the Government of India decided to set up the Department of Environment, which came into existence on the 1st November 1980 (Report, 1981-82).

The Department of Environment is a nodal agency for all environmental issues and it has a pivotal role to play in environmental management for sustainable development. There is a wide variety of tasks to be tackled, including the rational utilisation and management of natural resources; integrated management of land, soil, water and forest resources; pollution control; waste utilisation through recycling; conservation of wildlife and biological diversity; urban planning and the problems of slums; environmental awareness and education; environmental monitoring; and project-impact assessment. There is clearly a need to establish a rational order of priorities amongst these competing claims for attention.

The successful design and implementation of policies, and the successful completion of projects will have positive effects through boosting public confidence and winning ready co-operation. The tasks of environmental management and conservation are the responsibility of both the government and the people. Environmental problems and policies will have to be considered at the national, regional and local levels. Whilst the intentions and objectives of environmental policies in India are sound, their implementation and achievement (through various compulsions and constraints) have not been successful enough to restrain the decline in quality of the environment in the country.

However, there is hope that the future will see the gradual evolution of a sound integrated environmental policy and proper legislative and administrative measures to regulate wise use of all resources. It is hoped, moreover, that the directive principle of sustainable development will prevail through this evolution, and that a firm ethical bond between nature and society will be established.

THE NATURAL RESOURCE BASE

India is well-endowed with rich and varied natural resources. These can be broadly classified into:

(a) Renewable Resources like land and soil, water, forests and wildlife, and
(b) Non-Renewable Resources like minerals.

However, what is important is the proper use of natural resources and their conservation for sustainable yield. Much stress is laid on resource exploitation, but it is surprising that similar stress is not laid on resource conservation. The unenlightened exploitation of natural resources produces many adverse consequences. The damage to land, soil, water, natural vegetation, wildlife and recreational resources has been already severe and widespread. Unless adequate and timely measures are taken to conserve such resources, nothing but ruin will follow (Kayastha, 1970).

<u>Land Resources</u>
Land is the most important resource in India. Of the total land area, some 43.6 percent is agricultural or cultivated land; 14.6 percent permanent pastures; 12.2 percent cultivable waste; 10.7 percent forests; 16.4 percent barren and uncultivable; and 15.5 percent is urban and under other non-agricultural use. No information is available for the other 7 percent. It is estimated that up to 1.75 million km^2 (57.56 percent of the total area for which records exist) is subject to environmental problems such as erosion, waterlogging and salinization. In a country like India, where more than two-thirds of the workers are engaged in agriculture, the problems of land degradation must be tackled earnestly to ensure that agricultural productivity is adequate and that national food requirements are met. In reality it would be difficult to meet the required levels of agricultural production without safeguarding land and soil resources in the cultivated area of about 1.40 million km^2; nearly 60 percent requires soil conservation measures (Agarwal et al, 1982).

Of the total area of 1.75 million km^2 which is subject to environmental problems, 65.7 percent is suffering from serious water and wind erosion; 3.4 percent from waterlogging; 2.6 percent from salinity problems; 3.6 percent is wasteland needing reclamation; 1.4 percent suffers from liability to floods; 1.4 percent from alkalinity; and 1.7 percent is affected by shifting agriculture. Urbanisation and industrialisation are also taking away good agricultural land. Top soil is washed away and eroded, and the siltation of rivers, dams, estuaries and harbours adds another dimension to the problem. The bed of Ganga is estimated to have risen by half a metre in the past few years.

According to Vohra (1980) about 2.66 million km^2 need proper land management. Of this 53.75 percent is agricultural land and 46.25 percent is pasture, forests and uncultivated land. Within the agricultural land, the problems are distributed as follows:

(a) endangered by floods and canal irrigation - 9.40 percent
(b) degraded by erosion, salinity and waterlogging - 23.70 percent
(c) reasonably good agricultural land - 11.65 percent.

Within pastures, forests and uncultivated land the break-down is:

(a) cultural waste - 6.39 percent
(b) degraded forests and pastures - 18.05 percent
(c) fallow lands - 21 percent, and
(d) reasonably good forests and pastures - 13.16 percent.

There is thus little doubt that land and soil management have been far from satisfactory.

Surprisingly, a large number of planners, politicians, policy makers and economists still believe that there is little wrong with the manner in which India has managed its land resources. This is due in part to a lack of availability of detailed and accurate data and maps of land use, resources and land degradation. It also reflects a lack of organisation and trained personnel. Land is our most precious natural resource and keeping it in good heart is a basic requirement for national prosperity and culture.

Water Resources

Water is one of the most basic resources. It is necessary for all life, and is required for agriculture, settlement and industry. Because of the seasonal character of the rainfall in India - which is largely crowded into a few months - even areas of high rainfall pose problems of water supply (Kayastha, 1975). India has otherwise abundant water resource in its river systems and ground water estimated at 1,900,000 x 10^6 m^3, of which 1,645,000 x 10^6 m^3 is in all the river systems and 255,000 x 10^6 m^3 is in ground water.

The level of demand for water resources will doubtless increase with population growth, expansion of irrigation, and continued urbanisation and industrialisation. However the water resources base is likely to remain almost constant at 1,900,000 x 10^6 m^3. At the same time water quantity and quality are threatened by misuse and pollution of the resource base. Appropriate management will be required to avoid water crisis in the future (Grosvenor, 1980). There is a pressing need to treat water as a resource of great importance. Water resource management on a river basin basis, founded on the integrated use of available resources for industrial and domestic purposes, irrigation, power, flood and drought control, and inland navigation is urgently required.

At present over 80 percent of India's villages are without protected water supply (i.e. safe and clean) and only about 56 percent of urban population has this facility. Safe drinking water facilities are of prime significance as a health improvement measure. Considering all these, a thorough appraisal of water resource is necessary. The formulation of a National Water Policy will not only contribute to national welfare, but it would also be an appropriate step in the development of integrated use and management of this invaluable renewable resource (Kayastha, 1981).

Forest Resources

India possesses suitable geographical conditions for an extensive and diverse natural vegetation cover. During the long period of human habitation, much of the climax forest formations have been altered and large areas of forest have been destroyed for settlement, agriculture, industry and development projects. Heavy biotic pressure and inappropriate management practices have further damaged the remaining forests.

The paucity of forest cover is apparent in available data. Out of 0.75 million km^2 classed as forest lands, less than half is actually under adequate forest cover. An estimated 0.2 million km^2 of the forest land is affected by erosion.

No more than about 12 percent of the country's land surface is actually under adequate forest cover against the target of 33 percent advocated in the 1952 National Forest Policy. The distribution of forest is also imbalanced. Some 0.13 million km^2 is classed as permanent pastures but this area is devoid of any vegetation because of overgrazing or encroachment. The 1952 National Forest Policy has been described as a document of unfulfilled sentiment.

Deforestation produced instability in the Himalaya; forest cover here has declined from 60 pecent to less than 20 percent. The Indo-Gangetic Plain - the main base of agriculture and economy of the country, and the main axis of civilisation - could ultimately be transformed into a waste land. The results of such land use changes are also evident in Iran, Afghanistan and parts of Pakistan. Kayastha (1978) has therefore emphasised the tripartite nature of environmental management, with emphasis on resources, ecological conservation and technological institutional development processes. Such an integrated approach, he argues, may help to reduce the adverse impacts of development on forests in particular, and on the environment in general.

The average per capita forest area in India is only 0.14 ha in contrast to the world average of 1.19 ha. The contribution of forestry to GNP is as low as 1.6 percent. While the demand for forest products is increasing, the supply of forest resources is shrinking. The impact of human activities on forests has almost been an ecological disaster, resulting not only in loss of wildlife habitat but also in soil erosion, siltation, irregular stream flow, floods and droughts, fall in water level and land subsidence. Damage to forests has thus damaged the environment and economy of the nation. The forest tribes have suffered most due to deforestation. Since demand for wood and fuel outstrips commercial supply, illegal felling is commonplace. Altogether about 0.414 million km^2 of forest has been cleared between 1952 and 1976. In this manner, the forests will tend to diminish and disappear and the valuable renewable green gold resource will simply not be renewed.

Forest policies and practices need serious reappraisal. Social forestry and public co-operation should be encouraged. A package of measures is required, including location-specific technologies; programmes involving rational land-use and land-management; development of agro-forestry and social forestry; trained expertise; and a range of services to add new dimensions to forestry and to optimise productivity.

Other Biotic Resources

India has a wide variety of biotic resources which are rich in plant and animal life and provide sustenance to millions of people. It is of vital importance that biotic productivity be maintained through proper land and water management. Also important is the preservation of genetic diversity and the conservation of species and ecosystems for sustainable utilisation. Biotic resources and ecological habitats are rapidly disappearing or changing under the pressure of population growth and unplanned use of the natural environment. In India, 5 species of mammals and birds have become extinct in recent years and a further 103 species are listed as endangered. Our knowledge however is incomplete. The loss of unstudied organisms or ecosystems is a lasting loss to science, and often a loss of potentially useable resources.

Natural ecosystems are not only resources of economic importance. They also serve as design models for improving and managing existing and planned ecosystems. Representative areas with valued landscape and important fauna and flora, should be protected and preserved as areas of national heritage. Furthermore, the wanton exploitation and destruction of valuable marine ecosystems of the country must be stopped. The concept of Biosphere Reserves, evolved under the Man and Biosphere (MAB) programme, needs implementation. At present 10 National Parks and 202 Wild Life sanctuaries, covering 75,763 km^2, provide inadequate protection for endangered species and threatened habitats in India.

Mineral and Energy Resources

India is rich in metallic ores, has modest resources of coal and oil, abundant reserves of water power, and is somewhat deficient in non-ferrous minerals. There is abundant evidence of skill and industry in ancient India in the extraction and smelting of ores of gold and other metals. Although systematic mining and use of mineral resources began during the British Period, it was only after Independence (in August 1947) that the emphasis shifted markedly from the export of raw materials to the export of processed or manufactured materials.

Iron ore production has increased from 4.1 million tonnes in 1950-51 to 31.7 x 10^6 tonnes in 1970-71; the production target for 1984-85 is 60 x 10^6 tonnes. Similarly, coal production which was 33 million tonnes in the beginning of the First Five Year Plan (1951-56) rose to 104 x 10^6 tonnes by 1979-80. The production of various minerals - both ferrous and non-ferrous - will have to be increased to meet the growing demands of people and economy. However, mining production should be so planned as to ensure its maximum life and conservation of reserves, to avoid mining pollution, and to rehabilitate the derelict areas.

The energy resources of India consist principally of coal, mineral oil and natural gas, hydro-electricity, animal dung, vegetable waste and human and animal power. The energy consumption pattern is changing, with demand growing fast (in both absolute and relative terms) for commercial resources. Predicted requirements of minerals will grow by about four times, and those of energy by nearly eight times, by 2001 A.D. (Narain, 1980). There is an urgent need to formulate an integrated energy plan designed to utilise the energy resources in a rational way and to meet expected future needs (Kayastha, 1981). Any rational energy policy in India will have to devote more attention to renewable energy resources - such as biogas (methane); wood (with increased forestry on waste-lands and farms); solar energy; water power; and other resources that are abundantly available, such as mineral gas and combustible waste materials.

Both mineral gas and biogas have been neglected to date. In Bombay-High, some 4 x 10^6 m^3 of gas is used per day (equal to 1.4 x 10^6 tonnes of crude oil). The Calorific value of the 200 x 10^6 tonnes of cattle dung produced in India is equivalent to at least 20 x 10^6 tonnes of kerosene oil. If it was fed into biogas plants, it would yield over 300 x 10^9 m^3 of gas. This high quality manure would contain some 3 x 10^6 tonnes of nitrogen -

about 90% of the output of all the fertiliser plants in the country. There are only about 300,000 biogas plants in India, while there is need for some 8 x 10^6 units to improve the quality of life in the country.

The Government favours grand, capital-intensive energy schemes because it finds it easier to deal with a few large firms than with scores of municipalities, village organisations, small entrepreneurs, and even large numbers of rural or semi-urban householders. According to Khanna (1984), up to a point this is unavoidable. But if the authorities truly want to serve the ordinary consumer, they cannot take soft options all the way. Political compulsions and rising social aspirations demand that we produce and consume more energy in order to improve the quality of life of large masses. The distribution of energy consumption is the distribution of income and wealth; all are largely skewed in favour of urban areas. Energy policy appears to be a potent instrument in the promotion of development and social equality in the future. The policy options open to India are, inter-alia, in the choice of technologies, inter-fuel substition, pricing, energy allocation and environmental quality (Sethna, 1977).

The use and management of natural resources require policies and guidelines at the highest level to promote the effective utilisation, distribution and conservation of those resources. Nagchaudhuri (1977) has stressed the need for continuing information from resources survey and continuing information on the social, economic and technological aspects of resource use. This is essential, he argues, so that costs, social perceptions, environmental problems and the development of various technologies within the country and throughout the world are suitably noted. The task is sizeable and complex. But the challenge and the promise should motivate government, scientist and citizen alike to strive towards greater achievements in the rational use of natural and human resources for the benefit of both society and environment.

ENVIRONMENTAL POLLUTION

Increasing pollution of the environment gives rise to a range of problems relating to resource use, environmental degradation and human health. The main causes of environmental pollution, according to Sharma (1981) are:

> *rapid industrialisation and urbanisation, the use of fossil fuels, the construction of barrages and dams, the indiscriminate use of fertilisers and pesticides needed to sustain high yielding varieties in agriculture and finally increasing population which have led to the depletion of forests, over-congestion and waste accumulation, all in totality leading to drastic pollution of the environment in India.*

Industrial man has created a counter-productive environment for himself. Megatechnology has introduced the accelerative factor and Toffler (1970) has discussed its frightening consequences on the life of people. Misra (1983) has referred to disruption of ecological balances of the biosphere and pointed out some of the features of environmental pollution. Various forms of pollution degrade the environment and affect human health, including water, air, noise, land, radiation and odour pollution.

Water Pollution

Water pollution is a serious environmental hazard which affects human health. It is estimated that 70 percent of all available water in India is polluted. Nearly half of the diseases in India are water-borne, and the annual cost of treatment and loss in production is estimated at 6000 million rupees. Over four-fifths of the villages of India and about half of the urban population are without protected water supply. An estimated 7-8 percent of cities and towns have sewerage and sewage treatment facilities. The major sources of pollutants of water are community wastes and industrial effluents.

The levels of water pollution in most rivers, lakes and ponds have increased so much that they are not considered safe for human consumption without adequate treatment. For example, the Dal lake (the Pride of Kashmir) and the Holy Ganga are heavily polluted. Microbiological analysis of 61 samples of Ganga water in Varanasi revealed the presence of pathogens including cholera and typhoid germs. The national and state water pollution control boards have not been able to provide sufficient support for controlling water pollution.

Chaudhuri (1984), the Chairman of the Central Pollution Board, observes that to speed up the establishment of pollution control on the existing group of industries, the Board has evolved an industry-specific pollution control strategy. This has required a strenuous process of developing an industry-specific comprehensive industry document which covers numbers, sizes, geographical distribution, material inputs, process adopted, product mix by-products recovery, water consumption, various waste streams and their characteristics. The document describes the Industry Specific Minimal National Standards (MINAS), based on the evaluation of the costs of various levels of treatment, which covers water and other forms of pollution.

Air Pollution

Air pollution is related to the presence in the atmosphere of one or more substances introduced by man to such an extent as to adversely affect the welfare of humans and biotic life in the atmosphere. These pollutants may be solids, gases or liquids. In India, air pollution can be attributed mainly to industrialisation and urbanisation.

Air pollution is not confined to large cities in India; it has begun to affect even the small towns and villages where thermal power stations and large industries are being located. In a study of the Obra Thermal Power Plant in Mirzapur (which consumes about 5000 tonnes of coal per day), it was found that in the absence of adequate air pollution control measures there is emission of harmful gases and solid matter into the atmosphere. Leaves in adjacent forests show a covering of layers of waste material (Kayastha and Kumar, 1983). The Taj Mahal - a valued national heritage - is threatened by air pollution from a variety of sources, including the oil refinery at Mathura, thermal power plants, iron foundries and railway yards at Agra. The problem of acid deposition and acid precipitation starts with the burning of coal, oil and natural gas (La Bastille, 1981). Chembur, in Bombay, has the highest concentration of chemical industries in India, and it is widely regarded as a potential gas chamber.

The effects of air pollution are also evident in the increasing incidence of chronic bronchitis and lung cancer. Of what use is any type of development which deprives people of clean water and air for their well-being? Pollution affects biotic life, and even, soil, buildings and monuments. India has to take both legislative and enforcement measures to manage the air pollution problem before it becomes too widespread and serious.

Other Forms of Pollution

Noise pollution arises when the perceived noise level is in the range of 20 to 40 decibels (PNDB). In the absence of any preventive legislation, noise levels in Indian cities and towns are increasing. Calcutta, Bombay and Delhi are among the noisiest cities in the world. Threats to physiological and mental well-being arise from community noise, traffic noise and occupational noise (e.g. in factories). There is now a pressing need for comprehensive legislation to curb noise pollution.

Environmental pollution also arises from the leakage and mobility of radiation, and chemicals (including pesticides) which have serious effects on plant, animal and human life and may even cause genetic damage (Caspersson, 1981). The calamitous leakage of killer gas, said to be methyl isocynate, from the (U.S. owned) Union Carbide Pesticides Plant in Bhopal, on the 3rd of December 1984, is possibly the world's biggest environmental industrial disaster to date. According to official estimates over 2,500 people died from inhaling the gas and hundreds of thousands will suffer after-effects which may be long-lasting. The leak was caused by inadequate or lack of safety measures at the plant. According to one report, the same somewhat outdated plant had earlier been offered to and rejected by the Canadian Government. The disaster at Bhopal has sadly demonstrated that it is not only workers who are exposed to occupational hazards, but also others who live adjacent to such factories or plants. It is necessary to ensure that such a disaster is not repeated anywhere and that the victims get proper compensation. The Third World countries should not become the dumping grounds for machinery which is outdated or lacks adequate safety devices, or areas for experimentation with harmful chemicals (which would not be tolerated in developed countries).

However, every country has to look after its own environmental interests. Nearly 80% of the industrial establishments in India pose a threat to the environment as they do not meet the minimum standards of industrial safety set by the United Nations Environmental Programme (UNEP). Although the 1981 Air (Prevention and Control of Pollution) Act and the 1968 Insecticides Act have sufficient legal provisions, it is not sufficient to just have that. What is needed is their enforcement. Government officers who allow neglect by industries and other organisations, should be responsible for their actions.

There is, as yet, inadequate awareness of the hazards from environmental pollution. Legislation and implementation of acts are urgently required, along with increased public awareness and co-operation to successfully counter environmental pollution.

POPULATION, HUMAN SETTLEMENTS AND ENVIRONMENT

India has nearly 15 percent of the world's population squeezed into 2.4 percent of its total area. The population in 1981 was 684 million, giving an average density of 221 persons per km^2 across an area of $3.28 \times 10^6 km^2$. India has the second highest population total in the world, after China, and its population continues to rise. The decadal growth-rate during 1901-1911 was 5.75 percent and this had risen to 24.75 percent during 1971-81. Except for a slight fall in population total and growth-rate during 1911-1921, India's population has risen steadily during the century; the post 1951 growth-rate has been high. In absolute numbers, India's population increased by 136 million between 1971 and 1981, compared with 109 million between 1961 and 1971. There has thus been growing increase in population numbers despite the initiatives in family planning and population control. However, the decadal growth rate of population during 1971-81 was slightly lower than that of 1961-71, which was 24.80%. The birth rate is estimated to have come down to about 30 per thousand and death rate to about 15 per thousand in 1981, from the earlier 41 and 19 respectively in 1971. Thus there is little change in the crude growth-rate.

It is commonly accepted that rapid and large scale population growth adversely affects economic growth. Therefore the central objective of planning in India - "to initiate a process of development which will raise living standards and open out to the people new opportunities for a richer and varied life" remains largely unfulfilled. All Plans to date have been content with merely setting desirable targets for the rate of population growth; they have refrained from discussing possible ways of manipulating the demographic variables of births, deaths and migration and the principal economic or social means of influencing them (Mitra, 1974). The population policy has suffered accordingly.

Threats to the environment arise from lack of development, and lack of awareness, education, and action. The population of India - which is expected to touch the billion (10^9) mark by 2001 A.D. - will make even more demands on resources in the future. Consequently there will be even greater pressure on the environment. The reduction of poverty, which requires a slow-down in the rate of growth of population and probably a reduction in the size of population, seems to be a necessary pre-requisite for the achievement of long-term solutions. These will have to be combined with a programme of increased economic development, which must at the same time be tempered with an understanding of the properties (and dynamics) of ecosystems. The problems of life in human settlements (whether rural or urban) will have to be solved with the supply of more clean water and sanitation facilities, more and better housing, more efficient transportation and communication networks and, of course, better nutrition, health-care, education and employment opportunities (Khosla, 1974).

It is therefore within the framework of human settlements that the needs of the vast population must be catered for in a way that does not damage the environment, the resource base and the cultural heritage. There are in excess of 579,000 human settlements in India, of which more than 3000 are urban. In 1981 76.3 per cent of the population lived in rural settlements.

Environmental problems in the rural habitat often arise through over-use or misuse of natural resources, promoted by absolute poverty or lack of alternatives. Overgrazing by cattle and felling and lopping of trees cause deterioration of rural environments. A widespread absence of effective systems of community waste disposal has produced insanitary conditions and water pollution which in turn have had adverse impacts on human health. Chronic unemployment and under-employment in rural areas, coupled with the lack of economic viability of many land-holdings have encouraged large-scale rural-urban migration. This adds to the environmental problems in urban settlements. For the rural poor such migration means mostly the loss of an old world without the compensatory gain of the new. There is a pressing need for institutional changes in land ownership and integrated approaches to rural development with a package of services which would help to remedy the deteriorating situation in many rural areas.

According to the 1981 Census, 158 million (23.73 percent of the total population) were urban, residing in 3,245 towns. The decadal percentage increase in urban population was 46.02 percent between 1971 and 1981 (compared with 37.91 percent between 1961 and 1971). Over 60 percent of the urban population is confined to 216 urban agglomerations with populations of 100,000 and above (Class I towns). The urban population of India has grown from 25.6 million in 1901 to 156 million in 1981. There was an increase of 50 million in the urban population between 1971 and 1981. The phenomenal growth of urban population, without the provision of adequate urban facilities, has led to the growth of slums. The indiscriminate pressure on urban and urban-fringe land has strained urban services and seriously affected the quality of environment of many towns. Every urban settlement has expanded, devouring good agricultural land in doing so. The urban infrastructure, in both large and small towns, is unable to meet the requirements of increasing urban population. The infrastructure has thus become virtually overloaded and break downs in services causing inconvenience and urban environmental deterioration, are the norm not the exception.

To date attempts to improve the environment of human settlements have been piece-meal, confusing and haphazard. The use of local materials, personnel and technology must be re-examined; many problems have arisen through the unquestioned adoption of western technology and life styles, and through sheer neglect of indigenous conditions, resources and talents. Settlements, both urban and rural, have to be treated as an organic whole. As a nodal government agency for United Nations Centre for Human Settlements (UNCHS), the Department of Environment in India has to identify environmental imperatives in planning and in the development of human settlements, and to suggest ways and means of integrating settlement systems and natural ecosystems.

DEVELOPMENT AND ENVIRONMENT

Development and environmental issues, and the links between them, are of vital significance in India. The primary objective is to ensure adequate and appropriate development to meet basic needs of people, without causing unacceptable deterioration of environment and resources. In this context Biswas and Biswas (1981) stress the need to rectify earlier misconceptions that environment and development processes are incompatible. The concept of 'Environment-vs-Development" has to be replaced by the complementarity between 'environment and development'. Development, according to them, has to be sustainable over the long-term, otherwise it would become a self-defeating process. Sustainable development can only be assured if environmental issues are explicitly considered in the planning process.

It is essential to have a clear understanding of inter-relationships between society, development and environment for the formulation and implementation of any strategy that safeguards all concerned aspects. The crucial need is to plan development so as to enhance the quality of life and protect the environment. Mounting world-wide concern for the accelerated exploitation of resources for development inspired the U.N. Conference on the Human Environment held in Stockholm in 1971. In her address to the Conference, Mrs. Indira Gandhi (1972) pointed out that:

> *Environment cannot be improved in conditions of poverty and...we have to prove to the world that ecology and conservation will not work against their interests, but will bring improvement*

in their lives.

India shares many types of environmental problems with other countries but it also has its own specific problems. These include rapid population increase, urban and industrial developments, extension of agriculture on marginal lands, encroachment and indiscriminate exploitation of forests and other natural resources. The resulting environmental degradation is marked by widespread soil erosion, siltation, landslides, irregular river regimes, lowering of water level, pollution, floods and droughts. It is reflected ultimately in the deterioration of the quality of the environment and the quality of life.

The rural and urban poorer sections of society, the tribes and pastoralists have suffered most, as they have to live on an impoverished and polluted environment. The basic needs of the people - for food, shelter, employment, health-care and so on - have to be provided through the development of natural systems of the country which would include land, water, forest, fisheries, agriculture and industrial development (Kayastha, 1982). Poverty itself is a notable pollutant.

There continue to exist serious imbalances between the developed and developing countries. To correct these it is necessary to restrain unfavourable and harmful exploitation of resources in developing countries by external and internal vested interests. Developing countries have the opportunity to observe the experience of developed countries in selecting resource management strategies to suit their own interests. A number of developing countries - such as India and Tanzania - are in the process of considering alternative pathways to economic and social improvement, some of which involve the principles of ecological and resource conserving development (O'Riordan, 1978). The primary motivation for development after all is human welfare, which is also the primary motivation for environmental quality. Thus, the two motivations converge rather than conflict and this should encourage the search for optimal harmonious relationship between environment and development. The increased tempo of development promotes growing environmental deterioration. The needs of a large and growing population which suffers from poverty, the greed of vested interests and the careless application of technology have been the main causes of environmental degradation in India in recent decades. Environment suffers, not from development or from technology, but from lack of wisdom in directing and managing both growth and technology (King, 1975). The importance of environmental conservation is explicitly stated in the directive principles of Indian Constitution and Planning Policies for economic growth. In spite of this, there has been a marked deterioration in environmental quality due to the lack of interest and awareness, inadequate data, lack of planning and priorities, and indiscriminate exploitation of natural resources.

Examples of drastic environmental degradation are notable in the Himalaya, the Western Ghats, the plains and some coastal areas. Bamboo has disappeared from large parts of south India. Hydro-electric and other projects occupy large tracts of forest and agricultural land, and the rehabilitation of displaced peoples does not receive adequate attention. Half of all the energy used in India is for cooking purposes, but the Government has no Cooking Energy Policy and no integrated Energy Policy. Forest resources are shrinking due to increased demand for land and wood. The malady is well-advanced and needs immediate attention.

Since environmental conditions mirror the kind of society we have, the real goal must be to change our society so that it becomes non-exploitative (Chopra, 1983). Development should not represent both the triumph and tragedy of development and environment (Kayastha, 1983). An estimated 43 percent of India's population presently lives below the poverty line; their number is likely to increase to 470 million and unemployment will rise to 80 million. If suitable planned measures to generate employment and lift people above the poverty line are not introduced well in time, both will pose serious problems in the future.

Excessive livestock levels will be a further burden on the environment. By 2001 A.D., India will have to provide for the needs of a billion people and half a billion livestock. This task has to be achieved by enhancing rather than diminishing the productivity of land, water and forest resources, by appropriate scientific management. About

57 percent of the total area of the country is subject to problems of land degradation (including erosion). This proportion is likely to increase further if present trends continue. India is losing about 6000 x 10^6 tonnes of top soil per annum.

The frequency and intensity of floods and droughts has increased, and annual flood damage is estimated in the order of 10,000 x 10^6 rupees. Floods affect more than 50 million people and 40,000 km^2 of land each year causing destabilisation of the national economy. The problem of floods will have to be resolved within the larger perspective of a National Water Policy. By 2001 A.D. water demand will be in the order of 1,116 x $10^9 m^3$ per annum. Though there will be enough water to meet our needs, water quantity and quality are bound to be threatened by misuse, pollution and environmental degradation. Development must also allow the conservation of genetic variety of species and ecosystems for sustainable use. Soil erosion attracts attention in part because the effects are clearly visible; erosion of the gene-pool tends to go unnoticed because it is not directly visible. The diversity of biological organisms needs careful protection in their eco-systems.

There is clear evidence in India of a declining quality of life due to unplanned urbanisation, industrialisation and settlement. This deserves the urgent attention of planners, administrators, and environmentalists alike. Population control would reduce the pressures on environment and resources. To achieve this the birth rate will have to be reduced to 21 per thousand, the death rate to 9 per thousand and the infant mortality rate to 60 per thousand by 2001 A.D. With this continuing trend, a zero growth rate of population in India may be achieved by 2050 A.D. (Dutt, 1984).

Environmental impact analysis can assist in reducing adverse effects, through pre-planning. This task is constrained by lack of expertise, clear priorities, proper legislation and suitable mechanisms for the implementation of safeguards. In addition, the awareness and support of the population at large is necessary as an integral part of project formulation. The 'Chipko' movement is a striking example of people's role as protectors of environment. Not only is there a lack of reliable data, there is also a lack of well-defined environmental policy for management and forecasting.

National environmental policy in India appears to be implicit in the country's development policies. This would be acceptable if the policies properly co-ordinated both development and environmental protection. But they do not. The forest policy has an urban-industrial bias. As this implicit environmental policy is inappropriate, a new sustainable and environmental policy has to be formulated in India. At the same time concomitant changes have to be made in the national development policy. Effective environmental management for development will have to be based not only on a scientific and technological approach, but it will also have to take into account socio-economic factors and responsibilities. Greater use will have to be made of ground surveys and remote-sensing for map making and modelling, and organisational expertise has to be speeded up. The Department of Environment, the Planning Commission and some organisations are making valiant efforts to restrain the decline in environmental quality. Even if all possible steps are initiated now, it will be years before results begin to show. While environmental problems continue to grow, there is no room at all for complacency on this front (Report, 1980).

For integrated development and environmental protection, a wide variety of factors must be included, such as:

(a) the integrated management of land, soil, forest and water resources,
(b) the control of land, water and air pollution,
(c) the development of non-polluting renewable energy resources,
(d) waste utilisation through recycling,
(e) the conservation of biological diversity,
(f) the development of human settlements without congestion, with slum removal and environmental improvement,
(g) environmental education and awareness,
(h) population control and health-care, and
(i) individual and collective goodwill to rehabilitate and optimise both development and environment of the nation.

Environmental problems do not recognise political boundaries and their solution should involve the co-operation of all peoples and nations to maintain the planet earth as a common heritage. There is the hope that with the growing awareness of the need for co-operation for a planned development and healthy environment at international, governmental and people's level, the stage of co-existence will be attained for harmony, peace and progress.

ENVIRONMENTAL PERCEPTION, INFORMATION, INTERNATIONAL PROGRAMME AND RESEARCH

Perception and Behaviour

Individuals and groups relate to environmental problems through their perception of them (Blunden, et al, 1978). This is reflected in Anne Whyte's (1977) conclusion that man makes decisions and takes actions within the framework of his perception of elements and links within a problem, rather than any externally defined objects. Science and technology - in their contribution to economic and social development - must be applied to the "identification, avoidance and control of environmental risks and solutions to environmental problems for the common good of mankind" (U.N. Papers for Stockholm Conference, 1974).

The solution of environmental problems must be founded on clear perception of them. Without some understanding of the bases of perception and behaviour, environmental planning becomes a mere academic exercise, doomed to failure because they are unrelated to the terms in which people think and the goals they select (Lowenthal, 1967). Even well intentioned technological aid by funding countries has led to irreparable environmental damage of environmental opportunities and constraints in the developing countries. A 'Perception Gap' between farmers, agricultural advisers and governmental agencies was found to exist. This is illustrated in the perception, awareness and attitude of the flood plain dwellers in Lower Ghaghra Plain (U.P., India) which has important implications for their socio-economic development (Kayastha, et al, 1980). A sample of 150 respondents of both sexes, different age-groups and educational standards was interviewed; levels of perception differed from group to group. Another perception study in Calcutta Metropolitan Area, by Karan (1980), revealed that the perspectives of the individuals interviewed greatly influenced their cognition of environment at a given location.

The perception of environment needs to be developed through education and field studies, and propagated through appropriate agencies. At a higher level, research in perception of environment is valuable and should be encouraged. This will greatly aid in understanding attitudes towards the environment and concomitant environmental problems in India.

Environmental Education

Environmental education plays an important role in generating awareness of environmental problems amongst people at large, and amongst school and university students in particular. The approaches and types of courses have to be so designed as to meet the level of understanding in each group. Environmental education should be both formal and non-formal. The former will develop expertise in each discipline at the higher level, and the latter will develop awareness of environment. Environment should not be viewed only through a problem based approach; an ethical approach which develops a reverence and appreciation for environment is also required. This is offered in Aldo Leopold's plea for self-enquiry (cited in Gibbons, 1981) in the 1930s:

> *There is as yet no ethic dealing with man's relation to land and to animals and plants...The land relation is still strictly economic, entailing privileges but no obligations...obligations have no meaning without conscience and the problem we face is the extension of the social conscience from .people to land. No important change in ethics was ever accomplished without internal change in our intellectual emphasis, loyalties, affections and convictions. The proof that conservation has not yet touched these foundations lies in the fact that philosophy and religion have not yet heard of it. In our attempt to make conservation easy, we have made it trivial.*

The purpose of quoting this lengthy statement is to stress that environmental education should not be made trivial. In a detailed report on environmental education Narayan (1981) states that knowledge of how to maintain, protect and improve the human environment - through appropriate environmental educational programme - is needed to heighten environmental consciousness in all people. Acting upon the recommendations of UNESCO and the UNDP, the international programme in environmental education was initiated in India in January 1975. Environmental education has been introduced in primary and secondary schools. At the graduate and post-graduate level, emphasis is given to the understanding of concepts, techniques and problems, with special attention being devoted to project work on specific local environmental problems.

Environmental education is now receiving attention in educational institutions and disciplines in India. The University Grants Commission, the Indian National Science Academy, the Department of Environment and the Planning Commission at the national level, along with relevant organisations at regional and local level, are now involved in discussing and formulating programmes and policies of environmental education. The only constraint appears to be that the employment opportunities for environmentalists have not expanded alongside the evolution of these programmes of environmental education.

Environmental Information

The introduction of an Environmental Information System (ENVIS) for the collection, processing and dissemination of environmental information to help in the work of project planning, assessment and execution has been proposed in the Sixth Plan Period (1980-85). The system is expected to function on a distributed data-base system. The documentation and publication centre will publish status reports, case-studies and monographs. Resources and personnel inventories are also to be published. Such work can be carried out with the technical facilities presently available.

The work of the National Focal Point of INFORTERRA, located in the Department of Environment, has continued since 1976. ENVIS seeks to co-operate with other International Information Systems. The tasks of making comprehensive inventories of environmental resources will be done in phases, in collaboration with the environmental quality monitoring and environmental information systems programmes and other agencies such as the survey of India, the Botanical and Zoological Survey of India, the National Remote Sensing Agency and so on. Much data is available, but it is widely scattered and it needs to be collected together at sub-centres, regional centres and the National Data Bank Centre. It should be computerised so that it is available for specific centres and research institutions.

For research workers, there exists still a data-gap in environmental information. The data has to be collected in the field and then it may or may not be made available by institutions, industries and projects. Often the area analysis has to be based on sample surveys. Much of such painstakingly collected and analysed data which is presented through survey reports and dissertations, does not see the light of day and lies in store in libraries of universities and institutes; in the absence of adequate funds for publication much of it is simply never used effectively or disseminated widely. This is a national loss. It is suggested that selected environmental works that are of value should be published and made available.

<u>International Initiatives</u>

A range of international programmes and other activities relating to environment have been recently initiated. India participated in the Ninth Session of UNEP at Nairobi in 1981. Among the issues discussed was the programme, policy and implementation plan to combat desertification. In this work the Arid Zone Research Institute at Jodhpur has maintained collaboration with other research teams elsewhere. In the same year India participated in IUCN General Assembly session at Christchurch, New Zealand, where the review of implementation of World Conservation Strategy was discussed.

Collaborative programmes in the field of environ mental research have been initiated with USSR, UK, Japan, France, China, FRG and several other countries. The Physical Research Laboratory at Ahmedabad explored the scope of Indo-US Collaboration in research on biogeochemical cycles. India has also ratified the Asia Co-operative Environment Programme. Active Participation was the keynote of the UN Environment Programme Special Session, International Congress on Water Resources, the International Congress on soil science and various international symposia and seminars held by the Governmental bodies, universities and research organisations. Many scholars from India participate in international forums where environmental issues receive scientific attention. The publication since 1983 of the Indian Edition of Mazingira, the international journal for environment and development, is a welcome feature of international co-operation (Mazingira (1983)). Other activities include membership of Committees and expert groups dealing with topics such as Air Quality Monitoring, Air Pollution Control Tolerance Limits for Contaminants in Work Environment, Systems Analysis Techniques, and State Environment Committees. In addition, there are fellowships, research projects, awards, seminars, symposia, workshops and publications, many of which encourage active international co-operation and exchange of ideas.

Research Initiatives

Research provides basic data and analyses problems and trends in the environment. The associations between society and environment change through both space and time. Man's influence tends to grow with the increased use of science and technology, and the effect of transformed natural environments is greater than that of virgin or slightly changed nature (Gerasimov et al, 1975). This relationship is dynamic. Therefore continuing research is necessary to assess the changing relationships and the changing environment.

Since inception in 1981 the National Committee on Environmental Planning (NCEP) and its predecessor - the National Committee on Environmental Planning and Co-ordination (NCEPC), constituted in 1972 - have focused on the impacts on the environment of development activities. The major task was to promote research in environmental problems and to establish facilities for such research where they were necessary. The NCEP further implements its research programme and activities through the Indian National Man and Biosphere Committee (MAB), and the Environmental Research Committee (ERC). The Environmental Research Committee monitors environment pollution and its impacts, environmental aspects of human settlements, the rural environment and other related issues. The Man and Biosphere Committee studies the anthropogenic impact on natural ecosystems. More than 120 projects have been supported by MAB and ERC.

Work has also begun on the establishment of an Institute of Himalayan Ecology and Development, along with research on the control of desertification and on strategies for the conservation of fauna and flora. NCEP also sponsors research projects on the environmental impact of dams, mining operations and environmental pollution. In addition, the University Grants Commission, the Council for Scientific and Industrial Research, the Department of Science and Technology, and individual Universities and Institutes provide funds for research projects of environmental interest - the Himalayas, the Ganga, and the Western Ghats - several Universities have been involved in this work. Post-graduate students are assigned local environmental problems and undergraduate students are involved in social action programmes, such as afforestation, soil conservation and environmental awareness.

During 1981-82 the Department of Environment evaluated 23 proposals for thermal power plants from the perspective of environmental impact assessment. The Department also provides guidelines for research on environmental issues. The nature conservation programme has identified 19 areas as biosphere reserves. There are, in addition, various programmes involving research studies such as eco-development programmes. The Department and Government agencies still have to build up an adequate administrative machinery to monitor how the environmental protection or safeguards recommended are implemented.

ENVIRONMENTAL LEGISLATION AND PROTECTION

A number of laws have been introduced in India which are directly or indirectly related to environmental protection. In accordance with the Directive Principles of the Constitution of India, it is obligatory for the State and Citizens to protect and improve the natural environment. The concern for ecological well-being has been emphasised in the National Policy for Economic Development.

Recent environment legislation includes the Wild Life Protection Act (1974), the Water Pollution Cess Act (1977), the Forest (Conservation) Act (1980), and the Air (Prevention and Control of Pollution) Act (1981). Some of the older legislation is under review. In 1981, the Department of Environment took charge of pollution monitoring and regulation. Thus it is administratively responsible for implementing the 1974 Water Pollution Control Act, and the 1981 Air Pollution Control Act. The Department is undertaking the setting up of a legal wing to examine and draft the legislation required for establishing biosphere reserves, protecting grazing land, wet-lands and catchment areas of river basins, controlling toxic wastes and the exploitation of coastal waters. These developments are landmarks in the course of progress for environmental protection in India.

Numerous problems still remain to be tackled. As environmental protection is of paramount national importance, the government should provide legislation to cover all aspects of environmental pollution throughout the country in an integrated manner. Legislation is inadequate in certain areas relating to environmental protection. The inadequacy in environmental legislation includes measures to prevent over-exploitation of fisheries, a legal provision for taking over the treatment of industrial effluents by the Government, and the preservation of landscape of special significance. In addition, many laws promote resource-use and development without careful scrutiny of the potential short and long-term adverse effects on the environment.

Many existing laws for the management of environmental resources do not clearly define the social objectives to be attained. As a result, the administrative machinery responsible for implementing the laws is often not compatible with the intent and purpose of such laws. In some cases legislation enacted in one State may have deleterious environmental implications for an adjoining State. It is also true that where legislation is adequate, its implementation may be inadequate. As an example, the implementation of the Insecticides Act of 1968 has not strongly enough encouraged the move away from the use of organochlorine pesticides (such as DDT and BHC) which are criticised for their proven detrimental effects on many biological resources of the environment. Provisions in the Act for monitoring pesticides residues in the environment have been totally inadequate. Consequently increasing levels of pesticide residues are being recorded in food stuffs, animal tissues and human fat and even breast milk.

The implementation of the Water (Prevention and Control of Pollution) Act of 1974 has also been inadequate. Although the Act has already been adopted by more than adozen individual states, the central and state Boards for implementing this act did not receive adequate support, and they have become weak extensions of the Public Health Engineering Departments in the states. The same Board is required to implement the Air Pollution Control Act, which makes further demands on its limited resources and inadequate expertise. The offenders (i.e. polluters) cannot be brought to justice as the cases linger in judicial courts, while the pollution continues unabated.

The significance of implementing these laws of environment protection is not clearly appreciated by the administrative and management personnel or by the public at large, because of a pervasive lack of environmental awareness. The Tiwari Committee (1980) rightly remarks that in a country as vast and diverse as India, it will not be possible to achieve complete environmental protection solely through administrative measures. Many adverse environmental impacts can be mitigated or even avoided by an awakening of environmental awareness at the individual, communal and national level.

CONCLUSION: CHALLENGES AND TASKS

This account of various aspects of the environment in India makes it manifestly clear that only a beginning has been made to meet the challenges and tasks that confront the country. There can be some satisfaction but no complacency about the policies, programmes and achievements. The chapter has sought to point out all the significant aspects of environmental issues including policies, resources, pollution, population and settlement, Development-Environment Problems, perception, education, information, research, international co-operation, legislation and protection.

It remains to briefly sum up the challenges and tasks which will have to be considered in the years ahead. The first and foremost challenge is to disseminate awareness of the environment among all sections of society. The diffusion of an environmental consciousness is slow and tardy. Although it was recommended by a high level Government Committee that every Ministry should set up an environment cell, none so far has taken this step. The National Environmental Policy needs to be more clearly defined and more development-environment oriented, rather than being largely development-oriented. Sound national environmental management must rest on good,rational egalitarian resource management. The urban bias must go, as the majority of people in India live in rural areas, and a large section of society lives below the poverty line. The resource management policies need to be integrated, to embrace land and soils, water, forests and wildlife. The change from environmental deterioration to environmental protection will require a fundamental change in patterns of resource use and the integrated utilisation of available resources for social and economic development.

When most people begin to benefit from the environmental policies and programmes, then their voluntary co-operation will be more forthcoming. Of course, the people should not look soley to government for all this; community efforts should be made, if necessary, on a co-operative basis, in order to manage social forestry, community lands, water resources and other natural resources. The Government - for its part - admits with credit its shortcomings in the implementation programmes of environmental protection. In spite of wide-ranging efforts towards environmental protection, environmental deterioration continues and ways and means to stop this deterioration pose a central challenge on both government and people.

Who lives if the environment dies, and who dies if the environment lives? Therefore, a certain harmony and co-ordination has to be established between people, development and environment. Population control, egalitarian development and protection of environment are essential tasks. The environmental crisis is not confined to India. But each country has to solve its own problems. The environmental problems in India are urgent and pressing, but with goodwill and co-operation the environment can be protected and problems solved. Environmental problems may surpass national boundaries: the river and sea-borne pollutants of one country create problems of pollution for another country. These environmental aspects should unite us in an international co-operation aimed at solving the environmental crisis. Ward and Dubos (1974) conclude that "Today, in human society, we can perhaps hope to survive in all our prized diversity, provided we can achieve an ultimate loyalty to our single, beautiful and vulnerable planet, Earth".

REFERENCES

Agarwal, Anil, et al (1982) The State of India's Environment 1982, Centre for Science and Development, New Delhi

Agarwal, V.S. (1953) Geographical Data in Panini The Indian Quarterly, 29: 7-33

Ali, Muzaffer, S. (1965) The Geography of Puranas, New Delhi

Biswas, Margaret R. and Biswas, A.K. (1981) Environment and Development, In A.K. Sharma et al (editors) Impact of the Development of Science and Technology on Environment, Indian Science Congress Association, Calcutta, 107-114

Blunden, John et al (editors) (1978) Fundamentals of Human Geography, Harper and Row, London

Caspersson, Torbjorn (1981) Some Recent Biophysical Methods for Analysis of Genetic Damage in Man caused by Environmental Agents, In A.K. Sharma et al (editors) Impact of the Development of Science and Technology on Environment, Indian Science Congress Association, Calcutta, 95-106

Chaudhuri, Nilay (1984) Constraints and Conflicts In Pollution Control, Industrial Times, 26: 7

Chopra, Ravi (1983) The Politics of Development, The Statesman (New Delhi), 24.4.83: 7

Dutt, Prabha (1984) Losing Our Numbers, India Today (New Delhi) 9: 126-28

Gandhi, Mrs. Indira (1972) Address on Environment, Brochure, Ministry of Health and Family Planning, Government of India, New Delhi

Gandhi, Mrs. Indira (1984) Towards a Better Environment, Inaugural Address to NCEPC (April, 1972) in Indira Gandhi on Environment, Department of Environment, New Delhi, Report, Everymans Science, (Calcutta), 9: 274

Gerasimov, I.P. et al (1975) Man, Society and Environment, Moscow

Ghosh, A.K. (1981) Man and Environment: Reconstruction of Interaction Pattern in Pre-historic India, In I.P. Gerasimov et al (editors) Interaction of Prehistoric Man and His Environment, I.G.U. Commission on Environmental Problems, Mexico

Gibbons, Boyd (1981) Aldo Leopold: A Durable Scale of Values, National Geographic, 160: 682-708

Gilbert, M. Grosvenor (1980) Editorial Note on Water, National Geographic, 2: 143

Hora, S.L. (1937) An Outline of Field Sciences India, Calcutta

Karan, Pradyuman Prasad (1980) Public Awareness of Environmental Problems in Calcutta Metropolitan Area, National Geographical Journal of India, 26: 29-34

Kayastha, S.L. (1970) Conservation of Natural Resources in the Himalaya - A Vital Need, National Geographical Journal of India,16: 208

Kayastha, S.L. (1975) Resource Appraisal, In Walter Imber et al (editors) India, Kummerly and Frey, Berne

Kayastha, S.L. (1978) Regional Development in Special Areas: The Mountain Regions. The Indian Experience, Indo-Soviet Symposium on Regional Development and Planning, Tblisi-Baku-Moscow

Kayastha, S.L. et al (1980) Flood Hazard in the Lower Ghaghara Plain (U.P. India). A Study in Perception and Impact on Socio-Economic Development, National Geographical Journal of India, 26: 19-28

Kayastha, S.L. (1981) An Appraisal of Water Resources of India and Needs for National Water Policy, GeoJournal, 5: 563-564

Kayastha, S.L. (1981) Energy Problems of India: Socio-Economic Aspects, In R.P. Chaturvedi et al (editors) Socio-Economic Aspects of Energy, Cortland, New York

Kayastha, S.L. (1982) Perspectives on Environment and Development, National Geographical Journal of India, 28: 37-43

Kayastha, S.L. (1983) Population in the Himachal Region of the Himalaya: A Study in Population Characteristics, Pressures and Problems, IGU Commission on Population, Symposium on

Mountain Population Pressure, Kathmandu, (Unpublished)
Kayastha, S.L. and Kumar, S.C. (1983) Power Plant - An Environmental Problem of Air Pollution: A Case Study of Obra, Mirzapur (U.P.), Indian Science Congress, (Unpublished)
Khanna, K.C. (1984) Husbanding All that Gas, The Times of India (New Delhi) 17.4.84: 3
Khoshoo, T.N. (1983) India's Environmental Concerns, Mazingira, (New Delhi) 7: 9
Khosla, Ashok (1974) Population and Environment, In A. Bose et al (editors) Population in India's Development 1947-2000, Vikas, Delhi
King, A. (1975) The State of Planet Statement, First Draft, IFIAS
LaBastille, Anne (1981) Acid Rain: How Great a Menace? National Geographic, 160: 652-80
Lowenthal, D. (1967) Environmental Perception and Behaviour, Chicago
Mazingira (1983) Indian Edition, Editor: Asit K. Biswas, New Delhi, pp. 1-94
Misra, R. (1983) Ecology and Man, Proceedings of the National Conference on River Pollution and Human Health, Vranasi
Mitra, Asok (1974) Population in India's Development, In A. Bose et al (editors) Population in India's Development 1947-2000, Vikas, Delhi
Nagchaudhuri, B.D. (1977) Natural Resources and its utilisation, In Survey, Conservation and Utilisation of Resources, Indian Science Congress Association, Calcutta
Narain, Hari (1980) Resources, Environment and Economic Development, Special Issue on Environmental Perception and Problems. Editor: S.L. Kayastha, The National Geographical Journal of India, 26: 18
Narayan, Shanker (1981) Environmental Education: A Profile, In A.K. Sharma et al (editors) Impact of the Development of Science and Technology on Environment, Indian Science Congress Association, Calcutta, pp.119-131
Newbigin, Marion, I. (1968) Plant and Animal Geography, Methuen, London
O'Riordan, Timothy (1978) Environmental Problems of Resource Development in Developing Countries, Proceedings of the IGU Environmental Problems Commission and Working Group on Recreation and Tourism, Ile-Ife, pp. 33-35
Padmanabha, P. (1981) Provisional Population Totals- Series I India, Census of India, (New Delhi): 13

Pal, B.P. (1981) A National Policy on Environment, Department of Environment, Government of India, New Delhi

Report (1980) Report of the Committee for Recommending Legislative Measures and Administrative Machinery for Ensuring Environmental Protection, Department of Science and Technology, Government of India, New Delhi

Report (1982) Department of Environment 1981-82. Government of India, New Delhi

Saxena, D.P. (1976) Regional Patterns of Natural Vegetation, in Regional Geography of Vedic India, Grantham, Kanpur, pp. 23-30

Sethna, H.N. (1977) Survey Conservation and Utilisation of Resources, Presidential Address, Focal Theme, 64th Indian Science Congress Association, Calcutta

Sharma, A.K. (1981) Impact of the Development of Science and Technology on Environment, Presidential Address, 68th Session, Indian Science Congress Association, Varanasi

Spate, O.H.K. et al (1967) India and Pakistan, Methuen, London

Tiwari, N.D. (1980) Report of the Committee for Recommending Legislative Measures and Administrative Machinery for Ensuring Environmental Protection, Department of Science and Technology, Government of India, New Delhi

Toffler, A.C. (1970) Future Shock, London, p.517

U.N. Papers for Stockholm Conference (1974) The Environmental Challenge: A Compendium of U.N. Papers for Stockholm Conference on Human Environment, Macmillan

Vohra, B.B. (1980) A Policy for Land and Water, Department of Environment, Government of India, New Delhi, pp. 1-31

Ward, Barbara and Dubos, Rene (1974) Improving the Environment: Who should pay?, excerpted from their book, Only One Earth, by The American Review (New Delhi), 18: 64-70

Whyte, Anne V.T. (1977) Guidelines for Field Studies in Environmental Perception, MAB Technical Notes, UNESCO

Chapter Eight

ENVIRONMENTAL POLICIES IN JAPAN

Takamasa Nakano

INTRODUCTION

Many environmental problems in Japan stem from the combination of factors which has created a distinctly individual identity for the country - limited land area (75 percent of it hilly and unsuitable for building developments), large population (and hence high population density), rapid post-war industrial development and energetic economic growth, and a physical environment prone to flooding, landslides and other forms of natural hazards.

The population density on flat land in Japan is over 1000 people per km^2 (the average for Japan overall is 280 people per km^2), which is over 2.5 times that in the Netherlands (often taken as the country with the highest population density in the world). Such high densities give rise to crowded urban areas, and they promote complicated and high density land use patterns with fine grained land use mosaics. These in turn give rise to water pollution through the release of high loads of polluted waste water and contaminated waters into lakes and rivers. In recent years industrial wastes have been well treated, so that quite high quality wastes are now released into watercourses, but domestic wastes are still poorly treated in some urban and rural areas.

Stable and flat land resources are at a premium in Japan. Hilly terrain around urban areas has been transformed by terracing or regrading to produce lower land slopes suitable for building new housing on. Such reclaimed landscapes are highly susceptible to earthquake damage and disasters, to flooding and to landslide hazards in many areas. Essentially 'man-made' landscapes of this sort are becoming more widespread in Tokyo, Osaka, Nagoya and their surroundings where over two million people live.

<u>Background to Environmental Problems</u>

Problems of declining environmental quality have been experienced in Japan for many centuries. Early evidence dates back to the eighth century A.D., when the processing of copper ores using wood for fuel caused pollution of air and water resources. Forest habitats in the mining regions were destroyed by felling and polluted by sulphur dioxide gases, and rivers were contaminated with waste waters from the ore refining operations. Such pollution in the mining regions became even more acute after the seventeenth century.

Environmental problems have become more widespread and problematic since the Meiji Restoration in 1868 (see Table 8.1). Many forms of human activity have contributed to the deterioration of environmental quality, including the spread of coal powered railways, and the nuisances of smoke, noise, vibrations and offensive odours stemming from factories. The health of many industrial workers has also been affected by dust and particulate pollutants. Such problems have been complemented by reductions in landscape quality and changes in land use, most markedly in the mining areas and forests near the plains, where urban sprawl and industrial growth were concentrated on suitable flat sites.

With the exception of land subsidence environmental problems in the past have on the whole been limited and localised. Through time, however, there has been a reduction in environmental quality. This stems in part from continued land subsidence, most visibly in the lowland zones by the coast, where flooding from rivers and the sea has become more common. Subsidence has increased around Osaka and Tokyo and elsewhere during the Taisho (1913-1926) and Showa (post-1927) eras (Table 8.1). The chronology of increasing subsidence (Table 8.2) indicates that although concerted efforts to provide remedies for the subsidence have been made in recent decades, these have on the whole been too few, too small and too late to provide wholesale solutions to the problem.

TABLE 8.1 Background to Environmental Changes in Japan by Region

Era	Osaka	Tokyo	Others
Pre-Meiji (before 1867)	.flood repeated .change of river course .construction of port and canals .reclamation	.flood repeated .port facilities increased .canals .reclamation	.flood repeated .port at river mouth .reclamation .reclamation of wetland
Meiji (1868-1912)	.flood repeated .industrialisation .urbanisation .use of ground water .discharge channel	.flood repeated .use of ground water .discharge channel	.flood repeated .discharge channel
Taisho (1913-1926)	.land subsidence	.land subsidence .great Kanto earthquake .urbanisation .industrialisation	
Showa (since 1927)	.high tide .land subsidence .sea wall .decrease of land subsidence	.high tide .land subsidence .sea wall .decrease of land subsidence	.Isewan typhoon .land subsidence (natural gas) .land subsidence .land development .Miyagioki earthquake in 1978

Source: Nakano (1981b)

TABLE 8.2 Chronology of Main Periods of Land Subsidence and Related Events

Date	Events
1915	land subsidence due to pumping up of ground-water began in Tokyo area
1917	flood disasters due to high tide in Tokyo area
1923	great Kanto Earthquake and acute land subsidence in Tokyo
1932	abnormal land subsidence recognised in Tokyo and Osaka
1934	flood disasters in Osaka area due to Muroto typhoon; inland harbour plan for Osaka to prevent high tide
1940	pumping of ground-water as a major cause of land subsidence
1945	cessation of land subsidence in Tokyo and areas due to decreased pumping of ground-water; flooding due to earthquake, flood and tsunami in Kochi area (after Nankai Earthquake); flood disasters in subsided areas of Tokyo and Osaka
1950	land subsidence again in Tokyo and Osaka; land subsidence starts to appear in new areas
1953	deeper ground water use leads to further land subsidence; very acute land subsidence in Niigata area due to withdrawal of natural gas with ground water from below
1958	about 38 km^2 of land below sea level in Tokyo area
1960	over 200 km^2 of land below sea level in Nagoya area (described by Geographical Survey Institute); flood disasters in land subsiding areas in Tokyo (1958), Nagoya (1959) and Osaka (1960); control of ground-water use in Kawasaki, Osaka, Amagasaki Tokyo; separation of causes of land subsidence; control of natural gas withdrawal in Niigata area; increase and spreading of land subsidence areas in Japan; laws on controlling ground-water use issued and revised
1965	acute land subsidence due to withdrawal of natural gas in Funabashi area (in the vicinity of Tokyo)
1970	flooding of land below sea level in Kochi city

Table 8.2 (continued)

1971	Environmental Agency was established; natural gas fields of Tokyo and Funabashi areas were bought by local governments; acute land subsidence stopped
1975	1,168 km^2 of land below sea level reported by Environmental Agency; a total of 46 land subsiding areas in Japan

Source: Nakano (1976), Nakano and Matsuda (1976)

Many urban areas and industrial districts paid a heavy toll during the hostilities of World War Two - many were heavily bombed and burned, and the atomic bombs which fell on Hiroshima and Nagasaki left lasting legacies on the landscape. Both cities have been reconstructed since 1945, but urban sprawl was to progress beyond the city limits and affect landscape and environmental quality over a wide area. Other important post-war changes include the development of industrial districts along the coast (particularly after the Korean War, 1950-53), where new industrial facilities based on oil power developed rapidly. From about 1955 serious environmental pollution could be detected in and around the urban areas and industrial districts, and by the mid-1960s such pollution ('kogai' in Japanese) was to be the subject of new laws and statutory directives.

The Legislative Response

Against this background of changing environmental problems through time, the evolution of environmental legislation and administration in Japan has been a recent initiative. Most environmental laws have been passed within the last two decades (Table 8.3). The Environmental Agency of Japan, in its publication ENVIRONMENTAL LAWS AND REGULATIONS IN JAPAN (1976) claims that two general environmental laws provide the foundation for such legislation in Japan. These are Law 132 (Basic Law for Environmental Pollution Control) dating from 1967, and Law 142 (Law for the Punishment of Crimes Relating to the Environmental Pollution which Adversely Affects the Health of Persons), dating from 1970. The Environmental Agency publication describes appropriate laws and regulations

TABLE 8.3 Chronology of Environmental Legislation

Date	Legislation	Law No.
1948	Agricultural Chemicals Regulation Law	82
1967	Basic Law for Environmental Pollution Control	132
1967	Natural Park Law	161
1968	Air Pollution Control Law	97
1968	Noise Regulation Law	98
1970	Pollution Control Public Works Cost Allocation Law	133
1970	Marine Pollution Prevention	136
1970	Water Pollution Control Law	138
1970	Agricultural Land Soil Pollution Prevention, etc.	139
1970	Law for the Punishment of Crimes Relating to the Environmental Pollution which Adversely Affects the Health of Persons	142
1971	Offensive Odour Control Law	91
1972	Nature Conservation Law	85
1973	Pollution-Related Health Damage Compensation Law	111
1974	Waste Management Law	137

Note: Legislation on ground (land) subsidence is not included: land subsidence is dealt with in other laws on industrial water and building water.

Source: Summarised from Environmental Agency (1976)

dealing with a wide range of environmental issues, including the relief of victims of pollution, cost allocation, air and water quality, pollution of land resources by agricultural chemicals, waste products and materials, noise and offensive odours, and impacts on plants, animals and habitats.

These laws and regulations are closely related to the two main 'general laws' (132 and 142).

The Basic Law for Environmental Pollution Control (Law 132) defines 'environmental pollution" ('kogai') in the context of any situation in which human health and the living environment are damaged by air pollution, water pollution, soil pollution, noise, vibration, ground subsidence (except for subsidence caused by drilling activities related to mining), and offensive odours created by industrial or other human activities and affecting a large area.

The notable exception in this definition "environmental pollution" is subsidence related to mining activities; this creates certain problems which cannot be resolved by existing environmental law in Japan. Ground subsidence triggered off by underground mining is catered for partly in Mining Law and associated laws and regulations, but these are directed specifically towards the mining industry itself and not towards solution of the ensuing environmental problems. For example some regulations seeks to prevent land collapse above operating mines, but this is largely to prevent the collapse of the mining tunnel rather than to safeguard surface ground and permit development over the mining zone. Despite such regulations, land collapses are common occurrences, with the subsided areas often used as lotus fields. Houses cannot be built on the areas of collapse through risk of damage from differential ground subsidence beneath the properties.

A PERSPECTIVE ON THE ENVIRONMENT

All environmental problems must be set firmly into a space-time context, in what one might term a 'historico-geographical reality' (Nakano, 1983). This means that many environmental problems are closely related together in space and time, and a historic perspective is required to more fully understand how and why certain problems have arisen or been perpetuated.

In the example of land subsidence, related factors include mining operations, tunneling activities, inadequate infilling of redundant tunnels, changes of land use overhead, building of houses, and differential subsidence triggered off by imposed loads. The time context means that the monetary gains are enjoyed by the original land owners, the mining companies and the house builders, whereas the losses (in monetary terms and through inconvenience and risk) are met largely by the subsequent house owners. The cost-benefit evaluation is thus imbalanced in favour of the former groups, and against the eventual residents in the area. The time dimension also means that there may have been changes through time in the nature and powers of the administrative bodies responsible for the area, and other changes through time in laws, regulations and responsibilities for damage.

Environmental pollution and deterioration of environmental quality can be detected throughout Japanese history. Pollution of air, water and soil and destruction of forest habitat by fire occurred even in feudalistic times. Such trends can be seen today in many developing countries (such as India - see chapter 7). Shifting cultivation, an essential part of the lifestyle of many peoples in developing countries, promotes forest clearance. But the benefits are reaped more by peoples of developed countries, whilst indigenous peoples lose valued environments and suffer allied environmental problems (such as accelerated soil erosion).

Many environmental problems are now of global magnitude and concern. Typical of such problems are forest clearance for shifting cultivation, and the increasing use of natural resources (such as timber and minerals) in the developing world. Increasing atmospheric levels of carbon dioxide, promoted in part by the burning of fossil fuels, and desertification in arid and semi-arid areas promoted by natural climatic fluctuations and unsuitable land use and management, provide further examples.

Scales of Spatial Resolution

Because most environmental problems can be diffused spatially from one place to another, and because many small scale problems are so ubiquitous that they can create large cumulative impacts, it is useful to specify a spatial scale of resolution when formulating environmental policies. Six scales might be used:

(a) rural level problems,
(b) urban level problems,

(c) regional level problems,
(d) national level problems,
(e) continental level problems, and
(f) global level problems.

Clearly it will often be easier to establish links between environmental problems at one scale or level of resolution, whereas problems which transcend the levels are often more difficult to study and manage.

It is also useful to distinguish between direct and indirect causes of environmental problems. One illustration of direct causes would be forest clearance to create land for agriculture, whilst river channel instability promoted by increased sediment loads (perhaps triggered off by land use changes upstream - such as forest clearance) illustrates an indirect cause. Enlightened management of many environmental problems thus requires a blend of appropriate information from a broad range of studies, spanning legal controls of the environment, environmental changes (physico-chemical and psychological), reversible and irreversible types of environmental adjustment, strategies for environmental management, and links between environmental problems in developing and developed countries.

Some examples might be used to illustrate the links between spatial level (or scale) and direct and indirect impacts:

(a) at the rural scale, soil pollution can result from use of pesticides (direct) and harmful biota (indirect),
(b) at the urban scale, heating of overlying air to create an urban heat island can result from the use of various forms of fuel energy (direct), and this can be intensified by the creation of high density building within the urban fabric (indirect),
(c) at the regional scale, air pollution often results from emission of vehicle exhaust gases (direct), whilst delays in regional development and increased commuter traffic and longer hours of high density traffic (indirect factors) intensify the direct causes,
(d) at the national scale, water pollution often results from the production and use of synthetic chemicals (direct), whilst inadequate

technological assessment (indirect) does little to alleviate such impacts on environment,

(e) at the continental scale, wholesale forest clearance is promoted by the need for economic development (direct), which is in turn promoted by economic pressure exerted by developed countries (indirect) eager to trade resources,

(f) at the global scale, desertification can lead ultimately from increased use of oil (direct), which is influenced by industrial development, urban expansion, and changing agricultural practices (indirect factors).

Changing Environmental Quality

In Japan, the Environmental Agency has responsibility for monitoring and managing environmental problems. Each year it publishes a "White Paper on the Environment" in which different problems are highlighted and described. For example the White Paper for the fiscal year 1979 (April 1979 to March 1980) was submitted - in Japanese - to the 92nd session of the Diet, in pursuance of Article 7 of the 'Basic law for Environmental Pollution Control' (Law 132, 1967 - Table 8.3). In 1981 the Environmental Agency published a condensed version of the White Paper, under the title 'QUALITY OF THE ENVIRONMENT IN JAPAN, 1980'. The Preface to this review indicates marked changes in attitude and response to environmental issues over the last three decades.

The 1960s, a decade of rapid economic growth, population change and reduction of environmental quality, saw mounting evidence of more serious environmental problems and the state of the environment became a major social issue. During the 1970s the legal systems and administrative organisations for environmental protection (centred on pollution prevention) were established and improved. By the 1980s, the Agency reports that environmental policies were entering a new stage, and that demands were being made for further enhancement in the quality and scope of such policies.

There is evidence, however, to suggest that Japan is already making impressive headway in coping with environmental problems. This comes in two successive editions of 'TOKYO FIGHTS POLLUTION', published by the Tokyo Metropolitan Government in March 1971 and revised in March 1977. A marked improvement in environmental quality in Tokyo - widely thought to be amongst the worst cities in the world in environmental terms - is apparent over the six year period (1971-1977). The Preface to the 1977 (revised) edition describes some of the notable success stories. For example, land subsidence - which was a great problem in the eastern parts of Tokyo before 1970 - has been ameliorated substantially by controlled pumping of ground water. Air quality over Tokyo is also improving markedly, as reflected in the greatly improved visibility in and around the city. For example, the number of days per year when Mount Fuji (some 100km to the west) could be seen clearly from the city centre rose from 13 in 1968 and 18 in 1970 to 76 in 1975.

Whilst these signs of environmental improvement are well supported by available data, and there is doubtless evidence of great success in enhancing environmental quality through careful management, not all problems have been dealt with fully. For example, whilst rates of land subsidence have declined, this simply means that the problem has not been getting more acute. The areas which have already undergone subsidence cannot be restored to their original height without massive costs of landfill. Such areas are thus prone to flooding by rivers and by the high tides which accompany typhoons. Different environmental management strategies have to be used in such cases, and these centre upon disaster prevention measures adopted by local and national governments in Japan.

This highlights the need to consider environmental legislation in a broad context, because it spans both laws on environmental protection and laws on natural disaster prevention. The legal relationships between these areas of law in Japan are not clear. This is illustrated by the problems of dealing with man-made landforms around the great city areas. Many of these are associated with land subsidence which has been infilled to create sites for housing and industry. Inevitably such areas tend to be unstable, and they are prone to flooding and erosion by heavy rain and to earthquake damage in tectonically unstable Japan.

Natural disasters and environmental problems stemming from heavy rain and earthquakes are treated as natural hazards in Japan, and so they are based on different legal systems. Flood problems on subsided areas are also classified as natural phenomena. In both cases reconstruction is the responsibility of the Ministry of Construction and allied local government organisations, and the costs are met from taxes. The costs are broadly shared by the population at large (via taxes), and neither the developers nor the companies whose activities promoted the land subsidence have to contribute to the costs of dealing with the problems.

ENVIRONMENTAL INFORMATION AND AWARENESS

To some extent environmental planning in Japan has been hindered by a lack of suitable (and accessible) scientific observations on environmental quality and changes through time, and a shortage of efforts to integrate results from individual studies into a general overview. Continuous monitoring systems have been developed, and large observational data sets amassed. However such data are generally not used very effectively, and they are only processed in scientific studies if a particular problem is being examined.

National Surveys

National surveys of environmental quality are conducted every few years, and the results are released to the public. Such information is used more in public relations than in serious scientific enquiry, and the lack of general scientific surveys on the environment in Japan is to be regretted. In addition to the national surveys there have been basic studies on environmental improvement, focussing on a range of topics, and undertaken by government and prefectural government institutions. Such topics and studies are important, but little effort has been given to the integration of results.

Studies of the natural environment in Japan are normally carried out by natural scientists, and the human dimension is often overlooked. Natural environment is taken in government publications to refer to plants, animals, soils, lakes and reservoirs, rivers and the seas. The environment is rarely evaluated as part of a 'man-nature complex'.

Article 5 of the Nature Conservation Law (Table 8.3) requires that a National Survey on the Natural Environment be carried out every five years. The first was completed in 1973, and the second in 1978-79. The total budget for the National Survey (805.8 million yen) seemed high to the scientists involved, but it is very small when viewed alongside the budgets available for land development and disaster prevention. The Survey covers inland, freshwater and marine environments (Figure 8.1).

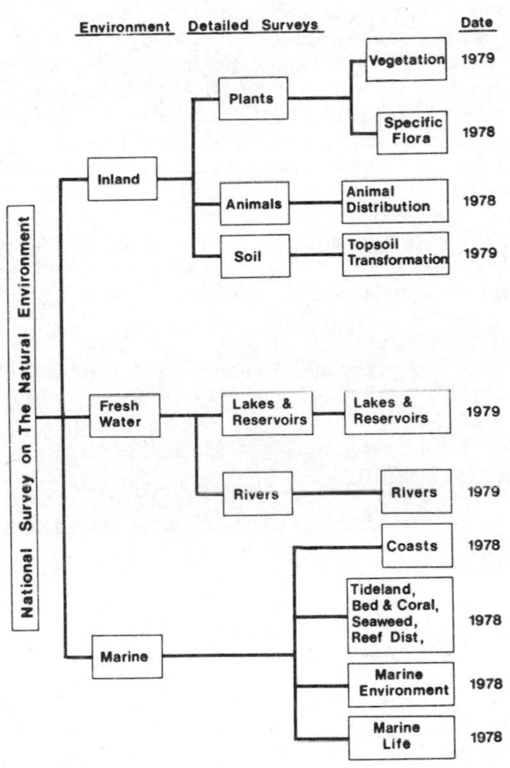

FIGURE 8.1: The Japanese National Survey on the Natural Environment (1978-79)

One product of the Survey will be the compilation of maps of present day vegetation in Japan, at a scale of 1:50,000. The maps will show the distribution of 'degree of naturalness' of the landscape, based on the extent of natural vegetation and the amount of man-made terrain, classified on a ten point scale. Degrees 1 to 3 represent artificial built up areas, and intensively used agricultural land. Degrees 4 to 7 cover man made grasslands, planted vegetation and secondary forests. Degree 8 represents semi-natural forest, and natural forests and natural grasslands are represented in degrees 9 and 10 respectively.

There are clear variations in the extent of land within the ten classes. Heavily man-modified landscapes (degrees 1 to 3) cover about 27 percent of the land area, mainly within lowland and drift-covered uplands. Moderately influenced landscapes occupy a further 45 percent of the land area, mainly in hilly areas, on volcanic piedmonts and on low or gently sloping mountain terrain. These are the land classes which are presently being subjected to development for non-agricultural land uses such as housing and industry (as encouraged by land development policies) - so that volcanic piedmonts are being artificially terraced to reduce gradients and paddy fields are being converted to industrial and residential areas through policies of adjusting rice production targets.

Environmental Awareness

Part of the initiative within environmental planning has aimed to improve general environmental awareness. To this end education about the environment has been included in the school curriculum, and environmental themes are covered on television and in the mass media. General awareness about the environment amongst the population at large seems to be seriously low, perhaps in part as a reflection of improved environmental quality. Environmental education should perhaps aim to mould attitudes about environmental quality and the links between protection and development, more so than it does at present.

One measure of environmental awareness is the number of complaints made about pollution. Roughly 41 percent of complaints lodged about pollution relate to noise and vibrations, and quite high numbers of complaints are received about offensive odours (26 percent), air pollution (17 percent) and water pollution (16 percent). Relatively few complaints are received about soil pollution (0.3 percent) or land subsidence (0.1 percent) at present.

But the situation changes through time - a larger percentage of complaints were received about land subsidence in past years, but complaints about heavy flooding in areas of subsidence appear to be increasing. Changes in the number of complaints about air pollution must be set against evidence of improved air quality in recent years. Annual concentrations of major pollutants (such as carbon dioxide and sulphur dioxide) have decreased markedly, but concentrations of nitrogen dioxide have increased (to between 0.03 - 0.04 ppm).

ENVIRONMENTAL PROBLEMS AND POLICIES

Environmental policies relate mainly to the management of land and water resources, but two problems make integrated environmental management more a goal than a reality in Japan at present:

(a) land use and water resources are dealt with by, and are the responsibility of, different organisations and are based on different laws and regulations, and

(b) conflicts often arise between development and environmental protection - which are carried out by different bodies, for different reasons, and with different views on the need for sustained quality of the environment.

Many of Japan's environmental problems stem from the fact that the evaluation of nature as environment (in its broadest sense) is overshadowed by the evaluation of nature for development. Financial gain is cherished more widely and strongly than fresh air and water resources and natural vegetation.

Water Pollution

Japan relies heavily on its resources of fresh and sea water. The former include rivers, lakes and swamps, and the latter include bays, inland sea and offshore sea. These resources have been affected by pollution from factories, farms and houses, although the adverse impacts have been spread unevenly across the landscape. The highest pollution levels, and accordingly worst damage, has occurred in the bays adjacent to the main industrial and urban areas and in the Seto Inland Sea.

Japan has a number of caldera lakes (caused by the flooding of collapsed volcanic vents) which are deep and have high water quality. Some are preserved in a pristine state, but some (such as Lake Toya) have been developed as recreation resources and they suffer from reduced water quality and shoreline erosion.

Rivers flowing through or near urban areas also exhibit problems of water pollution from contamination by waste materials from housing and industrial zones. Concerted efforts have been made by the government and prefectural governments to improve water quality, and these have been quite successful in many areas. Such efforts have reduced the incidence of offensive odours in many watercourses.

Water pollution is perhaps most acute in the bays and in the Seto Inland Sea, which receive waste products from industrial and urban centres. Data published by the Environmental Agency (1981) show a marked rise in the number of confirmed outbreaks of red tide in the Seto Inland Sea in the mid-1970s, followed by a decline in the late 1970s. Tokyo Bay has also experienced problems of pollution, particularly since 1959. Biochemical Oxygen Demand levels in the Bay have more than doubled since 1959 to over 2 ppm. Much of the pollution in Tokyo Bay derives from industrial complexes along the coast, but efforts have been made to improve industrial discharge facilities. Pollution also derives from the inefficient urban sewer systems of Tokyo, Yokohama, Kawasaki and other cities, which will require wholesale improvement of the urban structure before effective solutions emerge.

Pollution and Human Health

Results of surveys conducted by the Research Institute for Environmental Policy, of the Tokyo Metropolitan Government, illustrate some aspects of the pollution problem in Japan. For example there is evidence of the accumulation of abnormally high concentrations (in the region of 5,000 to

7,000 ppm) of nitrates in some vegetables sold in the city. Data published in the reports TOKYO FIGHTS POLLUTION (1971, 1977) also illustrate the magnitude of many pollution problems. For example, surveys have been carried out on mercury concentrations in the hair and blood of Tokyo residents (Table 8.4) and the results indicate much higher concentrations in men than in women, with highest levels overall amongst fish-eaters. High mercury levels have also been detected in new born babies (Table 8.5) indicating the link between mother and child. Studies of lead content in the hair and blood of Tokyo residents (Table 8.6) also reveal differences between men and women, and they indicate the greater exposure to atmospheric lead within the city centre.

Most of the legislation in Japan which deals with the impacts of pollution on human health is related to the Pollution-Related Health Damage Compensation Law (Law 111, Table 8.3), which was passed in 1973 and came into force on 1st September 1974. The Law seeks to provide speedy and fair protection for people suffering from health effects related to pollution. Under Law 111, governors of prefectures and mayors of designated cities are empowered by Cabinet Order to certify people suffering from such health effects, so as to allow them to receive compensation under the Law. Compensation is payable under seven classes of benefit:

(a) medical care benefits and expenses,
(b) disability compensation,
(c) survivors' compensation,
(d) lump sum survivors' compensation,
(e) child compensation allowance,
(f) medical care allowance, and
(g) funeral expenses.

Administrative response to health damage caused by specific pollution episodes has been very slow, and there is a feeling that negotiations between government, prefectural governments and private companies take far too long to reach sensible conclusions. This time lag is well illustrated in the case of mercury related water pollution in the Minamata area during the mid-1950s (Table 8.7). This case also highlights the problems of establishing causal links between pollution incidents and consequent human health impacts, and the even more difficult problems of negotiating

TABLE 8.4 Levels of Mercury in the Hair and Blood of Tokyo Residents

group		HAIR (ppm)			BLOOD (μg 100 g^{-1})		
		mean	st.dev.	sample size	mean	st.dev.	sample size
great fish-eaters	m	16.94	9.11	176	8.04	3.52	79
	f	7.05	2.05	2	6.2	-	1
islanders	m	11.94	6.99	104	4.01	2.36	92
	f	6.55	4.47	95	3.24	1.88	89
general residents	m	6.15	2.98	272	2.84	1.10	128
	f	4.45	2.37	396	2.19	1.37	283

Note: the great fish-eaters are a group of people believed to eat large quantities of tuna, other fish and shellfish; the islanders live on Oshima and Hachijo islands. m = male, f = female.

Source: based on data in Tokyo Metropolitan Government (1977)

TABLE 8.5 Levels of Mercury in Mothers and their New Babies in Tokyo

		TOTAL MERCURY		METHYL MERCURY	
	sample size	mean	st.dev.	mean	st. dev.
HAIR (ppm)					
mothers	90	5.26	2.86	2.30	1.36
new babies	90	5.57	2.80	2.17	0.86
males	41	5.92	3.14	2.34	0.93
females	49	5.27	2.43	2.03	0.76
BLOOD (μg $100g^{-1}$)					
mothers	90	1.74	1.02	0.70	0.41
new babies	90	3.02	1.89	1.52	0.79
males	41	3.10	1.45	1.61	0.74
females	49	2.95	2.19	1.45	0.82

Note: the blood of new babies was taken from the umbilical cord

Source: based on data in Tokyo Metropolitan Government (1977)

TABLE 8.6 Levels of Lead in the Hair and Blood of Tokyo Residents

group		HAIR (ppm)			BLOOD (μg 100 g^{-1})		
		sample size	mean	st.dev.	sample size	mean	st.dev.
great fish eaters	m	91	12.6	10.8	nd	nd	nd
	f	1	17	-	nd	nd	nd
islanders	m	nd	nd	nd	24	6.0	2.8
	f	nd	nd	nd	25	4.8	1.0
general residents	m	127	17.9	14.5	32	18.9	14.9
	f	111	20.9	17.3	20	13.8	7.2

Note: see Table 8.4 for notes on fish-eaters and islanders, nd - no data

Source: based on data in Tokyo Metropolitan Government (1977)

fair compensation payments when human health, welfare and quality of life are in question.

TABLE 8.7 Minamata Disease, Itai-Itai Disease and Chronic Arsenic Poisoning

Oct. 1955	Report on a strange disease of unknown cause at the 17th meeting of the Clinical Surgery Association - Itai-itai disease in the Jinzu River in Toyama Prefecture ('itai' in Japanese means 'pain')
May 1956	Report to the Minamata Health Centre (from the hospital attached to the Chisso Corporation Minamata Factory) regarding the occurrence of a strange disease - Minamata disease
Nov. 1962	Official recognition of embryonic Minamata disease
May 1968	The Ministry of Health and Welfare announces the view that Itai-itai disease is induced by such factors as pregnancy, lactation, irregularity of internal secretion, senility and calcium deficiency, combined with osteomalacia (which is brought about by kidney malfunction resulting from chronic poisoning by cadmium), and that the effluent of the Kamioka Refinery of the Mitsui Mining and Smelting Co. Ltd., is the only possible source of the cadmium
Sept. 1968	The Government announces that Minamata disease was caused by the ingestion of fish and shellfish contaminated with methyl mercury compounds discharged from the Minamata Factory of Chisso Corporation; Government announces that the waste water from the Ka Kanose Plant of the Showa Denko Co. Ltd., is the origin of the poisoning of Minamata disease in the Agano River Basin which was reported by the Medical Department of Niigata

Table 8.7 (continued)

	University to the Niigata Prefectural Health Department; Professor Tsubaski of Niigata University announced the occurrence of organic mercury poisoning cases
Dec. 1969	Minamata and the Agano and Jinzu River basins are designated as areas to which the Relief Law is applied
Nov. 1971	Environmental and social medical surveys are conducted in the area around the Toroku Mine, Miyazaki Prefecture, East Kyushu
July 1972	The Surveys report seven recognised cases of probable chronic arsenic poisoning
Oct. 1972	Solution of the compensation problem between the seven persons receiving medical relief and the Sumitomo Metal Mining Co. Ltd., at the mediation of the Governor of Miyazaki Prefecture; Toroku district is designated as an area to which the Relief Law is applied
Aug. 1973	Reports that seven persons in Au were considered to be suffering from chronic poisoning, five more were suspected and a further 19 need observation.
July 1974	The Sasagadani District in Shimane Prefecture is designated as an area to which the Relief Law is applied; Shimane Prefectural Government confirmed the evidence of environmental pollution by arsenic in the area surrounding the Sasagadan Mine and carried out a medical check up of residents in the district

Land Subsidence

By far the greatest environmental problems in Tokyo arise from land subsidence (Nakamo, 1970). The estimated cost of losses associated with subsidence accounts for nearly half of the total cost of environmental pollution, and it far outweighs the costs of air and water pollution (Table 8.8). Land subsidence in the Osaka area has been caused by the pumping of water and water-soluble natural gas. Such subsidence has promoted direct damage to structures such as buildings, dykes, bridges and underground pipelines, and this has been compounded by indirect impacts resulting from increased incidences of earthquake damage, severe flooding from heavy rains, and increased exposure to typhoon damage. Direct damage can be repaired by technology, which allows the recovery of the function of the structures. But - as noted earlier - the indirect damages are more costly and more difficult to 'repair' without wholesale landfilling to raise the lowered ground surface.

In the Osaka area land subsidence has been accompanied by increased flooding. Between 1925 and 1970 the area in question (which covers about 50 km^2) was flooded by high tides (produced by both typhoons and river floods) on 27 occasions. Nearly three quarters of a million homes were flooded in total over that period and nearly three thousand people died (largely as a result of high tides related to typhoons). The marked land subsidence in this area (so that some 35 km^2 of the land has now fallen below mean sea level) has been caused by the pumping of large quantities of ground water since the 1920s.

The average cost of supplying water to the city over the last ten years has been about 20 yen per m^3. A more realistic costing would include the cost of direct and indirect impacts arising from the land subsidence (through flooding, inconvenience, danger and death), and ideally also the cost of infilling the subsided areas to restore ground surface levels to their original positions. The cost of supplying ground water resources, if they reflected these allied environmental costs, would be extremely high (they would, in fact, more than double).

Pollution mitigation

A range of measures have been introduced with the aim of controlling if not reducing the problems and consequences of environmental pollution in Japan. These have arisen from the initiatives of many parties, including government and prefect-

TABLE 8.8 Estimated Cost of Environmental Pollution in Tokyo, by Sector and Form of Pollution

Units are millions of yen, for one year, at 1972 prices

Sector	Public sector	Business sector	Family finances sector	Total
Air pollution	24	1,059	1,758	2,841
Noise and vibration	70	406	1,027	1,503
Land subsidence	8,391	399	987	9,777
Water pollution	379	-	-	379
Compound pollution	-	588	4,056	4,644
TOTAL	8,864	2,452	7,828	19,144

Source: based on data in Tokyo Metropolitan Government (1977)

ural governments, autonomous bodies and private companies. They can be classified into seven broad categories of measure:

(a) policy making,
(b) improvement of legal system,
(c) administrative enforcement,
(d) continuing surveys and monitoring of pollution,
(e) national surveys over extended time scales (years),
(f) basic studies on environmental improvement, and
(g) initiatives within education.

Much of the inertia within environmental planning in Japan can be traced back to the political decision-makers. The Liberal and Democratic Party - the dominant political party in Japan - is conservative in its approach to pollution prevention. This conservatism is carried over into central and local governments, which are slow in their response to pollution problems. Many small problems are allowed to grow and coalesce, until major problems develop which are costly if not impossible to solve. Many aspects of pollution problems are woven together into complex inter-relationships, so that effective management must tackle the entire system rather than just the more visible components.

The suite of problems related to motor cars illustrates this complex holism of many environmental problems. The dominant problem is doubtless the air pollution promoted by emission of exhaust gases from cars and lorries, but this is locked into an assemblage of related issues such as oil taxes, the structure of the motor vehicle industry, road construction, technological developments in dealing with exhaust gases, increasing numbers of cars on the roads, narrow roads in congested urban centres, and so on. It would be impossible for any one organisation to successfully tackle such a wide range of problems.

Individual components of the overall problem tend to be dealt with by different organisations, and these have their own policies and administrative regimes which are not always compatible with those of other oranisations dealing with the same problems.

GLOBAL SCALE ENVIRONMENTAL PROBLEMS

Whilst there has been detailed consideration of national problems of environmental quality within Japan in recent decades, this has not been entirely to the exclusion of global considerations. The first serious attempt by central government to explore global environmental problems came in 1981, when a special commission was set up to discuss the global scale problems. The commission reported in the 1981 WHITE PAPER ON THE ENVIRONMENT, in which it isolated three main problem areas:

(a) global scale dispersion of pollutants,
(b) diminishing wildlife resources, and
(c) removal of forest cover and desertification (especially in developing countries).

The commission recognised the need for concerted international co-operation to tackle these major problems, and for collaborative efforts between Japan and the developing countries to help them to tackle their own problems.

The commission was also very aware of the difficulty of compiling a balanced data base on which to assess the nature and scale of the global problems, faced with a markedly uneven availability of data (and this of uneven quality and quantity) from different countries. Its assessment of problems of air pollution (with a focus on increasing concentrations of carbon dioxide) was based on foreign data, as was the review of declining wildlife resources and loss of species and habitats at the global scale. The commission's study of ocean pollution was based on observations from the Indian Ocean and from the West Pacific Ocean.

One important omission from the report by the commission was any consideration about what role Japan might most usefully play in resolving or managing these global problems. This must be a high priority theme on the agenda of environmental debate, because Japan - as one of the most highly developed economies in the world - is closely linked to most other countries through international trade in natural resources (such as animals, timber pulp, iron ores and oil) and in manufactured products (such as cars). As one valuable contribution, Japan might sponsor and carry out basic studies on the causes and character of desertification, and it might offer appropriate technical and financial assistance to developing countries presently facing the costs, problems and constraints of desert expansion in marginal areas.

CONCLUSIONS

It is clear that certain steps have been taken in Japan in an attempt to control if not reduce environmental pollution, to preserve if not enhance environmental quality, and to cope with environmental hazards. On the whole these initiatives have been based almost exclusively on technological solutions to environmental problems. Such approaches are doubtless basically sound, but technological solutions might not be the only nor necessarily the best strategy to follow.

Technological developments and initiatives are not without limits - they are costly in time, effort and resources, and they are not always capable of dealing suitably with all aspects of a given environmental problem. Moreover, technological developments can be strongly influenced by sales policies of the companies engaged in research, development and marketing of the technology. Indeed, often new technologies either create or contribute to problems of environmental quality.

The case of motor cars in Japan illustrates well this precarious position. Japan produces between two and five times as many cars as West Germany, the United Kingdom, France, Canada, Italy and many other car-producing nations. Many of these cars are built specifically for the export market, but a large number are also sold in Japan. An increasing number of Japanese cars are contributing to environmental problems within the country - through air pollution stemming from emission of vehicle exhaust gases, congestion in crowded city centres and use of resources in manufacturing and running the cars. Various strategies to reduce these problems might be followed. Urban renewal to widen heavily used roads might reduce problems of congestion, but this is a long term solution which is costly and would require wholesale reshaping of the urban fabric. The control of cars within cities offers an alternative option, but this would reduce personal mobility and it would be unpopular. The best prospects seem to lie in technical improvements in car engines, which would reduce exhaust gases - but again this is a long term solution that requires forward planning, considerable resources and legislative backing.

There are clear links between economic growth and environmental quality in Japan as elsewhere. But the links are complex and two way. Economic growth is required to generate the capital needed for environmental protection programmes, and to promote research and development in technologies applicable in dealing with environmental problems. But in turn economic growth often promotes a reduction in environmental quality through heavy resource use and the search for economic success in preference to environmental stability. Economic growth can also promote the very technologies which contribute to declining environmental quality and increased pollution (such as cars).

The paradox linking development and environmental quality is well articulated by Professor Tokue Shibata, an economist and former Director of the Research Institute for Environmental Protection (Tokyo Metropolitan Government). He writes (Shibata, 1983):

> *All of the environmental problems in Tokyo today are generally concerned with the city structure and the economic structure themselves. This is true in cases of photo-chemical smog, garbage, red tide, neighbour noise and other problems. From this point of view, Tokyo still faces a severe situation, and is coming to a turning point in the context of environmental policy. The task must extend from the war on individual cases to the war on finances and the war on congestion. Now, there are many citizens who are aware that while they are enjoying economic prosperity, they are losing something more valuable. In other words, the citizens are convinced of the urgency to control economic activity so as to maintain a healthy and comfortable environment; and are reminded again of the Tokyo Metropolitan Environmental Pollution Control Ordinance that declares 'the dignity of men has priority over economic*

freedom'.

Whilst the views articulated by Professor Shibata are doubtless well founded, they are not shared by all.

In final analysis environmental policies will be formulated amongst decision-makers with different views on the environment. At present the dominant view is pro-development, and environmental protection assumes a minor position. The enforcement of rational land and water use management policies and strategies must be stressed. Socio-economic perspectives must be included in environmental policies alongside scientific and technological ones. The key ingredient should really be "environment for all".

REFERENCES

Environmental Agency (1976) Environmental Laws and Regulations in Japan, Environmental Agency, Tokyo

Environmental Agency (1981) Quality of the Environment in Japan 1980, Environmental Agency, Tokyo

Nakano, T. (1970) Lands below sea level due to subsidence in the urban areas of Japan, In Japanese Cities: A Geographical Approach. The Association of Japanese Geographers Special Publication Number 2, pp. 237-43

Nakano, T. (1980) Methodological systematisation of anthropogenic transformation of natural ecosystems, In Study and Control of Natural Ecosystems, International Geographical Union Symposium of the Commission on Environmental Problems, USSR, pp. 65-73

Nakano, T. (1981a) Geographical consideration on land and water use, GeoJournal 5/6

Nakano, T. (1981b) Land and water in Japan - the general situation and problems of its development. Geographical Reports of Tokyo Metropolitan University, 16; 95-100

Nakano, T. (1983) Historico-geographical systematisation of environmental problems. In Special Publication Number 14, Research and Sources Unit for Regional Geography, University of Hiroshima, pp. 21-26

Nakano, T. and Matsuda, I. (1976) A note on land subsidence in Japan, Geographical Reports of Tokyo Metropolitan University, 11; 147-61

Nakano, T. et al (1980) Recent characteristics of flood disasters in Japan, The National Geographical Journal of India, 26; 1-16

Shibata, T. (1983) Environmental control in Tokyo - Environments and man's control of them, In Special Publication Number 14, Research and Sources Unit for Regional Geography, University of Hiroshima, pp. 45-62

Tokyo Metropolitan Government (1971) Tokyo fights pollution, Tokyo Metropolitan Government, Tokyo.

Tokyo Metropolitan Government (1977) Tokyo fights pollution (revised edition), Tokyo Metropolitan Government, Tokyo

Chapter Nine

TOWARDS A GLOBAL ENVIRONMENTAL STRATEGY

J. Richard Sandbrook

INTRODUCTION

Since 1972 - the year of the United Nations Conference on the Human Environment in Stockholm - there has been a crescendo of concern about environmental degradation worldwide. This has been manifest in a variety of declarations, strategies, resolutions, plans and programmes. But where has it led? What, if anything, has changed? Is there a real crisis that justifies a global strategy? To answer it is helpful to review who has been making the environment an issue over the last decade, and for what reasons. Some clarity on these points then allows the questions to be considered.

THE ENVIRONMENTAL MOVEMENT SINCE 1972

Perceptions of the state of the world environment were markedly different in 1972 from what they are today (Earthscan, 1982). The early alarm was directed towards the rising tide of population, pollution and 'excess' resource use. Conference resolutions of the period (including Stockholm) reflected this perception and focused almost entirely on the purely 'environmental' dimension of the global problem. Other documents of the time - such as Limits to Growth (Meadows et al, 1972) and Blueprint for Survival (Goldsmith et al, 1972) - did not feature poverty, human misery, resource conflicts and a score of other currently fashionable issues as major components of their environmental 'problematique'. In effect much of the so called 'environmental movement' has moved on from a preoccupation with the externalities of economic growth (pollution and the upper limits of resource use) to more fundamental human-centred concerns.

Reducing the mass of environmental literature that has poured out since the early seventies to a few clear cut directions and lines of thought is difficult. This is primarily because a hallmark of the movement since Stockholm has been the gathering of strength by way of increasing diversity. That diversification has, in turn, led to a highly varied, widely dispersed, and at times openly conflicting set of references. In effect, the environmental crusade has long ceased to be a simple add-on concern to, say, local government policy making, radical politics or industrial planning. It is now central to each, with many faces and characteristics appropriate to each.

Nevertheless there are major groups in the movement which can be broadly described. These give an insight into the issues of concern, the goals that are sought and some of the methods employed. The five broad groups are:

(a) The Environmental grass roots (e.g. The Friends of the Earth network),
(b) The Conservationists (The IUCN network),
(c) The Environmental pragmatists or proceduralists (e.g. The Environmental law and administrative network),
(d) The Globalists (e.g. the policy studies network), and
(e) The Sustainable Developmentalists (The new network).

In reality these are not mutually exclusive groupings. They represent a constantly shifting body of individuals who move around from category to category dependent upon opportunities, place of work and changing conviction.

But because there are different groups with very different approaches to problem solving, any attempt to set out a global approach to the 'environmental issues' of the day is bound to be incomplete and superficial. In effect there cannot be only one way to meet our global problems, and the choice of 'best' amongst a range of alternatives must reflect the selectors niche within the five broad groups.

ENVIRONMENTAL GRASS ROOTS

The 'grass roots' category is a somewhat amorphous mixture comprising of people operating in their own community at the local level. Typically in Europe such people are engaged in attempts to improve the quality of their place of living and work, fighting 'not in my backyard issues', or using environmental issues as a root for political influence and power. The issues range from local pollution hazards, through local planning decisions, to broad alternatives based on recycling and renewal economic activity (see chapters 4 and 5).

In the developing world, the typical grass root environmentalist reflects (and often champions) a spectrum of concerns that includes overcoming poverty, improving human rights, as well as highlighting environmental problems and issues. The separation of environment from development is less marked in the Third World (see, for example, chapter 7).

In effect, the grass root environmentalist North and South is very much a creature of his or her own circumstances; looking for small improving steps on a pathway to a more equitable future which is nature conscious and sustainable.

CONSERVATIONISTS

In the niche above the 'grass roots' are the organised conservationists. Most of them have moved on from local issues to considering how they can protect species and habitats from the destructive impacts of economic advance. The International Union for the Conservation of Nature and Natural Resources (IUCN) provides a co-ordinating network for such groups and people.

As with the 'grass roots' level, however, there is no grand plan beyond improving matters locally or at best regionally. Thus IUCN's recent environmental blueprint - the World Conservation Strategy (IUCN, 1980) - reflects an aggregation of local conservation concerns classified by habitat type (such as watersheds, wetlands, drylands, forests and oceans). The resultant 'strategy' focuses upon priorities that are a product of local concern. It is <u>not</u> a global recipe for sorting out issues and priorities, or for building a new political consensus between rich nations and the poor nations.

World conservation Strategy

The Strategy (IUCN, 1980; Allen, 1980) set out three broad global objectives:

(a) the maintenance of essential ecological processes and life support systems (agricultural systems, forests, coastal, freshwater systems, the oceans and the atmosphere),
(b) the preservation of genetic diversity, and
(c) the sustainable use by humans of species and ecosystems.

It assumes that it is in the interests of all peoples to pursue these objectives, not least because the condition of the earth is ultimately of concern to all of us.

One suspects that if the authors of the Strategy had attempted to reconcile national development and environmental practice with global conservation goals, then the document would have been far more controversial. Such a reconciliation would be impossible without addressing difficult questions, and without making choices on how best to answer them. Four key questions are:

(a) At what point does an environmental problem cease to be only a concern of the nation-state which claims or exercises jurisdiction over the affected resources? For example, the UK may object very strongly to the way in which Brazil treats tropical rain forests, but at the end of the day current law and practice indicates that the forests are under Brazil's jurisdiction, no matter what the UK may think or say.
(b) To what extent is bad environmental practice and resource-destruction merely a reflection of the underlying economic position of nation-states? The strategy only goes to the point of claiming that long-term sustainable development is better than the short-term 'go for growth' approach. It also concludes that attention should be focused on the ingredients of the Third UN Development Decade. But any useful or realistic analysis of the reasons for natural resource-destruction would have to include questions of wealth distribution within and between nations.

In turn, this implies the need to examine the terms of trade between nations. This is required not only to isolate direct environmental effects (such as the clearing of rain forests to make way for export-led stock rearing), but also indirect effects (such as poor balance of payments position that arguable leads to over-use of wood as fuel with great consequential environmental damage). Alternatively, the falling price (in relative terms) of key commodity crops arguable increases the use of land for these rather than food crops; this in turn increases food imports into countries that should be self-sufficient. The interactions are endless.

(c) How capable are many nation-states of managing their environments, even if they wanted to? Do they have the necessary laws? Are the laws enforced or even enforceable? Does corruption or simple neglect make them valueless in practice? Does the country have the technical 'infrastructure' to monitor, assess and control problems? The answers to such highly significant operational questions will clearly vary considerably from country to country.

(d) Do people place the same value on environmental goods - and hence make the same choices about environmental policy - as the authors of the Strategy? What significance does different creeds, political ideologies and priorities have in moulding environmental attitudes and influencing priorities? The Soviet Union, for example, does not appear to have the same attitudes to the exploitation of fish stocks, nor the Japanese to the exploitation of great whales, as do many western countries.

Answers to these and similar questions were avoided in the Strategy, in the interest of presenting global conservation issues in a crisp, engaging and non-controversial manner. In short, the World Conservation Strategy is a very valuable propaganda tool, but it is not the type of global strategy that the problems demand.

PRAGMATISTS

Faced with all these obvious pitfalls, the conservation movement has effectively split into two groups in recent years. On the one side is the 'species and habitat' group, and on the other the rising class of environmental pragmatists.

Environmental pragmatists are to be found in government, industry, academia, and interest groups. They are not so much concerned with global trends as with what can be done <u>now</u> within current political and economic constraints. They have been working in three priority areas:

(a) the development of national and international environmental law,
(b) reinforcing the institutional capacity to think, plan and conduct environmental work on the ground, and
(c) altering the international flow of funds and investment toward 'global' good housekeeping.

<u>Environment and Development Programmes</u>
The aid and environment debate is a useful example of the pragmatists in operation (see O'Riordan, 1981).

The recent Nordic (1982) report on Environment and Development within the development assistance process took public analysis of the issues and the response to new heights. Never before has a group of governments collectively reviewed all aspects of their policy (in this case their development assistance or aid policy) so exhaustively from an environmental viewpoint.

The efforts within other national governments to define a workable and comprehensive Environment and Development Programme also illustrates that the idea of linking the two issues has firmly taken hold, not least because it is popular with the taxpaying public so to do. Nearly everyone is in favour of good aid - why not good environmental aid?

The Nordic (1982) report lists a series of straightforward recommendations under the headings of bilateral assistance, multilateral activities, research and surveys, training and information, and administration. In many respects this follows the format of other reviews such as the independent study of the 'United Kingdom's Overseas Environmental Policy' conducted as part of the UK World

Global Conservation Strategy Review (Sandbrook, 1982). Its conclusions are also very similar. But perhaps it is fair to suggest that if any 'pragmatist' in the OECD area who has closely followed the aid and environment debate for the last five years set about the task of the Nordic group, then they too would arrive at broadly similar conclusions and advice.

Amongst this 'like-minded' group of pragmatists the view generally prevails that there are six overall environmental objectives in the development assistance process:

(a) to raise indigenous capabilities in environmental/natural resource management by way of clear technical assistance agendas and work,
(b) to build upon existing expertise in the North so as to realise the full mutual advantage to both the donor and the client state,
(c) to ensure that environmental planning is not left out in development planning or in the aid project cycle,
(d) to gather sufficient hard data of an environmental kind (taxonomic, ecological, geological, etc) to enable sound environmental/development planning to occur,
(e) to inform the public (North and South) of what is at stake, and
(f) to concentrate on those systems which are particularly at risk - be it deserts, watersheds, moist forests or urban growth.

There would be some disagreement within this group of pragmatists, over technical issues. For example, some would prefer formal Environmental Impact Assessments (see chapter 2), whilst others would favour looser reviews. Guidelines would be variously employed (or not). There would also be differences in identification and selection of target problems and priorities. But overall there is a fair degree of consensus and resolve amongst the practitioners of the business.

This is not to say the pragmatist group have succeeded. For despite the analysis and review of the last five years, most development agencies are still far from realising the defined targets of the 'like-minded' group, or even in some cases from showing a basic inclination to change. For example, if we take a simple checklist and apply it to multilateral and bilateral sources of finance, how many of them can realistically claim to:

- have a high level environmental/natural resource policy?
- have staff and internal resources, or even a focal point, for environmental purposes?
- have enforceable environmental reviews?
- have effective environmental planning guidelines?
- have any training for staff in environmental planning?
- conduct research into environmentally sound projects and development options?

Many - particularly the multilateral banks - have made noises in the direction of all these. In part many have moved forward. But, in truth, we are still some way off broad and visible commitment to environmentally sound development.

This review of aid and environment hides the equally pragmatic and - to date - successful work by legal and administrative practitioners in the North. By now there is a rolling programme of environmental legislation in each OECD country (see Malanczuk, 1980; Haigh, 1984; also chapter 4). The question is now whether the regulatory approach can go much further, given the increasing resistance to it by entrepreneurs and the 'right of centre' governments that they elect. The answer to the limitations of pragmatists' approaches perhaps lies with the 'globalists'.

GLOBALISTS

The slow progess of formal procedural and administrative reform arises in part because of lack of awareness and political will. To meet these problems another major group (again principally of the North) has come into existence - the Globalists.

The most highly researched but conservative of the Globalist group is the Organisation for Economic Co-operation and Development (OECD) secretariat (see, for example, OECD, 1982). But there are many more. The UN Environment Programme (UNEP) UNESCO, and others in the UN family (including the Food and Agricultural Organisation) all produce global analyses trends and difficulties (see Holdgate, Kassas and White 1982). A characteristic of all these agencies is their attempt to change the level of political will and commitment attached to environmental issues by way of global studies.

Such changes have been attempted in part by way of generalised tracts on the major trends in environment and, more recently, development. The emphasis is upon the holistic approach, in which everything is related to everything else. Thus, for example, the recent World Resources Institute (1984) "Global Possible" conference was sub-titled Resources, Development and the New Century. Its rational was deep in 'global speak'. The summary report of the meeting includes the following:

> *Are world resource challenges serious enough, and broad enough in effect, to warrant the wide attention the Conference has urged?. The answer is surely "yes".*
>
> *Those of us now living allow natural systems to be abused, ignored, or destroyed at our children's peril. The resources under stress today are vital to tomorrow's economic development and growth in the many ways that the papers prepared for the Conference make abundantly clear. Sustainable development, in turn, by providing the means to earn a livelihood in a non-destructive manner, will reduce the pressures that people in poverty exert on natural resources. It can also stimulate the expansion of export markets and investment opportunities. Although much of the worst resource deterioration is occurring today in the Third World, the industrialised nations must come to terms with these issues and support better resource management around the globe: they are the dominant consumers of natural resources, and their economic futures are bound to the resources the planet's thin envelope of land, air and water provides.*
>
> *International security is at stake too.*

> *There will be many more people on this earth soon. Without the changes urged here, a large portion will join the legions who already live with constant hunger, illness, and illiteracy. If we allow their numbers to grow, if we allow economic development that is unsustainable, and the pressures of people on resource increase, political tensions and conflicts will rise. The effects will be felt in every sphere of political relations, from waves of "ecological refugees", to conflict over scarcer land and water to increasingly isolationist trade and then foreign policies.*
>
> *For all these reasons the actions suggested in the accompanying agenda would make an enormous different to the world's welfare over the next ten to thirty years. If we take the needed initiatives and take them now, widespread human suffering can be alleviated, threatened natural resources can be protected, and the vital groundwork laid for both international security and renewed - and sustained - economic growth. The new century can be much brighter than frequently supposed, but only if our actions match our aspirations.*

The global strategy that followed was equally broad in scope. It dealt with a wide range of items, including:

(a) population, poverty and development,
(b) the urban environment,
(c) fresh water,
(d) biological diversity,
(e) tropical forests,
(f) agricultural land,
(g) living marine resources,
(h) energy,
(i) non fuel minerals,
(j) atmosphere and climate,
(k) international assistance and the environment,
(l) business science, and
(m) the citizen.

What is the average politician to make of such a charter? Does the global approach - in its attempt to be comprehensive - overload an already over complex international agenda?

Certainly such attempts help to clarify the priorities of the UN system and of bureaucrats in government. But one suspects that they are so far removed from the lives of taxpayers, voters, small-scale farmers, entrepreneurs and the poor that they just pass by largely unnoticed. The world does not appear to be in the mood to change gear by way of bold over-riding initiatives.

In fact it is probably true to say that we are all in great danger of becoming bored with the restatement of the problems on a global scale. The slogans, catch words and metaphors are beginning to lose their attraction and effectiveness. How small is beautiful? What future shock and when? Limits to whose growth and of what kind?

Many have come to see that it is time to start work energetically on some of the components of the _solution_, rather than merely to talk of the problems of population growth, resource management and the inequitable distribution of wealth.

SUSTAINABLE DEVELOPMENTALISTS

The environmental agenda of the North has become progressively more concerned with minutiae (laws and procedures), or with global generalisations. In contrast, the agenda of the South has been increasingly overwhelmed by poverty and human rights' issues, and by the rush to achieve economic take-off at any price (Brandt, 1980). Pure conservation - in its isolation from economic reality - is doomed to fail in all but the most privileged circumstances.

Crisis of Confidence

These trends have led to a crisis of confidence in the environmental movement worldwide, particularly with respect to the Third World. New funds, people and ideas are in short supply. The facts are all too familiar; the problems are well-known but progress on the ground is not evident. Many of the actors have been fooled by their own success at generating media attention, foundation grants and popular support.

But in reality very little has changed in terms

of the trends that concerned them in the first place (see chapter 1). More people are hungry today than a decade ago. Deserts continue to spread. Forests and the genetic stock they contain disappear at alarming rates. Soil erosion mounts year by year. The atmosphere is still polluted. Hazardous wastes still cause problems and damage.

So what is the current environmental agenda, given that human activities continue to severely prejudice the long term survival of nature as much as they did a decade ago?. It is at this point that the committed either give up or change direction. The change of direction is now becoming evident.

The New Crusade

The "new crusaders" live under a novel creed. Gone are attempts to construct global or even regional agenda for action. Instead there is a fresh awareness that the approaches taken to problem solving are more important than recognising the global 'problematique'. Why bother to aggregate problems when all that results is an all prevailing sense of gloom? Merely recognising problems solves nothing.

One component of the realignment is the attempts to formulate national conservation strategies, to build-up the local voluntary sectors and reinforce institutions and science, and to get involved in the physical business of improving the environment and living conditions. The pluralism mentioned at the beginning of this chapter has become the strength of the movement.

It is now recognised that this is what must be built upon, rather than yet more international 'global speak'. Hundreds of thousands of small but contributory activities are being carried out at the very point where the environmental problems are most evident (see, for example, Stokes, 1978). In effect to many environmentalists the intergovernmental agenda has become an irrelevance, it having failed to make any real difference.

There are a number of key components to the new crusade which compliment the past, but which also set activity firmly in the real theatres of difficulty (as opposed to the corridors of power in Washington, New York and Geneva). These components add up to a global approach but not a global strategy. The consensus is spreading step by step in the Third World.

In essence, five points are being integrated into the spirit and wording of thousands of initiatives which spread well beyond what has traditionally been called the 'environmental movement'. The points are that development must:

(a) Reach the poor - is the result of projects equitable?
(b) Mobilise and motivate people - is the result of projects practicable?
(c) Achieve long-term biological productivity - is the result of projects environmentally stable?
(d) Spread appropriate technology - is the result of projects efficient?
(e) Generate income - is the result of projects economic and productive?

The world of development assistance geared to these objectives would be a better world for all concerned. An emphasis upon these objectives would meet the goals of the conservationists, the developmentalists, even the dispossessed and the helpless.

It is possible under each of the goals or approaches to set out key characteristics. Reaching the poor must involve securing land tenure for them, respecting their culture, improving their life expectancy and meeting their basic needs. Mobilising and motivating people will not occur unless local administrations are reinforced, decisions decentralised, education emphasised and leadership rewarded. Biological productivity - in the long term - implies a level of integrated ecosystem planning, using local skills and traditions, researching sustainable yield potentials, and keeping future resource options open.

The choice of technology, to be appropriate, must reduce reliance on external expertise and energy, it must meet basic needs, it must involve resource thrift and recycling. Repair renewal must feature, and scale must be appropriate to place and time. The economic criteria are less easy to define but they should include a proper evaluation of externalised costs, long run income generation and net benefits to the economy as a whole.

CONCLUSION

The global approach to environmental problems has changed significantly since the United Nations Conference on the Human Environment in 1972. Then the primary concerns were about the externalised costs of industrialisation in the 'North' and poverty in the 'South'. Now there is far more concern about how development can include good environmental stewardship - how can development be sustainable?

The chapter briefly reviews this shift in thinking by way of the major groups of activists who are involved. It considers, briefly, the activist or 'grass root' movement, the 'conservationists', the 'environmental pragmatists' and the 'globalists'. Finally it considers the new coalition largely concerned with putting sustainable development into practice of the community level. The overall conclusion of the chapter is that 'global strategies' are rather a thing of the past. There is now a distinct inclination to stop talking in generalities and to get down to the particular.

REFERENCES

Allen, R. (1980) How to save the world, Kogan Page, London
Brandt, W. (1980) North-South: A programme for survival, Pan, London
Earthscan (1982) Stockholme plus 10. International Institute for Environment and Development, London
Goldsmith, E. et al (1972) Blueprint for Survival, Penguin, London
Haigh, N. (1983) EEC Environmental Policy and Britain. Environmental Data Services Ltd., London
Holdgate, M.W., Kassas, M. and White, G.f. (1982) The World Environment 1972-1982, Tycooly, Dublin
IUCN (1980) World Conservation Strategy, IUCN, Gland, Switzerland
Malanczuk, P. (1980) Development - European Community. Environmental Policy and Law 6; 186-9
Meadows, D. et al (1972) The Limits to Growth,

Earth Island, London
NORDIC (1982) Milo och bistand, NORDIC Report
OECD (1982) Global Economic and Ecological Interdependence, OECD, Paris
O'Riordan, T. (1981) Problems encountered when linking environmental management to development aid. Environmentalist 1; 15-24
Sandbrook, R. (raporteur) (1982) The UK's Overseas Environment Policy. Report No. 6 in Earth's Survival: A Conservation and Development Programme for the UK. Nature Conservancy Council, London.
Stokes, B. (1978) Local responses to global problems; a key to meeting basic human needs, Worldwatch Institute, Washington.
World Resources Institute (1984) The Global Possible: Resources Development and the New Century, World Resources Institute, Washington

INDEX